METAMUSIC VERSUS THE SOUND OF MUSIC

A Critique of Serialism

MetaMusic versus The Sound of Music
A Critique of Serialism

William Thomson

With a Foreword by
David Butler

The Edwin Mellen Press
Lewiston•Queenston•Lampeter

Library of Congress Cataloging-in-Publication Data

Cau

Thomson, William, 1927-
  Metamusic versus the sound of music : a critique of serialism / William Thomson ;
with a foreword by David Butler.
     p. cm.
  Includes bibliographical references and index.
  ISBN-13: 978-0-7734-3807-1
  ISBN-10: 0-7734-3807-6
  1. Music--20th century--Philosophy and aesthetics. 2. Twelve-tone system. 3. Music
theory--History. I. Title.
  ML3845.T57 2010
  781.3'3--dc22
                                    2010015374

hors série.

A CIP catalog record for this book is available from the British Library.

The Edwin Mellen Press
Box 450
Lewiston, New York
USA 14092-0450

The Edwin Mellen Press
Box 67
Queenston, Ontario
CANADA L0S 1L0

The Edwin Mellen Press, Ltd.
Lampeter, Ceredigion, Wales
UNITED KINGDOM SA48 8LT

Printed in the United States of America

Table of Contents

Foreword

Although it has been part of our artistic culture for more than a century, post-tonal music still presents us with a number of conundrums. One of the most intriguing of these is the disconnect between the music's perceived historical significance and its relative scarcity on the musical performance stage. On one hand, post-tonal music—and especially that of Serialism—long has been considered by most academic musicians to be pivotally important in the history of twentieth-century music, and it has inspired a large body of theoretical and analytical literature, with contributions ranging from mere cleverness to true brilliance. Yet with all the attention this musical genre has been paid by music theorists and critics, it has never drawn a proportionately large audience in the concert hall.

Over the years, William Thomson has assembled an increasingly persuasive explanation for the failure of post-tonal music to develop the kind of significant listener base that would match the historical and critical attention it has drawn. His proposal, in the simplest possible terms, is that tonality provides a time-based pitch syntax that acts as a perceptual "glue" for listeners who have grown up within that tonal culture. Post-tonal music steps beyond that syntactical boundary.

The evidence that leads Thomson to this position is broad-ranging: a combination of critical and theoretical commentary, historical and anthropological research, and empirical evidence drawing primarily from results of perceptual experiments recently completed in the relatively young research area of music cognition. Few writers could pull such disparate information together into a coherent and convincing package, but Thomson has been mining this vein for a long time; his dissertation on musical tonality was completed well over a half-century ago, [1] and he is internationally known for his articles and books on tonal and post-tonal music.

In *MetaMusic versus the Sound of Music: A Critique of Serialism,*
Thomson extends and buttresses several central lines of inquiry launched in his
seminal book, *Schoenberg's Error,* [2] and he broadens the perspective of his
discussion to include intriguing parallel developments in various visual and
literary arts contemporaneous with the zenith of the Second Viennese School.
MetaMusic deals with a complex and controversial topic that could easily
intimidate most readers. But it's evident that William Thomson made a real effort
in *MetaMusic* to minimize the use of undefined technical terminology and
academic harrumph; as a result the book is very accessible—almost
conversational in tone. It is a welcome addition to his influential series of
contributions to music and arts criticism.

David Butler

David Butler is Professor Emeritus of Music Theory, The Ohio State University.
He is author of *The Musician's Guide to Perception and Cognition* (G. Schirmer,
1992) and hs served as Editor for the College Music Society *Symposium.* He was
founding Editor of the website publication *Empirical Musicology Review.*

---

[1] In *A Clarification of the Tonality Concept.* Ph.D. dissertation, Bloomington, Indiana:
Indiana University, 1952.

[2] Schoenberg's Error, 1991.

Acknowledgments

The value of this book is in large part derived from my many years of attention to the work of persons who pursued their goals with the tenacity demanded for unearthing truth. I have done my best to follow in their paths, to profit from their wisdom. Prominent is the late Leonard B. Meyer, as well as David Butler, Diana Deutsch, Don Gibson, Erkki Huovenen, Earnest McClain, Eugene Narmour, and Steven Pinker. Their individual and collective contributions to our understanding of human perceptual processings for music have nudged my own pursuit of conceptual clarity, my struggles to explain what makes music tick, what makes it valuable for us, what does not, how the musics of the world bear demonstrable marks of basic kinship.

I wish to thank the Norris Foundation of the University of Southern California for underwriting costs for quoting certain materials. Hearty thanks also are due to the Huntington Library in San Marino, whose vast holdings of early 20th century documents—including the complete collection of Eugene Jolas's classic periodical *transition*—were made available to me for rummaging through the days of the heralded Arts Revolution.

Permissions Granted

Excerpts from Arnold Schoenberg's *Opus 11, No. 1*, page 187, and *String Quartet No. 4*, page 175-176, granted by Belmont Music Publishers

Ezra Pound's complete *Canto XLIII*, page 77, granted by New Directions Publishing Corp.

Excerpt from *The Collected Essays of Milton Babbitt*, page 174-175, granted by Princeton University Press

Notation of the songs *Kuro 'I Nye*, p. 71, and *La mintso*, page 127, granted by Northwestern University Press

Excerpt from *Windswept Peaks* by Wen-chung Chou, page 210, granted by C.F. Peters Publishing Co.

Excerpt from *Arabesque*, page 201, by Paul Nauert, granted by the composer

Notation for the African song "*Ta Avo na Legra*," page 112, granted by W.W. Norton Publishing Co.

Notation for the song "African Women's Duet," page 44, from *Africa, Journal of the International African Institute*, 1928, granted by the International African Institute

Prologue
METAMUSIC VERSUS THE SOUND OF MUSIC:
A CRITIQUE OF SERIALISM

A curious anomaly persists today in the world of art theory and criticism. An issue of belief, its home base is most firmly planted in academe. Its epicenter resounds with dissonances between theory and practice, between description and reality, forcing a rift between a world fancied and a world confirmed by human perception. This conflict between conceptual categories and human experience is a product of ideologies born of the 'Revolution' proclaimed for the arts early in the 20th-Century.

Making and enjoying some kind of art has been a part of the human scene from times beyond documentation. Cave paintings and Stone Age flutes preserved today provide reminders of people communicating with each other over and beyond the humdrum needs of everyday life. Indeed, anthropologist Ellen Dissanayake reminds us that our ancient predecessors gave special homage to such frivolous activities and their produce. For them they were special, "associated with magical powers; their makers were heralded as special kinds of people because they had access to those powers."[1] Evidence abounds that a weakness for such forms of communication has pervaded humanity.

Until the late 19th century the creation of music or literature or visual images was a relatively outgoing operation. Artists enjoyed special skills and used them to communicate inner images with an established audience. They spent little time worrying about how, why, or for what broader purpose this seen or heard artifact was being wrought. That straightforward approach began to alter noticeably for some artists by early in the 20th century, when a persistent self-consciousness of the creative act began to dominate the scene. To be *modern*

---

[1] *Arts and Intimacy*, 169.

became the charge, and one path boasted of wholly rational, objective motivations. As David Harvey describes the mood, "the aims of modernity . . . were to develop objective science, universal morality and law and autonomous art according to their inner logic or internal structure."[2]

Such craft-searchings fostered a climate of introspection, a time when *How* it was done often became at least as important as *What* resulted. Even when the *What* was the object of concern, its accompanying descriptive effluvia frequently dominated the scenario. Extrinsic ideologies and self-conscious guides at times outweighed confirmable properties and values; *style* became a greater concern than *content*—at times it became an embarrassing excess baggage. The pretentious descriptive overlay often negated the communicative claim of the object, whether painting, poem, or sonata. A predictable result of this galloping self-consciousness is an impressive conjunctive population of art theorists and critics.

WHEN ART OBJECTS REQUIRE EXPLANATION

The *Thing* no longer suffices to fill the bill; it requires heavy wordplay to achieve the desired result—perhaps even to be understood. Whatever the medium, the total mix sometimes exceeds perceivable realities, things presumed to convey artistic images to a perceiver. At rare times it seems to consist exclusively of lexical overlay, critics talking to themselves to create meta-criticism, theorizing that is "more concerned with its own methodology than with the aesthetic substance of art." [3] When this mix of object and overlay prevails, *MetaArt* is the result.

There is no evidence that Michelangelo nor Titian fretted over the personalizing elements of their styles nor how they interrelated; it's unlikely that medieval composer Ockeghem nor classicism's Haydn worried for a moment of

---

[2] *The Condition of Modernity*, 9.
[3] I am indebted to Roger Kimball for coinage of the term *meta criticism*. (*Tenured Radicals*, 104-106.)

their tuneful careers about how to "compartmentalize," how to pre-fabricate note collections within a motet or a minuet. Nor did renascent Shakespeare and romanticist Balzac waste much time theorizing over how the emotional power of their words and sentences might be enhanced by their exact placement on the page. Just such concerns loomed large in the consciousness of some New Age artists.

Symptomatic of the times was G.B. Shaw's coinage of the epithet *Sardoodledom*. It was his fancy putdown for dramatic scenarios in which technical concerns outweigh attention to the realities of dramatic characterization.[4] It was an infection as prevalent in painting and music as in the theater. Today it's a condition dominated by scholars and critics, especially those attached in some way to higher education, where even the most arcane ideas can enjoy the comfort of non-debate. A common product is its development of a special language, "an insider language unintelligible to the uninitiated." [5]

Our overarching concern here is twofold. First come simple reminders of guidelines for judging the legitimacy of artifacts intended for human consumption as Art, works of any medium that can pass the most minimal tests. Our conclusion may be regarded as iconoclastic. It holds that some highly praised artifacts of our past don't—or barely do—pass the test. And then our second concern is to examine the relevancy—in some instances verifiable truth—of several of the more immodest tracts of 12-tone music, the major product of 20th-Century Serialism. It was the basis for music's most celebrated form of *MetaArt*. Our quest will be dominated by it, with brief side glances at other art media for a broader perspective.

But I wince as I utter that word *Art*, reminded that it is loaded with potential vagaries that can send chills through a body. What separates *Art* from all else? Or what is *beautiful*, and what is "fine" about *Fine* Arts? Is the "taste" of learned

---

[4] Shaw fashioned his word from the name of French playwright Victorien Sardou (1831-1908).

[5] Daniel Flynn, *Intellectual Morons*, 243.

connoisseurs actually and demonstrably "better" than that of the curious citizen who looks and listens carefully? A prize *New Yorker* cartoon of many years ago hit an oblique blow at such rhetorical questions of value. Showing two men in conversation within one's living room, the owner says to the other: "I may not know art, but I know what I like." The surrounding walls are hung with portraits of himself.

I once had the profound pleasure of meeting and chatting with philosopher Bertrand Russell.[6] In the course of our exchange I asked him: "Lord Russell, you have written about almost every subject under the sun, so why have you never written about aesthetics? His response was even more pithy than expected: "Eesthetics? [with was his British pronunciation] "No one knows anything about *eesthetics*!"

Our discussion here will attempt to avoid the dangers of individualized "eesthetic" values, skirting the epistemic chasms that threaten such discussions *per se*. My thrust will be more pragmatic, my goals more definable, more reachable. My initial concern is with conditions central to the inescapable demands for any artifact that it be regarded as experientially admirable, in and of itself. What attributes are demanded to pass the most elemental tests of *'tis* or *'tain't*. Beyond that line in the sand our concerns need not step. Our criteria nonetheless enable us to recognize that some motivations and practices in the arts of the past century's touted 'Revolution' were doomed to failure, and for a simple reason: they fell short of or they exceeded the bounds of what can be experienced *qua Art*. They were victims of practices derived from flawed ideologies. And thus they usually entered the Valley of *MetaArt*.

Can one reasonably make such a claim? Or is this just another irresponsible value judgment made by a highly experienced crank? Since we need to begin this journey together, let us test its validity together. Carefully study the latest of my

---

[6] This was in Bloomington, Indiana, at the University, around 1951, where he had just given a lecture about world population control.

cherished creations: *Thomson, 2009: Silent Southern California Rectangle in Black and White.*[7]

Can it be called art? If your answer is something like "We must first consider all pertinent semiotic angles and intentionalities before drawing a conclusion," then I suggest that we part company now; further discussion would be fruitless. If, on the other hand, the answer is a simple and immediate "No," then we at least begin together. We can agree that, although loaded with heavy *intentionality*, my artifact is but a rather barren context of severely limited parts. Its pairs of horizontal and vertical lines (*parts*) do form a rectangle (*context*), but that's as far as it goes. Art it is not. Art objects project multiple layers of context, words forming clauses that form sentences filling out paragraphs, *et al.*

Our later discussions should confirm that I am not just airing some cramping prejudices. Indeed, there are, sufficient "art objects" from the past hundred years, lauded as supreme creations of sheer wonderment, whose actual content make my argument not only relevant but overdue.

A vital issue necessarily emerges: regardless of a creator's *intent* or a critic's luxuriant explanatory overlay, some properties are no less vital to art objects than fingers to a hand. In art they fulfill basal needs of human cognitive/perceptual operations. And, after all, art objects are created for human consumption.

My point is not that the content of successful art objects cannot alter in many ways over the years, so that what is admired today must resemble and be wholly

---

[7] True (as only art historians may note), my style is excessively influenced by the "Voids" of Kasimir Malevich's *Supremetism.* Those who know Andy Warhol's *White Painting* of 1964 may detect further kinships

consistent with what was admired in the court of Louis XIV. It is rather that successful transformations nonetheless adhere to certain demands of human experience. We still do not inhabit the "Free Land" so joyfully touted by several sloganeers of the early 20th century (and frequently repeated later). The land we do inhabit—regardless of one's culture or era—imposes dimensions dependent upon established biological functions and their limits. The *Here* and the *Now* are not sole determinants of human behavior. A more realistic appraisal honors psychologist Steven Pinker's conclusion that

> the mind is equipped with a battery of emotions, drives, and faculties for reasoning and communicating and they have a common logic across cultures, are difficult to erase or redesign from scratch, were shaped by natural selection acting over the course of human evolution, and owe some of their basic design (and some of their variations) to information in the genome.[8]

The Meta-Problem in Music

Although the more specious ideologies and consequences of the last century's heralded Arts 'Revolution' are of great concern here, recurrent focus is on the inherent musical and conceptual problems posed by the dodecaphonic detour launched by Arnold Schoenberg and Mathias Hauer in the 1920s. Its role as an epiphany of modernism cannot be overstated. It offered something wholly lacking in struggles for *The New* in other arts: a *system.* That system's uniquely seductive effluvia eventually spawned something that at times replaces the music it was developed to produce: a supreme example of *Theory* replacing *Practice*, of *Words and Numbers* replacing *Tones*. This extra something makes special and unique music's role in the arts revolution, although its path was largely consistent with those taken by some painters and writers of the times.

---

[8] Pinker, *The Blank Slate*, 73.

The fullest flowering of Serialism over the past half-century became an insiders' *cause célèbre* for academics, forming the spine of books, scholarly presentations, class lectures, articles in learned journals and graduate seminars. But despite its broad appeal, the system's basic claims suffer deep problems, pesky thorns in the conceptual flesh. They are rarely acknowledged in print. Similar flaws of ontology haunt the visual and literary arts, but in a far less systematic way. And therein lies the supreme fascination of *MetaMusic*.

Ideologies can be gloriously beneficial. They also can pose dangers, especially when they develop from flawed premises, then ignore contrarian views. Daniel Flynn states the case well when he argues that exposing ideological falsehoods "tends to inoculate would-be dupes against succumbing to future lies." He wisely opts for an atmosphere of free debate and honesty, "conditions that cultivate thinking rather than programming." [9]

Those ideological problems posed by Serialism become evident in music after hard looks at two broad yet commanding facts of history. The first relates to the fate of actual music produced via rigid applications of 12-tone technique. The "market" aspects of modern painting can keep artifacts derived from any questionable approach alive (and expensive), but the music and literary markets are not so accommodating; some of the highly touted masters of the early *avant* have not fared so well. And thus arises the question, "How has music's celebrated New Way, the Serialism of Schoenberg and Hauer survived, as revered theory if not as practice?"

And then there is that second problem. It bears an even more threatening prospect. As later chapters here document, we humans are stuck with those "faculties for reasoning and communicating" claimed by Pinker, basic ways by which aural machinery and brain operations feed our consciousness. Many early champions of a drastic overhaul in music chose to believe scenarios to the contrary. That touted process called *evolution*, they argued, enables ambitious

---

[9] *Intellectual Morons*, 245.

listeners to develop more agile and deeper listening talents. After all, music has demonstrated an evolutionary path through history. Or, alternatively, maybe John Locke's old *tabula rasa*[10] explains it best, leaving our perceptual doors wide open for anything new: whatever comes along can work for us—if blessed by sufficient conviction and reams of justifying words. Both answers are handy copouts. They continue to be honored by some highly intelligent people.

As we shall observe in later discussions, no evidences from history or from studies of cognition and perception confirm either alibi. The pitch property of tonality, for example, wasn't a culturally-imposed condition, an idiosyncrasy developed for minuets and powdered wigs of 18th century Western Europe. Although widely held, such a view is as naive as that which holds that the forces of gravity awaited the conceptualizing genius of Newton.

We shall unravel evidence showing that much of the continuing cascade of prose explaining serialized procedures—*qua music*—tells of little more than illusions. It feeds unwary readers with elaborately precise descriptions of *notes* rather than of *sonic realities*. It is a condition destined to be remembered as a snug fit for Charles Fair's classic description of the *The New Nonsense*: "contemporary ideas which, although widely discussed and taken by many with the utmost seriousness, either lack support from existing evidence or are clearly contradicted by it." [11]

Those misconceptions in music demand heavy and focused discussion; they are so primal to coveted ideologies that they are hard to recognize, much less to dislodge. It's a strange condition when theories of Art ignore basal human needs, going on to elaborate and extol objects unable to fulfill the functions respectfully provided for them. But it happens.

Fragments of this story have been told before, [12] although not with the holistic approach adopted here. One fascinating aspect of the Arts-in-Revolution

---

[10] The idea itself spread widely after Locke, passed on by such as Rousseau and Freud.

[11] P. 33.

[12] In *Schoenberg's Error* of 1992, and *Tonality in Music* of 1999, for example.

tale has never been linked to a more general and ancient human foible, a trait that casts dark shadows on Aristotle's claim of humanity's rationality. I call that trait *The Schizo Syndrome*. It is defined and illustrated in our first chapter. It will return often as a touchstone of sobering reality, one of the elemental forces behind all *Meta-Arts*.

Chapter 1

SETTING THE SCENE

The Arts were not alone in that 'Revolution'. The whole of scientific inquiry and society in general heralded an aura of discovery, all motivated by the growing conviction that things were not what they had been thought to be, a sense of imminent—and forced—overhaul. As Arthur Koestler summed up the era many years later, the mood was one "of transition and awareness of crisis, which embraced the whole human spectrum of activities, social organizations, religious beliefs, art, science, fashions."[1] There had been nothing like it since the age of Copernicus.

The 18th-century conception of the universe as *plenum formarum* (with its variety of life fully accounted for) began to crumble. The notion of a universal stuffing called *ether* was demolished in 1905 when Einstein redrew the basic plans for physics. By 1910 Ernest Rutherford and Neils Bohr had proposed an astounding similarity between the dynamics of our vast solar system and the tiny atom; within the same decade Sigmund Freud urged that human behavior originates in such netherworlds as the unconscious mind and irrational impulses, regions and events previously unimagined, much less explored.

As for the arts, new ways were sought for dealing with chosen crafts, whether in the act of creation, explanation or reception. Fifty years earlier the very word *artist* had begun to acquire more the meaning it has today. These special people, the artists, developed idiosyncratic interests unknown in times past, yet their job descriptions bore similarities with those of ancient times, that

---

[1] *The Sleepwalkers*, 510.

aura of magical powers anthropologist Ellen Dessanayake described for art makers of prehistory. [2] Those who dominated the ideological front were usually driven by wholesale acceptance of *Tabula rasa*. But it was a blank slate with a dollop of Rousseau's and Swift's Noble Savagery thrown in for drama. They were further comforted by the image Nietzsche had drawn, the artist as cosmic prophet. Maybe Ortega y Gasset over dramatized it all but caught its spirit in claiming that[3]

> the new art was but a part of a larger societal confirmation. It was a pathway toward helping . . .the elite to recognize themselves and one another in the drab mass of society and to learn their mission which consists in being few and holding their own against the many.

Whatever the approach taken, whatever the medium, personal expression was the dominating force, replacing royal or religious motivations invoked in ages past. If one retains the overall notion of inspiration and discovery, of art as self-expression and communication of emotion, one arrives at Karl Popper's designation of Art as "a kind of theology without God . . ." And this was something quite new, for "now the artist inspires himself." [4]

Darwin's ideas provided a fresh new perspective, a "scientific" reason for change. The old slate may appear to be blank, but something is driving culture down a particular path, and its goal must be recognized as *Progress*. It was an encompassing canon of change consistent with the organic postulate developed by Herder and Goethe in the late 18th century. Conditions of *Now* were derived from conditions of *Before*; they will in turn provide the core for a *Future*. By 1880 the idea of Evolution was an accepted (and often misunderstood) thesis among the intelligentsia. For many the implicit conviction was simple: any truly *modern* work was by definition virtuous. The commanding atmosphere of the day was

---

[2] *Homo Aestheticus: Where Art Comes From and Why.*

[3] "The Dehumanization of Art," 7.

[4] *The Unended Quest,* 66. Popper also avers that the self-expression part of it is "utter triviality."

epitomized in Steven Vincent Binet's leitmotif for the Pilgrims of his *Western Star*: "We don't know where we're going, but we're on our way."

This sense of ordered change fit well with historian Arnold Toynbee's imagery of "creative barbarians," those who must come along periodically as the brooms that sweep the stage clear, ridding it of a tired culture's debris. And for brooms swept by artists, Darwinism—as understood by these evolutionary opportunists—was a happy endorsement of the doctrine of progress. Whatever the reigning ideology, the New must be found. The proclaimed artistic past was recognized as but shards of the West's Spenglerian decay.

Philosopher Hegel had pronounced the very end of Art early in the 19th century, noting the impossibility of surpassing the produce of classical Greeks, medieval and renascent Europeans. And look at what followed Hegel! The decay recognized by him and Spengler was real, but that was then; now it must be replaced if "progress" were to prevail.[5] All one needed was the will to seek, then bring about the needed realignments. So by the 1900s a pop narcissism and megalomania, derived via Rousseau, Nietzche, Freud, and Marx, had fomented a monumental pressure for remodeling the world. One extreme refuge was the Theosophy movement, which became a haven for several prominent artists; its scenario was derived from the conviction that modern science could help renovate human institutions—so long as contact with a "divine" basis was retained.

Even the expression *L'art pour l'art*, introduced as early as 1804 in reference to ideas of philosopher Immanuel Kant, had entered the elitist lexicon by mid-century.[6] Its basic implication continues to echo for many today: utilitarian motives and goals pervert art. It nonetheless was a perspective often tempered by an opposing egalitarian twist. Ideas and motives often straddled an

---

[5] Fervent arguments were made as late as mid-20th century that a continuing *improvement* of the human lot was a 'scientific' fact of evolution. Classic of the genre was Lecomte du Noüy's *The Road to Human Destiny* of 1955.

[6] See "The Genesis of the Theory of 'Art for Art's Sake' in Germany and England," *Smith College Studies in Modern Languages II* (1921), no. 4. and Wilcox, "The Beginning of *L'Art Pour L'Art*."

ideological fence: artists were of the elite, but they could still speak directly to "the masses." A Blaise Cendrars "elastic poem" of the period begins suggestively with "*Les fênetres de ma poésie sont grand' ouvertes sur les boulevards.*" ("The windows of my poetry are grand openings on the boulevards.") But Cendrars's gaze isn't just out toward the masses; he's also looking into his own psyche, objectifying his personal motivations and goals. His "looking out" is matched by a "looking in," the kind of self-consciousness that had begun to reign.

The NewWay was not always a clean break with tradition; many artists remained consistent with the past. The streams of consciousness fabricated by James Joyce and Edith Wharton may at times be jolting, but they draw from raw materials directly observed in a human world. It's unlikely that Marc Chagall's painting *The Musician* of 1912-13 was ever mistaken for actual images from real life, but one does not doubt that it represents an identifiable world, from the foreground cellist and violinist to the crude background signs. The music of Alexander Scriabin or Charles Ives or Alban Berg can at times lack a clear sense of key or even an identifiable tunefulness, yet it still bears ties to a sound world of the past. That past was by no means lost.

Confused Categories Along the Way

The big story nonetheless reveals that some byproducts of ideological brooding resulted in alien conditions, hopeful theories could lead to the creation of questionable—or at times outrageous—products. Even when invoked within a parent art by people of proven skill, some results could be compellingly different in intent, subject matter, and treatment. The self-consciousness endemic to the early revolution led to overtime theorizing about "How to." How can I create something new, something different from the past, something uniquely expressive of myself?

This theorizing atmosphere led to the production of extensive explanatory prose accompanying the artifact, sometimes by the artist, at other times by a critic/theorist. The condition was a prime mover in the struggle for progress and it led to a change in the nature of the "artifact." Now it was a combination of art object plus descriptive baggage, making that unique mix we call *MetaArt*.

The *Dada* splinter of Tristan Tzara and Marcel Duchamp begun in the late teens was a prime example.[7] Derived from a narcissistic will to shock, it could corral novel ends and means with its readymade fruits, leaving tenuous any legitimate kinship or parentage. Even today we read in the tabloids of *Dada*-inspired art, of its paintings and sculptures, its "constructs" and "conceptualizations," its "found " objects which, consistent with *Dada's* ideology, usually repudiate valid artistic mores in both subject matter and treatment.

Bastard child though it may have been, *Dada* has enjoyed a long and newsworthy life, a successful splinter in the pop wing of art. Whether in visual, literary, or musical products, it can nudge us into confusing our categories of value; its direct appeal lies in the massage rather than the message. At best, what it projects can be amusing, fully engaging. At worst it bears a message of erected middle-finger mockery, whether of social, political, religious, or artistic origins. Its images are not motivated by *aesthetic* properties, by elements uniquely resident in the object. There is an imbalance—if not total confusion—of categories, a vital contributing factor in the creation of any genre of *MetaArt*. It is a result of what I call the *Schizo Syndrome*.

So What's the Schizo Syndrome?

It's a human weakness for confusing categories. Its origins—to my knowledge unobjectified before—lie in our unique talent for expanding or contracting, rearranging or replacing things in attempts to make a better world.

---

[7] The term probably came from a comment by painter Gaugin in a letter from Tahiti. He felt the urge to revert to more personal and primitive images like those of his childhood rocking horse, which he called *Dada*.

But potential traffic jams inhere. Aristotle wasn't spouting pure fictions when he claimed the rationality of man; he just overstated the case a bit.

The *SS* is not some esoteric malady of the post-Freudian psyche; it's both simple in nature and ancient in heritage. One humble example helps us comprehend its basal nature. The crossword puzzle's goal is to lure you into supplying all of the "across" and "vertical" words thought up by the puzzle's creator, maybe even baffling you in the process. But note something extra.

1.1 Crossword mat

8/18/09

The mat bears a property "over and beyond;" it's a special non-verbal message. Note the visual symmetry. In the total outlining box, every "above" space duplicates an obverse image of its "below" mate, every "right hand" space duplicates by obverse image its "left hand" space. How fetching! But what do these fancy spatial deployments have to do with things lexical?

Nothing. The visual symmetries are pure appendage, decorative excess baggage. They may project a high degree of ocular delight—if noticed at all—but they play no role in the word-world of acrosses and downs. It's a benign cancer; its addition poses a bit of pain for the puzzle's creator during diagnosis and surgery, but no damage to vital organs. More profound manifestations of the *SS* show up in surprising places.

As it did in the automobile industry when "styling" became a competing—not to say controlling—part of the design process, at times to the detriment of safety and ecological progress. It may well have initiated the early 21st-century gloom of American automakers. Or think for a moment about what we call *Showbiz.* The *SS* trait thrives in segments of contemporary theater, film, sports, politics, and other human pastimes, including even religion. We speak often of "stardom." And how is that unique status evaluated? Not always by critical analysis of relevant work accomplished. Columnist Walter Scott once probed the criteria-for-celebrity in *Parade* news magazine.[8] Hitting the Looking Glass a shattering blow, he calmly states the bare facts: such rankings are weighed "by a formula that takes into account a celeb's earnings, marquee value and the number of times that he or she appeared on major magazine cover stories in the period ending June 30."

As Showbiz star Cher once opined, "I understand how people with very mediocre talent can be the most famous people in the United States. I was already famous . . . before I tried to do anything good." [9]

A thorough review of *SS* manifestations could fill a book. I trust that the basic condition is understood by now. We could turn to the stellar role of advertising in our news media. My daily "news" paper consists of more ink

---

[8] September 7, 2003.
[9] *Los Angeles Times*, Oct. 19, 1987.

devoted to sales pitches than to unbiased news,[10] and as lovable curmudgeon Andy Rooney once confessed, even the famed CBS "newsmagazine" *60 Minutes* averages no more than 40% of the real thing. The other twenty minutes go to the highest bidders.

So what does all of this have to do with music? Surely nothing so monumental as the *SS*s of *Showbiz* could have infected the super-sophisticated world of serious music. Perhaps something less imposing? Something more on the scale of the crossword puzzle's visual symmetries? We shall review conditions in the Arts that, sadly, are more on the profound side. I have no desire to separate "low-brow" from "high-brow" art. One can nonetheless establish an elastic fence between *Showbiz* chic and artistry, even to recognize that the fence can be misleading. For example, it yields a common basis for recognizing the silliness of a dance "performance" by *HighArt* composer Pauline Oliveros compared to a captivating routine by Gene Kelly of the *Showbiz* world.

Some Basic Ground Rules

The irreducible criteria for art I'll observe here are simple; they are embedded in our discussion of my "Silent Southern California Rectangle in Black and White" of the *Prologue*. They number only two, but their implications can be found in seven drawn up by philosopher Dennis Dutton,[11] whose worthy target is to explicate "the signal characteristics of art considered as a universal, cross-cultural category."

Art, first of all, is communication; whatever the medium, its artifacts must convey meaning of some kind. This is an *inherent meaning* created by one human psyche and unraveled by another. It is a meaning projected by discriminable parts-within-parts that cohere to make an experiential whole, a *context*. Any

---

[10] Advertisements are "news" of a special utilitarian kind, but they miss the criterion of "unbiased."

[11] "Aesthetic Universals." William H. Gass also develops an imposing set of generalized partitions for the avant-garde ("Vicissitudes of the Avant-Garde."). They exceed the narrower needs of this study.

aesthetic experience is more than just a simple, direct recognition of external things. It instead involves "an imaginatively reconstructed percept. . ." Its "contextual qualities cannot be perceived without the aid of the imagination." [12] In music those qualities are products of sonic events, in painting of visual, in literature of words.

This demand for context entails cohesions at more than one dimensional level. The classic example is that of tones and chords making phrases that make sections which fill in movements, and so on. The resultant whole within any medium may convey a *referential meaning*, or it may be a meaning confined within, as audiated or visualized by a perceiver, but its cues must be inherent. This embodiment of context, this projection of structure, satisfies a human need for perceptual containment, a condition Donald Kuspit tells us[13] "signifies perfection through the luxury of unity or self-integration it enjoys within that formal containment." Nelson Goodman fleshed out the same meaning with his coinage *repleteness*, comparing the barren jagged line of an electrocardiogram with a rich Hokusai drawing of Mount Fuji. [14]

And then there is our second criterion. It holds that to be art there must prevail an evocative power motivated by those inherent cues, power that reveals evidence of *artistry*, a mastery of skills exceeding those enjoyed by most of us. As art historian E.H. Gombrich explained long ago, it is present "whenever anything is done so superlatively well that we forget to ask what the work is supposed to be, for sheer admiration of the way it was done."[15] Added to our first, this criterion gives us a rock bottom base for appraisals of the most rudimentary kind. When we hear claimed the creation of Art (even when verified by esteemed critics), of how the naked "artist" climbs up poles and cables, with Vaseline liberally applied to bodily surfaces and orifices, we are justified in taking pause to

---

[12] Andrew Ushenko, *Dynamics of Art*, 25-26.
[13] *The Cult of the Avant-Garde Artist*, 16.
[14] *In Language of Art: An Approach to a Theory of Symbols*.
[15] *The Story of Art*, 477.

ask: Which of the two basic requisites of art, if not both, is manifest here, and how?

Let us take note of just one other human frailty that aids and abets public acceptance of "artworks," regardless of the problems they may pose for comprehension. Like Hyacinth of the great British TV series, we scramble to "keep up appearances." We avoid admitting that we find an object less than moving because we don't understand it, especially when it is said to fulfill some noble ideology. And thus intellectual cowardice becomes a pernicious enabler for questionable art. Henri Laboit objectified the basic trait without even mentioning the word "cowardice."

> Many of those who contemplate an uncomprehended or (more precisely) incomprehensible work will not want to appear not to understand it, and besides, the appearance of understanding it places them outside the common rut. Outrage, even without art, . . . will always find a snob public to appreciate it. [16]

This weakness must be regarded as a part of our accommodation of aesthetically barren objects, especially when they possess some form of extrinsic notoriety. We find it easy to laud things for their representation of a passing peccadillo, objectified trend, or even historical era. Objects are suspected of being especially *valuable* if a critic or theory-spinner has lavished barrels of prose in expounding their unique content and supreme excellence. Critic Jed Perl once expressed it in reviewing a show of Jasper Johns paintings: "it was a hit because it satisfied an audience that believes aesthetic experience is a form of historical experience." [17]

Fine. But we do need to keep our categories straight.

---

[16] Laboit, *Loc. cit.*, 210.
[17] *Gallery Going*, 47.

The What, the When and the Where

A precise date for the beginning of the arts *Tsunami* that sired the *MetaArts* can't be named. There was none. It was on its way—in painting more than in other arts—by the 19th -century's end. Virginia Woolfe's visit in 1910 to a London gallery, a show filled with recent Cézannes, Picassos, and van Goghs, led her to declare that year—in fact *December* of that year—as the date "when human nature changed." The date was evidence more of Ms. Woolfe's personal epiphany than definitive for the whole of art, but 1910 isn't a bad marker. Our later discussion of music's hand in it all will confirm it a best-of-all-possible compromises.

The sweeping tide's epicenter is usually identified as Paris, but for *The Arts* as a whole that's over simplistic. Both Vienna and Berlin were robust fellow-contenders, especially Vienna in painting and music. The reigning atmosphere of revolt nonetheless had large scale repercussions in countries of less stabile social and political conditions. A passionate public Russian broadside of the times echoes a widespread attitude. [18]

> The academy is a moldy vault in which art is being flagellated. Gigantic wars, great inventions, conquest of the air, speed of travel, telephones, telegraphs, dreadnoughts re the realm of electricity . . . The new life of iron and the machine, the roar of motorcars, the brilliance of electric lights, the growling of propellers, have awakened the soul, which was suffocating in the catacombs of old reason and has emerged at the intersection of the paths of heaven and earth.

Germany's Weimar announced in 1919 that the Academy of Arts, along with the Academy of Building and the Prussian Provincial Art Commission, were to be dissolved. The goal: "Enlivenment of the museums as education establishments for the people." [19]

---

[18] "Cubism and Futurism to Suprematism: The New Painterly Realism," in *Russian Art of the Avant-Garde: Theory and Criticism, 1902-1934,* 87.

[19] Kandinsky: *Complete Writings on Art,* II, 488.

Wherever and whenever it all started, a notable aspect of the Revolution was the sharing of ideas and artifacts by its movers and shakers over a large part of the European landscape. Succinct evidence of arts interbreeding of the times is found in a review by Elliot Paul of George Antheil's *Ballet Mechanique* in an early edition of Eugene Jolas's *transition*. [20] For Paul it was the most important music composed since Stravinsky's *Le Sacre du Printemps* of 1914. Why? Because "Antheil works with the time-space inside his musical structure," and this reminds Paul of the way Picasso deals with visual objects. He then broadens his imaginative canvas by noting that "Surely it is more than an accident that painting and music should take this turn in the age that Einstein's theory of relativity was promulgated." And then Paul caps his observation by noting that writers James Joyce and Ezra Pound were both staunch supporters of Antheil's music.

So Music's 20th-Century revolution was a special time, a time when guiding figures struggled to create a new reality, in some way achieving what Gerald Heard called *Superconsciousness*, what Arnold Toynbee knew as *Etherialization*, what Pitirim Sorokin termed the *Ideational Culture*. All fit. But let us observe that the results were not always successful. Some guiding ideologies in all of the arts developed from a shaky basis. The more severe manifestations led to artifacts of negligible—if any—human relevance, yet they spawned ancillary critical and scholarly tracts that dwarfed the parent. Those instances of excess—those *MetaArts*—remain today as poignant reminders of Charles Fair's claim that "revolutions seldom realize their avowed aims." [21]

---

[20] *"Zukunstmusik,"* April, 1927, 148. Paul doesn't mention that Pound produced a pamphlet in 1927 entitled *Antheil and the Treatise on Harmony.* (See *transition, loc.cit,* 150.) Rumor suggests that it told little of Antheil's conception of harmony.
[21] *The New Nonsense,* 19.

Music's Path to Revolution

The three most prominent art genres shared motivations and veerings in their early 20th century struggles, and yet disparate features were prominent within the whole mix. Of the lot, music possesses the most complex remnants of 'revolution'. Virginia Woolf's Eureka! year of 1910 is an especially apt marker for music. [22]

Debussy had composed most of his "Impressionism;" compatriot Ravel was a youthful 35 and in the midst of his new opera, *L'Heure espagnol*; Italian Ferruccio Busoni was touring his own jolting NewAge piano sounds throughout Europe and America. Russia at the time was resonating to ethereal sounds from Alexander Scriabin and Nicolai Rozlavetz, while sophisticated down-home Americana flowed from the Charles Ives pipe organ in Connecticut. All of them were exploring sonic worlds that vaulted the Bach-Beethoven-Brahms-Wagner frontiers. As if to officially cap off an era, two notable holdovers from the past would soon die: Austrian Gustav Mahler in 1911, German Max Reger in 1916.

By the century's second decade nobody in touch with art music could avoid a single powerful conclusion: for those of the creative edge, the past was more revered than imitated. That yearning for self-consciousness in music dictated that "I, Composer X, must create music unmistakably different from (and newer than) that of Composer Y." Arnold Schoenberg expressed a majority sentiment of his contemporaries when he confessed that this inner drive for renovation had led him "...to examine the up-to-dateness and up-to-futureness of their [other young composers] and my creations." [23]

Widely celebrated as the most abstract of the arts, the art most directly entwined with the emotions, music would seem readymade for the role of ascendancy, the art destined to express philosopher Ludwig Wittgenstein's

---

[22] Allen Forte opts for 1908 as the marker in music, Schoenberg's *George Lieder*, op. 15 his proof of "profound change." I find Op. 9, the *Kammersymphonie* of 1906 as apt for signs of extreme departure from tradition, *Opus 11* perhaps even more fitting.

[23] *Style and Idea*, 92.

proposition at the end of his *Tractatus*: things of real value are things that can't be *gesagt* [said], but only *gezeigt* [demonstrated]. [24] The more embarrassing excesses of late German Romanticism specially primed music for serious attention to a few basic issues. Style became a major issue, a conscious motivator for change. Long-established structural expectations like periodic melodic phrases—even melody itself—pat musical forms, uniform meters, and the tension-release auras of consonance/dissonance were too reminiscent of a passé past. They fit only the expectations of the masses seated in the grandstands.

One choice of replacement was the extended sound montage, short motivic/harmonic perorations replacing the extended tunes of yesterday. Debussy was an early master, his *La Mer* of 1903-05 a decisive example. Richly furnished with fragmentary motifs in ravishing orchestral sounds, even those fragments are mostly derived from arpeggiations of chic "new" chords rather than from extended melodic thrusts. There is arguably one truly lyrical "tune' in the whole work, the fifth theme of the first movement. It is an aural signal for the sun's arrival overhead at noontime.

Example 1.2: "*De l'aube à midi sur la mer*" from Debussy's *La Mer*.

Similar evidence of this move away from *de rigeur* melody can be found in short motivic/harmonic perorations like those of Charles Ives' *The Unanswered Question* of 1908,[25] while severely a-melodic conditions dominate Scriabin's richly chromatic *Poème D'Extase* of the same year. They also reign in such

---

[24] Leaving one to wonder—if true—why any painter, composer, or writer (including Wittgenstein) would bother to say anything.

[25] Ives (1874-1954) was one of the most experimental composers of his time; there were few new mixes he didn't try. Except for so-called *bitonality*, most of them, including quarter-tone tunings, and simultaneous multi-metric schema, didn't become stock-in-trade.

sound-for-sound's-sake creations as those by Edgar Varese after 1914, works such as *Arcana* and *Ionization* (the latter scored for an ensemble of sirens and percussion).

It was not a one-track race. Some composers were less radical in their approach, supplanting déclassé properties of tradition simply by retreading them, often in blatant ways, at other times reflecting a "folk" basis. Crunching loudnesses and piquant dissonances, aping the world of machines, as in George Antheil's *Ballet Méchanique*, could herald the sassiness of a chic new milieu. Yet another path sought a difference by borrowing from other cultures, even the jazz sounds of Black America. Ernst Krenek's pre-serialist claim to fame, *Jonny spielt auf*, was a classic of the genre; George Gershwin's whole concert oeuvre, piano preludes to *Porgy and Bess*, flourished as a style hewn from borrowed sounds of an "alien culture."

The discovery of musics in remote lands, Thailand, Bali, India, and China, offered even more exotic sources, leading to some wild shots at a kind of East-West sonic bonding. Painter Picasso found Iberian arts provocative; writer Ezra Pound reveled in ancient Chinese poetry and culture. Composers were similarly seduced by the strange sounds of far away places: Hungarians Béla Bartók and Zoltan Kodály collected folk musics from a broad spectrum of cultures, Bulgarian, Moroccan, and Rumanian as well as Hungarian. Both published their ethnographies, as well as incorporated tunes and stylistic idiosyncrasies in their own concert works.

Again, Debussy was a revered guide. He had succumbed to the enchanting sounds of Javanese music at the Paris Exposition in 1889; by 1893 a rare kind of historicism (for the time) entered his sound world, the Phrygian mode coloring the first theme of his *String Quartet*. Several other works, like the *Pagodes* and *Soirée dans Grenada* from *Estampes* (1903) and *Images* (1905), echoed sounds from remote lands and cultures. The specter of something even more remote, medieval organum, stamps his prelude *La Cathedrale engloutie* of 1910. His lead was followed; [26] similar tonal ingredients harking of the past would later play a vital role in coloring folk-inspired works by compatriot Ravel,[27] Italian Ottorino Respighi, and Englishman Ralph Vaughan-Williams.

The yen for a detectable difference led several adventuresome composers to mystical ideologies. Russian composer Scriabin, like several painters of his time, merged into just such an exotic world, yielding a tinge to his sounds that reflect anything but a Russian basis. [28] His music sported harmonies that bypassed distinctions of consonance/dissonance, jumping the gun on the kind of 12-note chromaticism that later would make Arnold Schoenberg famous. His *Seventh Sonata* (1913) is probably the first music on record bearing evidence of pitches organized via serial strategies. [29]

Scriabin's saturated pitch palette was a hit commodity of the time; much of the probing new music produced early in the 20th century was woven from as many of the twelve notes as could be crammed into a texture. This trend toward greater pitch diversity would become music's most celebrated release from bondage, replacing the antiquated tonal perspective provided—as the cliché went—by the 7-note major and minor scales and shadings of consonance/dissonance. At last, the 12-tones of the chromatic scale could be freed, marking an evolved revolution: from 5 to 7 to 12!

And the Revolution Goes On, and On, and . . .

Let us recall that those volunteers in the *avant guerre*, were not seeking just a shift of style: they were *liberating* their art from shackles of the past. In 1907 Busoni wondered aloud how music might "be restored to its primitive natural

---

[26] For Schoenberg this sort of pitch exploration was proof that "tonality was already dethroned." *Style and Idea*, 104.

[27] As one simple and direct example, No. 3 of Ravel's *Mother Goose Suite*, "Empress of the Pagodas," draws from its four-hand piano setting both timbres and pitch structures alien to West-European norms.

[28] Stravinksy asks, ". . .frankly, is it possible to connect a musician like Scriabin with any tradition whatsoever?" (*Poetics of Music*, 98.)

[29] I find no record of Schoenberg even mentioning him or his music.

essence . . . how it can be freed . . . from architectonic, acoustic, and esthetic dogmas. . . to be pure invention and sentiment." [30] True, he was carried away with the passion of the times, yet composer Mel Powell would echo the same sentiment some eighty years later upon receiving Music's 1990 Pulitzer Prize: "I subscribe to atonality because it's egalitarian. It cancels hierarchy and creates anarchy, the ideal musical state." [31]

Powell's words reflect the naïve mix of Marxian idealism with Freudian fancy that had soared in the consciousness-expansionist age of the 1960s, when devotees of such gurus as Joseph Hart, Aldous Huxley, and Timothy Leary sought ways to escape the "prosaic games" of Western culture. [32] It was the era during which *MetaMusic* began to establish its hold in academe. As Roger Kimball has observed of those times, America's social revolution touted a "demand for absolute freedom together with the promise of absolute ecstasy." [33] It was nothing new for the Arts. Russian painter Kandinsky's repeated mantra from 1912 bore the same message: "There is no 'must' in art, which is forever free." [34] It was a sentiment that would have brought tears of joy to Rousseau's eyes.

With freedom as its conscious goal, it is ironic that a systemic approach to creativity might be chosen to achieve it: Serialism. It's a path that poses an irony: a complex system is developed to free the captive. Much of that system's fascination lies in the riches it was claimed to offer, and by 1910 one composer was ready to begin the delivery.

Most historians agree that Arnold Schoenberg (1874-1951) was the heaviest ideological force in art music from early-to late-20th century. For many, his ideas would qualify as the pre-ordained direction taken by that evolutionary

---

[30] In "Sketches of a New Aesthetic of Music" (*Entwurf einer neun Äesthetik der Tonkunst*. Trieste, 1907).
[31] *Los Angeles Times*, 14 April, 1990, F5.
[32] See Joyce Milton, *The Road to Malpsychia*, p. 87.
[33] *The Long March*, 173.
[34] "The Spiritual in Art," *Complete Writings on Art*, Vol. I, 169-170.

condition that gave credence to a true "Revolution." [35] It's hard to disagree with Carl Dahlhaus's ruling that even his move to atonality early in the century was "the decisive event in the music of the first half of this century . . ." [36] It represented a recasting of some central musical properties and it laid the foundation for the most elaborate attempts at music's overhaul known. His ideas had profound ideological effect on other artists as well, especially on Russian painter Wassily Kandinsky. But his long-term legacy was musical.

Schoenberg's gifts have enjoyed some of the most florid praise known by any modern musician. That praise extends from claims that he was as much a creative reactionary as progressive [37] to claims that he was the singular creator of modernism in music. British musicologist Anthony Payne's paean of 1968 is one of the most glowing appraisals of his creative and theoretical bequests. Payne's judgment meshes with that of Dahlhaus: Schoenberg *was* the new direction for music. His biography (*Schoenberg*) is dedicated to extolling "the extraordinary ways and means by which he renewed musical language and feeling at the beginning of this century." [38]

Payne's praise was far from unique. It is echoed with undiminished admiration four decades later in Ethan Haimo's thorough examination of the early period of change between 1899 and 1909, *Schoenberg's Transformation of Musical Language*. It is continued with undiminished ardor in Allen Shaw's *Arnold Schoenberg's Journey* of 2002

Schoenberg was anything but averse to the mission of leading his art into a new promised land. Nor was his influence narrow. By the 1920s he had supplied music's remake with something special, the *pièce de résistance* no other art could boast. Here was a formulaic method, a definable "system" rather than lofty generalizations and passionate manifestos. He was fiercely motivated. At times

---

[35] Schoenberg rejected the term *Revolutionary*; Debussy had rejected the term *Impressionism*—for equally specious reasons.

[36] *Schoenberg and The New Music*, 8

[37] Such as J. Peter Burkholder's "Schoenberg the Reactionary."

[38] *Schoenberg*, 9.

his actions suggest a sense of cosmic purpose, of extra-terrestrial guidance. A recurrent thread prevails within his lifelong comments: cosmic controls are out there. They are available to the creatively blessed.

Indeed, his perspective harks of Friedrich Schelling's convictions of a spiritual world in which the truly proper life is directed toward an existence of sublime perfection. [39] Even the dramatic use in his 2nd *String Quartet* [40] of Stefan George's phrase "*Ich fühle Luft von andern Planeten*" ("I feel air from other planets") fits with more direct hints that he felt specially anointed. [41] It's an image consistent with a comment made by his long-time friend Walter Rubsamen that "his credence in numerology belies the character of a man who seems in many ways to have been a reincarnation of the Gothic philosopher speculating about mathematics, astronomy, and the music of the spheres." [42]

There were more earthly influences as well. He was a musician of his time, and Wagner was the most luminous recent figure of that world, the most popular prophet. In Schoenberg's mind it was he who had affected a change in the very "logic and constructive power of harmony." He had made evident the crumbling state of tonality, then Debussy's moods and pictures of Impressionism had thoroughly "dethroned" it. [43] Payne's biography finds a wealth of credible Wagnerian inheritance for Schoenberg, especially in *Tristan* and *Parsifal*, "where lines leapt and twisted in response to the anguish of the dramatic situation, frequently avoiding contact with the notes of the underlying harmony in an additional bid of acute expressive tension." [44]

Schoenberg also was impressed by non-musical trends of his times, like the angst for ornamentation Viennese friend Adolf Loos developed into a trademark.

---

[39] With Hegel, Schelling (1775-1854) was one of the most influential writers of his century.

[40] Last movement.

[41] From George's poem *Entrückung* in the collection *Der Siebente Ring*. Kandinsky heard the Quartet in Munich in 1910, overwhelmed by what he inferred to be its message.

[42] Quoted in Ashton, *Op. Cit.*, 101.

[43] *Style and Idea*, 104.

[44] Payne, *Loc. cit.*, 10.

Architect Loos's struggle sought innate aesthetic controls, which he considered to be endemic to all the arts. [45] They fostered conditions of art the formidable Mdme. de Stael had tagged in earlier days with lofty terms like *désintéressement absolu*, and *esthétique transcendentale*. Active as Schoenberg was as a composer, he nonetheless was a recognized intellectual figure within his culture, joining with Alexander Zemlinsky to organize Vienna's *Vereinigung schaffender Tonkünstler* (United Composers). His role as a mover and shaker in the city's cultural affairs was feted in 1924 by an observance of his fiftieth birthday, the Mayor presiding.

Self-taught, he was a composer of proven genius prior to our fence of 1910. A stream of exceptional works flowed from his imagination, beginning in 1897 with his first *String Quartet*. The stream included his capping work of that era—probably the best known of his compositions—*Verklärte Nacht* (1899). Despite a corrosive Viennese anti-Semitism, his music was well received, confirming him as a composer of exceptional merit. By 1901 he had completed most of his massive *Gurre-Lieder*, its monumentality alone proof that this young man was more than a journeyman craftsman.

Schoenberg's success was assured. He nonetheless showed signs of champing hard on the old bit of tradition as early as the *Kammersymphonie* of 1908. His *String Quartet No. 2* of that year abuts atonal with tonal passages in a unique stylistic mix. And thus began an early search for ways to preserve music's aural sense yet replace the time-worn ways tones had been mixed to project it. Pitch context, known as *tonality* or *key*, became his prime target. By 1909 he was on the threshold of a personal epiphany. In a letter to fellow musician Busoni he asserts nothing less than a will to escape music's past.

> I strive for complete liberation from all forms from all symbols of cohesion and of logic. . . away with 'motivic working out'. Away with harmony as cement in bricks of a building. [46]

---

[45] Loos made a distinction: products of the Fine Arts were answerable to none; those of architecture to everyone.

[46] *Ferrucio Busoni: Selected Letters*, 389-390.

It seemed a credible story, especially when given a trendy evolutionary twist, but its implicit position depends upon a questionable premise. That premise ran something like this: In a past era a "new condition" had evolved from the modes of medieval cathedrals, the *Dorians* and *Phrygians* of ecclesiastical rite. That condition slowly hardened into the major/minor keys of Handel-to-Brahms. It then began losing ground with the advent of composers' portrayal of emotional states—especially of the Wagnerian kind—rather than the fleshing-out of pre-established forms like sonata and rondo, minuet and trio. The bricks of the music building were changing drastically, century-by-century!

Schoenberg was captivated by music-theoretic intricacies, by arguments of esthetic value. [47] His conceptualization of music's properties derived from revered music theorists of earlier times, such as Simon Sechter, or via some of his contemporaries. [48] For the most part they were thinkers who had encased their structural descriptions within the major/minor, consonant/dissonant mix that ruled their times. As we now realize, those conceptualizations were crampingly narrow.

Theorists who formulated them knew little or nothing about music before 1700 or music from other than the central European cultures they inhabited. Their explanations lacked the reductionist simplicity of truly scientific theorizing. They nonetheless provided the bedrock of Schoenberg's ideas. And since in Schoenberg's opinion the conditions of music's pitch organization were mostly a product of *Art* rather than of *Nature*, it was his artistic duty to remove them as expectancies from the musical fabric. Like many others of the times, he was impressed by Hegelian propaganda, how history is set on an inescapable path that leads only forward, a path that only the most prepared can discover. For him that path's direction for music was obvious, and he was prepared to lead the way.

---

[47] "Aesthetic Values" were a big thing in turn-of-the-century Vienna. See Janik and Toulmin *Op. Cit.*, 44.

[48] Such as Alois Haba, Heinrich Schenker, and Hugo Riemann. Despite his reliance on some of Riemann's ideas, he publicly stated his distaste for them, and Riemann returned the favor. See David Bernstein, "Schoenberg contra Riemann" for a thorough discussion of their theoretical spats.

Chapter 2

MUSIC'S EPIPHANY:
"THE MOST ABSTRACT OF THE ARTS"

Schoenberg's perspective on music's past centered upon the condition of pitch centricity—whether one calls it *tonality* or *key*, *pitch vectoring* or *auditory perspective*. In his judgment it hadn't existed before 1701. Before then, modal music prevailed. And thus his concentration on a newly-minted condition for twelve notes represented yet a later and *improved* human capability. He alluded to it with references like "As the ear advanced . . . ," [1] on to his conclusive pronouncement that "tonality has been revealed as no postulate of natural conditions. . . it is a product of art."[2] And this is a significant conception, for it denies the pitch structuring of the Mozart-Brahms era as a part of the "natural" human condition.

This "art as cause" colors some heavy thinking in the art world today, a basis for the cliché that no "human nature" exists, that all change—indeed all meaning—is derived from social dynamics. Its corollary postulate, "advancement of the ear," was an early addendum to music's NewAge canon. Pianist-composer Busoni wholly endorsed it. In his 1907 *Sketch for a New Aesthetics of Music* he averred that "Only a long and careful series of experiments and a continued training of the ear will render the unfamiliar material approachable and plastic for the coming generations and for art." [3] As we shall note in later discussions, it was

---

[1] *Style and Idea*, 277.
[2] *Ibid.*, 284.
[3] We might think of that state as *Sonic Expansionism*.

an idea that would color the perspective of many converts to early atonality and Serialism, a principal issue of the new art of *MetaMusic*.

Ears ready or not, by 1908 Schoenberg had set out to add that third condition to music history's modal-to-tonal chronology, whether it is to be called *atonal*, *pantonal*, *neotonal*, *post-tonal*, or *tonally ambivalent*. Music historian Bryan Simms traces this early development, noting that Schoenberg's atonal music [4]— and Simms prefers that term—was motivated by much the same angst felt by other artists of the times. But his music at that time gradually "lost its spontaneous and emotional character, and it came to rely on methodic controls in the fashioning of its materials...." [5]

Virgil Thomson's observation that Schoenberg's music "on the inside was just good old Vienna," [6] suggests that he basically was just tending the same old kitchen with slightly different recipes. But Thomson's pithy pronouncement is misleading for most works composed after 1910, even though some, like the Op. 42 *Piano Concerto*, echo a kind of old-world Brahmsian romanticism. Schoenberg was fixed on nothing less than remaking the way one goes about composing, and thus, necessarily, how one must perceive it. In an essay of 1931 he proudly credits himself with "having written truly new music which, being based on tradition, is destined to become tradition." [7] Most important for our story, Schoenberg's itch would make the world of music scratch.

American composer George Perle later caught the same "release from bondage" spirit in a mid-century resonation of Schoenberg's role. "Atonality originates," he observes, "in an attempt to liberate the twelve notes of the chromatic scale from the diatonic functional associations they still retain in

---

[4] Some academics decided after 1950 that the term *atonal* was too severe for such music, opting instead for *non-tonal*, even though the latter is like replacing the word *fat* with *non-slender*. Schoenberg himself refused the term *atonal*, sidestepping the accepted meaning of *tonal* ("possessing tonality"): His music consisted of *tones*, so in his judgment it could not properly be called *atonal* (*Style and Idea*, 263). See the further discussion of *atonal* in Chapter 7.

[5] Simms, *The Atonal Music of Schoenberg*, 3.

[6] *American Music Since 1910*, 71.

[7] *Style and Idea*, 174.

'chromatic' music'." [8] This iconic claim was firmly embedded in Schoenberg's beloved phrase "The Emancipation of Dissonance." Or as Pierre Boulez would put it, "the series dilutes the opposition between horizontal and vertical, just as it creates a universe where consonance and dissonance are abolished." [9] Music must caste off the shackles imposed by the value-relatives of *Consonant* and *Dissonant*.

The Dodecaphonic Detour

By 1923, in piano pieces Opus 23 and Opus 24, Schoenberg had developed his ideological yen into a full blown theory. He opted for the word *method* rather than *system*. His approach was straightforward. Music's irreducible sonic bits, he argued, are most readily and fully represented as a collection of twelve different notes. [10] Like adding to the primary colors of painting, music's basic hues have been increased. Hereafter, the well known chromatic scale must *as a totality* provide the raw basis for human ears. [11] This dodecaphonic (or *12-tone*) method would replace the "free atonality" of works he had composed between 1908 and 1923. In Allen Shawn's description, this prefabrication of pitch content had a specific and perceivable function. It was

> a method for establishing the tonal (tonal meaning "tones") world of a specific piece out of the twelve notes of the chromatic scale. Once it is established, one must then create a piece of music in this tonal world.

With many others (including Schoenberg), Shawn further attributes functional conditions to a row, in that "the ear would hear any other version of the same

---

[8] Perle, *Serial Composition and Atonality*, 1.

[9] *Boulez on Music Today*, 132.

[10] Or more precisely, twelve *pitch-classes*.

[11] Each of the twelve is duplicable at other pitch levels (*octaves*). In practical terms, music's pitch gamut extends from the contrabass fiddle's (extended) lowest C (around 33 cycles per second) to the piccolo's highest c (around 2112 cps). Electronic synthesizers readily increase that range.

succession of the intervals created by these tones as belonging to the same tonal family." [12]

Within the next half-century the 12-tone method would become the talk of sophisticated musicians everywhere, the cutting edge of musical theorizing.

Schoenberg was above all else an original, a creative thinker, but he wasn't the only proponent of such a compositional approach. Fellow Austrian Joseph Matthias Hauer (1883-1959) devised a similar method around the same time,[13] but Schoenberg's intellectual fire and superior compositional talents cemented his claim to the invention. Like the great Renaissance proponent of Harmony of the Spheres Johannes Kepler, he enjoyed proving everything he believed and he believed everything he proved. For his more fervent disciples, his system meant gravitating "from a mere compositional technique to a new law."[14]

Readers already familiar with the dodecaphonic approach might well skim through the next few pages. For those unfamiliar with it, a brief exposition can be helpful. It is in essence quite simple, although its full fleshing out can become monumentally complex. As we'll observe in detail later, its explication and application has busied some musicians well beyond anything its inventor might have foreseen.

Although the twelve available notes form the raw basis, Schoenberg was fully aware that soundings of nothing but up and down chromatic scales would fall short of aesthetic delight. [15] His overhaul fixed all the twelve into a matrix, a *Row* (or *Ordered Set* or *Series*) in ways unlikely to project any one note as more important, ways that might suggest a sense of pitch hierarchy. This set of 12 provides a raw note-jig for composing. And thus the chromatic scale can be reordered [16] into something like that shown below. Remember that each note

---

[12] Quotes are from *Arnold Schoenberg's Journey*, 198-199.

[13] *Zwölftontechnik, die Lehre von den Tropen*, 1926, was Hauer's most notable contribution.

[14] Payne, *Op. cit.*, 40.

[15] It works, of course, for Don Giovanni's descent into hell, creating a sense of fluid-like fluctuation.

[16] The available permutations of the 12-note set = 12^{12}, or 479,001,600.

represents all other notes of the same *pitch-class*: note *B* represents any *B*, high or low; note *F*-sharp represents any *F*-sharp (or *G*-flat).

Example2.1: Chromatic scale and derived row

Scale   **Row**

They're all there, and such an ordering wards off suspicion that any single note is more important than another, a condition of denial that is elemental for the method. As Schoenberg tells it, his

> method of composing with twelve tones substitutes for the order produced by permanent references to tonal centres an order according to which, every unit of a piece being a derivative of the tonal relations in a basic set of twelve tones, *the 'Grundgestalt', is coherent because of the permanent reference to the basic set.*[17]

This basal claim of *coherence* as a product of the set looms large in our later discussions. It is repeated in another essay when Schoenberg explains that "Composition with twelve tones has no other aim than comprehensibility."[18] So the row imposed a pre-packaged democracy, 12-note set replacing the despotic 7-note sets of the major/minor scale tradition.[19] But although a pitch "democracy," the row is fabricated in a way (or so-claimed) to project its own unique pitch context as a perceptual condition.

The alleged *Grundgestalt* condition, as a source of structural power, has played a key role—although usually implicit—in the serialist canon over the years. One of Serialism's most venerated exponents, Pierre Boulez, added his

---

[17] "My Evolution," *Style and Idea*, 91. The italics are mine, for future reference.

[18] *Style and Idea*, "Composition with Twelve Tones," 215.

[19] Remember Schoenberg's conviction that major and minor scales were *causes*, not *results*, of tonality. As we shall note presently, this was an unfortunate conception.

emphatic confirmation in discussing how a row must be ordered to achieve desired results:[20]

> The internal structure of a series is crucial in the development of its organizational potential; consequently it should not be left to chance; on the contrary, it is necessary to foresee the precise direction in which these powers are to be deployed.

Schoenberg's initial chore in composing *Klavierstücke Opus 33a* (1929) was mapping out a note recipe. Its ordering is paramount.[21] There are no joinings of pitches underived in some orderly way from that initial mapping.

Example 2.2: Row Derivatives from Row of Ex. 2.1

Transpositions (or T)

(Inversions (or I)

Retrogrades (or R)

Retrograde-inversions (or RI)

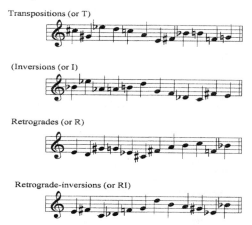

Opus 33a begins with the chords shown next. Note how they are culled from the primal and retrograded transposition matrices.[22]

---

[20] *Boulez on Music Today*, 70.

[21] Schoenberg never fully explained the *Grundgestalt*, but he was certain the row performed a central role in achieving it. Josef Rufer struggled faithfully to clarify the concept in his *Composition With Twelve Notes* (p. 18 ff), and his translator (Humphrey Searle) even tried valiantly to sharpen the edges further. Perhaps it is best classified under the old Wittgensteinian *Ungesagen*!

Example 2.3: Opening, Schoenberg's *Opus 33a*

2.3 continued

And thus the entire pitch structure of *Opus 33a* is derived from the single series, a veritable jigsaw of pitch coagulations. The work reveals how a 12-tone DNA can be transformed into unique musical offspring, every moment's pitch content derived from a pre-determined order. [23] And don't forget a fundamental assumption of it all: an inherent unity is manifest in the ordering, the alleged *Grundgestalt* providing "comprehensibility." It's a unity that prevails, regardless of reorderings such as *I* or *R* or *RI* applied to it. It's hard to avoid drawing parallels between this notion of a pitch organicism and 17th/18th-century images of organic structure, of prototypes generating transformed relatives, when a cell develops and then every developmental phase gives birth to a variation of the

---

[22] Nachum Schoffman has argued with good cause that the work's "series" resides in these chords rather than in a linear succession—a *row*. ("Schoenberg Opus 33a Revisited," 40.

[23] Loudness, texture, rhythm, timbre--remain as potential shaping agents. Several mid-20th century composers (Boulez, Babbitt, *et al.*) serialized time, texture, and loudness, achieving what was triumphantly hailed as *total serialism*. These works represent more historical toys today, yet as our final chapter chronicles, some current pre-compositional recipes are similar to their creative procedures.

prototype, producing a new version of a universal plan. Every new level gives birth to yet a successive level. [24]

And herein resides one of the thorniest questions leftover from music's revolution via the 12-tone set: Can such a collection, in and of itself, actually engender a sonic context, one that serves the grounding function claimed for it? Or was that just hopeful speculation, a case of aims justifying means? Despite Schoenberg's assurance that pitch comprehensibility is the product, the question of a row's fertility to engender it remains unknown. It has been framed obliquely by musicologist Rose Subtotnik when she asks if other musical elements "are able to engender musical intelligibility in the same autonomous—that is, intra structural—and general sense as classical tonality seems able to do it." [25] Leonard B. Meyer voiced similar skepticism almost a half-century ago, a time when Serialism was enjoying its ascendancy in the United States. His doubts raised few other voices. He concluded that permutations of a series, the Is and Rs and RIs, "cannot be perceived as variants of a model given earlier, particularly of a model in the pitch domain, but only as new events in themselves."[26]

Among others, Leonard Bernstein was one who resisted history's temptation to adopt serial procedures in composing his own music. He avoided condemning the method or even the results, as a whole, but he expressed grave reservations about it as an approach to creating a sound world.

> The trouble is that the new musical "rules of Schoenberg are not apparently based on innate awareness, on the intuition of tonal relationships. They are like rules of an artificial language, and therefore must be learned. . . form at the expense of content—structuralism.[27]

In the meantime, several decades of empirical studies of music perception have ensued. As we shall note in detail in Chapter 6, that central claim of a row's

---

[24] As in Jean Baptsiste Robinet's ancient classic *De La Nature.*

[25] *Developing Variations,* 196.

[26] *Music, the Arts and Ideas,* 284. Those powers are even more remote in music of total serialism.

[27] *The Unanswered Question,* 285.

power to induce coherence remains an alluring idea, but it is built on an unconfirmed teleology. For this reason we may be forced to understand a row as a source for pitch unity only in Wittgenstein's sense of the unsayable. And then, of course, a remaining potential conclusion is that the claim is in fact baseless. Whatever may be the eventual answer, no other medium of our art world endured a similar systemic overall as that known to music.

Meaningful parallels are easily drawn between Schoenberg and his Viennese colleague Freud, as trail blazers in their respective domains. In fact, the composer readily comes to mind in reading Morton Hunt's conclusions regarding the psychologist's long-term mark on history.

> After all the assaults on his character, the philosophic arguments
> about his theories, and the laborious efforts to validate or
> invalidate them, the measure of the man and his ideas is their
> impact on the history of psychology and on Western civilization.[28]

Like Freud, Schoenberg raised the curtain to an enormous stage, leading to dramatic rethinkings of music and the mixing of its elements. In this sense, as composer/theorist he opened up vast areas of the musical unconscious that had long awaited recognition and objective evaluations on their own.

The Music, the System, the Tell of Time

Schoenberg's method turned out to be a "most persuasive theory." But an irony hid behind the scenes: his serial *method* rather than his serial *music* lit a more enduring fire in the 20th century music world. American composer John Adams summed up the condition in 1989. As he put it, the music world's expectations that Schoenberg's orchestral works would become standards in the repertoire

---

[28] *The Story of Psychology*, 205

never came to pass. It was his judgment that Schoenberg's music "will permanently be avant-garde works, always difficult to approach." [29]

Here was something really new, a planned approach to the creative act, an "objective" path to the sublime that had been so coveted. Unique within the arts, it nonetheless bore at least one kinship with others of the times: Schoenberg's theorizing—perhaps at the expense of his musical output—reflected the heightened self-consciousness of technique that marked that era, the early days of *MetaMusic*. In that sense it was thoroughly "modern."

His *Suite for Piano*, Op. 25, was the maiden voyage into 12-tone composition, [30] to be followed just five years later by *Op. 33a*. Within a decade his music and his method had become highly marketable coinage. Noteworthy converts were his star Austrian pupils Alban Berg and Anton Webern. Before mid-century, international ranks included England's Humphrey Searle, Italy's Luigi Dallapiccola, France's René Leibowitz. His move to the United States in 1934 further confirmed an international image. His students and his disciples were an informal yet devoted coalition, and they were a force regarded by many as the anointed source for music's evolution. The 12-tone method was prime ticket to the main show, the catholicon for music's future.

A major feature of that show was the row's utility for modeling pitch content, and in this sense it was a handy addition to the creative toolbox. That it negated pitch as a purveyor of unity—unless it really could project that *Grundgestalt* function touted for it—was its most troubling point of contention. If it lacked such contextualizing potency, all music so-composed must depend exclusively on other musical properties such as timbre, rhythm, contour, loudness, and texture for its shaping. Except for simple differentiations of higher and lower, louder and softer, pitch would be a no-show in that game. And that's easier to regard as a loss than as a gain.

---

[29] In an interview with Greg Warner, *Los Angeles Times*, February 14, 1989.

[30] All of this composition was 12-tone, unlike the single movement in the *Serenade* of 1923. Curiously, Schoenberg's method was first publicly explained in 1924 by pupil Erwin Stein. ("*Neu Formprinzipien*," September issue of the *Musikblatter des Anbruch*.)

This new found joy in the method didn't fully eclipse testimonials for the music. Some products of Schoenberg's pen were recognized as gems by several of the world's star performers. Ironically, they usually bore innuendoes of shortcomings along with admiration. Typical is a tribute to the 1942 *Piano Concerto*[31] by Alfred Brendel. The famed pianist admits that the work contains passages that suffer "occasional lack of focus," then opines with an air of regret that it "may never become fully domesticated." But, alas, in his judgment the *Concerto* as a whole justifies its problems. Further testimonials of support—usually limned with similar reservations—convey the presence of a hidden criterion: the performer's evaluation of a composition is in part colored by the sense of gratification felt in "having it under wraps," of having developed the manual skills required to perform it. [32]

Non-performer jurists of academe, however, are the most active in continuing support for these early departures from pitch mores. Historian Bryan Simms admits that even today "Schoenberg's atonal music remains as elusive as it ever has been, still among the most complex phenomena in the entire world of art." But then the Simms perspective seems to shift when he says that "the music endures . . . Schoenberg's atonal works continue to grasp and hold the musical imagination, speaking plainly to a state of human consciousness." [33] He does not help us reconcile the phrase *remains as elusive* with the nearby claim of *speaking plainly*; and therein resides one of the continuing contradictions—assuming the appropriateness of both claims—of this music's history. Nor do such assurances stack neatly with the indifference voiced by most listeners.

For even the most ardent fans, an aura of blood sweat and tears colors explanations of hearing Schoenberg's more adventurous serial and pre-serial atonal works. Claims of value made by true believers project the kind of challenge

---

[31] *New York Review of Books* XLII, Feb. 16, 1995, 27-29.

[32] A pianist friend of mine, champion of contemporary music Walter Robert, once told me that at first he very much disliked the Ernst Krenek *2nd Piano Sonata*. But once he "got it under his fingers," he "warmed up to it."

[33] Simms, *Op cit.*, 6.

of "work-harder-to-enjoy-more" implied by Simms. Anthony Payne's mid-20th century paean spoke of practical barriers of a kind that resonate with Wittgenstein's classic *Ungesagt*; his words of praise describe rather murky musical waters. In parts of Schoenberg's last five Orchestral Pieces, No. 3 of *Opus 11*, and the *Enthauptung* and *Mondfleck* songs of *Pierrot Lunaire*, he confesses that so much is going on that "part of the expressive idea would seem to be to provide a symbol of something impossible to perceive direct." [34]

Of course, Payne's intent is to praise Schoenberg's willingness and ability to create an "appropriate representation of an experience almost too bewildering for the human mind to encompass." Some of it was program music whose scenario celebrates what then was a newly-formulated Freudian world, like it or not, accept its accuracy or not. And perhaps in this sense Payne is right. Schoenberg knew how to do it, scenario or not.

Two decades after Payne's encomium, American composer Charles Wuorinen paints a testimonial to *Pierrot* with the same palette of gratifying toil. Great as the 80-year old work may be, he admits that "abruptions still make it difficult, even at this late date; listening to it occasionally reminds one of attempts to befriend a porcupine."[35] His brief synopsis of *Pierrot* even opens with a preemptive justification that portends of heavy listening: "The art of every age contains a few works that we all must confront." So for him the aesthetic justification for *Pierrot's* songs lies in their "inner strength, as well as the historical moment that they reflect." [36] In other words, this music possesses a unique kind of undefined structural power; and regardless, you *must* listen to it anyway, for it came at a pivotal time in music's history. In this Wuorinen echoes Carl Dahlhaus's argument [37] that a work's newness "as a historical event" is just as important as its directly perceived content. And thus historicity looms large as

---

[34] Payne, 33.

[35] *"Pierot Lunaire,"* Op. 21," in the notes for the CD *Arnold Schoenberg : Pierrot lunaire and The Book of the Hanging Garden.*

[36] "Interiority" and "inner strength" are terms fetishized by critics in the visual arts too.

[37] *Schoenberg and the New Music*, 12.

a determinant for aesthetic impact. We are reminded of Jed Perl's succinct putdown of a Jasper Johns exhibit mentioned earlier: "it was a hit because it satisfied an audience that believes aesthetic experience is a form of historical experience."[38]

The historicist criterion is not rare today. In evaluations of music, thorny auditory obstacles are regarded as secondary to an artifact's achievement of success in cultural history, particularly if it possesses some extrinsic degree of notoriety. Such a view dismisses the sonic essence of a work as principal criterion of value. Rheinhold Brinkmann lays out such a perspective in a discussion of Schoenberg's early (1909) *Kammersymphonie* (which happened to be one of Schoenberg's favorites, his "ewe lamb"). Recognizing the work's off-putting nature, he argues that its very constitution, its "compression," holds the secret to that condition.[39]

> It is this constitution that legitimizes the work's historical and aesthetic importance. The historical place of the work—a place it fills consciously— determines the difficulty of the encounter precisely because of the work's uncompromising embrace of the notion of difficulty itself, as defined by comprehensibility.

Quite an argument! As difficult to understand as it is to accept at face value. Others are even more colorful.[40]

Composer Charles Wuorinen adds greater objectivity to the regimen, instructing listeners that one's historically-sanctioned attentiveness to *Pierrot* must be directed toward "inner workings" of the whole, [41] the "moment-by-moment continuity, the shifting complex of pitch and rhythmic relations, the play of instrumental sonorities, the progress of the text." His guide is less *avant-garde*

---

[38] *Gallery Going*, 47

[39] "The Compressed Symphony," in Frisch, *Schoenberg and His World*, 141.

[40] Allen Shawn (*Arnold Schoenberg's Journey*, p. 59) argues that "the best way to get an intuitive grasp of Schoenberg's 1902-12 music is to view his paintings of that time.

[41] Notes to the CD *Pierot Lunaire* . . . Wuorinen doesn't explain how "internal" elements are distinguishable from what he later calls "external."

than he seems to think. In fact, it directs us toward those things we normally attend to in careful auditions of any music. We are never told precisely what in *Pierrot's* songs manages to pique our enlightened sense of sonic delight. Although this proposed work regimen is fraught with "many obstacles," they should be taken in stride for historical reasons: in this music Schoenberg is polishing off the replacement of tonality with his special "autonomous structural principle."

The picture painted by such approvals is gratuitously foreboding. Here is a composer seeking that new path to music's Promised Land: whatever may be the produce of his search, it is justified by the imposed creative struggle itself. And then listeners must follow suit by engaging in that struggle to fully appreciate the object and its role in history. It's a hardscrabble aesthetic, as strange as it is ironic. We shall encounter similar grueling guides for Art Appreciation in our brief encounter with painting and literature in Chapter 3. They confirm close *MetaArt* ties among the media. With a chuckle they recall a predictive scene in G.B. Shaw's biting satire *Caesar and Cleopatra*, when the Empress questions her court's reigning musician about learning to play the harp. Her principal issue: how long will it take? The maestro answers: "Only four years. Your majesty must first become proficient in the philosophy of Pythagoras."

Schoenberg was aware of the experiential mine fields he was laying, but he handily pre-confirmed the guidelines provided later by Payne and Wuorinen. He also bolstered his self defense by claiming that contemporaries are never final judges of an art's worth. And furthermore, although his music "seems to increase the listener's difficulties, it compensates for this deficiency by penalizing the composer." And then comes the justifying *coup-de grâce*: "Only the better-prepared composer can compose for the better-prepared music lover."[42] Let us not miss the built-in insurance this truism promises the listener: those who approve

---

[42] Schoenberg, "Composition with Twelve Tones," 245.

the music are assured of being the "better prepared music lovers." Even greater pressure not to admit disapproval!

Growing Signs of a Failed Revolution

High level blessings or not, endorsements by serious listeners and performers for serial music occurred less frequently as the years rolled by, especially for works composed after 1907. By century's end few concert-goers were yearning for "An Evening of Schoenberg," and "Classical Music" radio stations throughout the U.S. seem to disdain anything he composed after *Verklärte Nacht.*[43] One highly praised pre-dodecaphonic work, the monstrous *Gurre-Lieder* of 1901,[44] merits distinction as music's counterpart to Howard Hughes' renowned "Spruce Goose." It is heard only on those rare occasions when the required massive resources (soloists, mixed choir, expanded orchestra) are available and Handel's *Messiah* has been performed too recently.[45] This seems to counter the sermons of Brinkmann and Payne and Wuorinen; his music remains a relatively untapped reservoir of our history—despite its "fame." A blunt scene was painted by composer-critic David Schiff when he said that even eight decades after it was composed, "audiences still find Arnold Schoenberg's *Variations for Orchestra* a self-conscious magnum opus to be as charming as an industrial park. . ."[46]

Nor does his music go unheard alone. By the 1950s, doggedly serialized music by any composer was not grasping and holding the ears of an impressive segment of the listening public—not even in academe. Fewer than 15% of American composers today use a 12-tone approach in their composing, and those

---

[43] Let us note in passing, however, that such "classical" stations are seldom champions of *any* kind of music composed since 1900. One critic tagged them collectively as "The Baroque Ghetto."

[44] First performed in 1913.

[45] One ambitious proposal made back in the 1980s would have mounted a *Gurre-Lieder* performance in the Los Angeles Dodger Stadium. It didn't happen.

[46] David Schiff, *Sound Check* , 26.

who do shy away from its tighter strictures. Even the music by recognized masters suffers indifference when it is dominated by serial procedures.

Apologists for the music created via Serialism were quick to find the problem's seat in the "unprepared listener." One went so far as to suggest in mid-century that to appreciate serial music one must hear it with "a contrapuntal ear"[47]—whatever that might mean. And there was Milton Babbitt's serious recommendation back in 1960 to the effect that serial music demanded a different perceptual approach to be properly understood by listeners. In his words, "it imposes new demands of perception and conception upon the composer and listener." [48]

He no doubt was right. But such claims necessarily bring to mind those reviewed earlier about the advancement of our hearing talents, even the achievement of "natural essences" longed for by Busoni back in 1907. It is also reminiscent of the super-consciousness, via drugs or mystical trance, sought in the American social revolutions of the 1960s. Both of those perspectives hark back to an obsolete form of psychological Behaviorism of the John B. Watson variety, the blank slate version that produced such claims as: "Give me a dozen infants and my specified world to bring them up in and I'll guarantee to train them to become any type of specialist I might select . . ." [49]

True, Schoenberg was not the only forgotten composer of our history. Should we recall—for better perspective—the relative neglect of Bach's music until Mendelssohn reintroduced it to the masses in 1829, long after the master's death? Are these conditions of neglect for serial music further confirmation of Schoenberg's ruling that contemporaries are never the final judges of value? Are they but another example of lagging taste, unwashed masses immune to values known and revered by the elite? That could be a part of it. On the other hand, it's possible to find more probable causes in less ingenuous sources. We must observe

---

[47] Hans Keller, "The Audibility of Serial Technique, "*Monthly Musical Record* 85 (Nov 1955).

[48] "Twelve-Tone Invariants as Compositional Determinants," 55.

[49] In *Behaviorism* (revised ed.), 82.

that the concert world and the availability of music today are quite different from what existed in the 18th century's final decades, when Bach was as good as forgotten.

Whatever the ultimate cause, an aura of quiet neglect has developed over the years, a veiled yet unmistakable recognition that dodecaphonically-conceived music lacks a record of *musical* validity. This conclusion has been expressed by many reputable musicians from diverse segments of the music world. Once asked his opinion of Schoenberg, film composer Miklos Rosza described him as "the Alchemist of Music." For him the 12-tone approach was "a stillborn idea." He nonetheless admitted the method via a back door in the early 1960s when he turned to a row for portraying the Devil in his score for the film *King of Kings*. As he put it, the conditions he wished to portray were best achieved by the "spirit of negation" provided by that technique. [50]

The iconic Russian Stravinsky was even more pointed in a later reference to the pre-serial *Pierrot Lunaire*: "I do not feel the slightest enthusiasm about the aesthetics of the work, which appear to me to be retrogression to the out-of-date Beardsley cult." [51] Despite his unsympathetic regard for Schoenberg's music, Stravinsky nonetheless gave credence to and personalized the 12-tone system in his later years, in *Agon* of 1953-57, more thoroughly in *Threni* of 1957-58. Both works exist today more as historical mementoes than as admired music. As David Schiff has observed, despite its monumental nature, *Threni* "languishes unperformed and barely remembered."[52] Such music can be understood as late displays of a great composer showing he can keep up with the times.

Aaron Copland voiced his lack of enthusiasm with a bit more insight and breadth.[53] In his words, "One gains the impression that it is not the music before which the commentators are lost in admiration so much as the way in which it lends itself to detailed analysis." He shared Richard Franko Goldman's earlier

---

[50] Both quotes are from Rosza, *Double Life,* pp. 99 and 180.

[51] *An Autobigraphy*, 43. His allusion is to Aubrey Beardsley, 1872-1898.

[52] Schiff, *Loc. Cit.*

[53] *Music and Imagination*, 69.

fears of meta-criticism, that the flood of words surrounding serialism would "succeed in analyzing music out of existence."[54] Copland's main concern was the way a particular style seemed to be imposed by the system—"principles and theories of composition leading to complete aridity." He considered Schoenberg's *Wind Quintet* of 1924 to be "weird," an outstanding failure, although he admired *Moses und Aaron* and the late String Quartets.[55]

But as with Stravinsky, irony reigns supreme. Copland's diagnosis of systemic illness didn't preclude trying out the method in his own compositions. It shows up in limited doses as early as the *Poet's Song* of 1927, then evidences of full-scale serial procedures appear in scattered works as the years rolled on. By the time of his *Piano Quartet* of 1950 and the orchestral *Connotations* and *Inscapes* of the 60s, he had managed to incorporate rows in thorough ways. [56] Those serial intrusions did not fully negate his own inimitable sound, but they produced works that are far cries from trademark successes like *Rodeo*, the *Clarinet Sonata*, and *Appalachian Spring*.

American composer George Rochberg was a thoughtful musician, a seasoned professional, a gifted composer. Like many budding American talents of the 1940s, he converted to Schoenberg's way of doing things. He did, that is, until his dramatic apostasy not long after mid-century. [57] His summing up of serialist shortcomings, as carriers of auditory fulfillment, is compelling.[58] In his judgment the approach's fatal flaw stems from excessive systemic rigor, at the expense of what can be heard as coherent musical content. In Rochberg's mind adherence to the system leads to an absence of perceptual bunchings. Even when the greatest of rhythmic coherence is assured, sound-bits don't coagulate into meaningful contexts. He likens Schoenberg and his musical role to that of Hermann Hesse's

---

[54] *The Musical Quarterly*, April 1960, XLVI No. 2, 262-64.

[55] Both quotes from Pollack, *Aaron Copland*, 65.

[56] Both orchestral works are the least celebrated of the Copland oeuvre.

[57] Rochberg said he felt unable to communicate his feelings musically in the 12-tone system after the tragic death of his son in 1964.

[58] "Reflections on Schoenberg," *Perspectives of New Music* 11 (1973), 56-83.

fictional character Harry Heller, who also was "caught between two ages." He was "a kind of Steppenwolf," unable to fully relate to the traditions from which he came, compelled to leave behind whatever security those traditions offered—yet always longing for them.

As for stylistic ramifications of the dodecaphonic approach, turncoat Rochberg concluded that it rendered for music a "decreasing profile of identity" compared with earlier music, including Schoenberg's. The 12-tone works were reduced

> to a music entirely lacking in any aurally meaningful, identifiable characteristics. In short, from a music that can be remembered, to a music which can be remembered but with varying degrees of difficulty, and finally to a music which utterly (or almost) defies memory.[59]

Rochberg was responding to the same inherent danger voiced earlier by Copland, the hazards of any "system" doggedly imposed upon the creative process.

Isolated segments of the music establishment reacted with predictable wrath to Rochberg's apostasy. In an interview of 2001 he revealed that he "was accused of betraying in the following order, the church and the state. I was a traitor, a renegade."[60] But the bigger picture reveals that American composers from George Gershwin, Walter Piston, Leonard Bernstein and William Schuman, to Carlisle Floyd, John Adams, and John Corigliano wholly ignored the presumed "challenges" of a postulated musical evolution. They didn't buy the idea that the 20th century's pitch world need be radically different from what it was in Josquin's time. Their music has enjoyed a healthy life; it seems destined to last.

All such negative observations of the serial scene have not been so kind. Indeed, the atonal cat was most publicly let out of the bag in the United States over a decade ago by music critic Donald Henahan. In a brief essay that pulls no punches,[61] he begins with the observation that

---

[59] In an interview, *Philadelphia Inquirer*, 2001, quoted from *The Los Angeles Times*, June 1, 2005, page B10.
[60] *Ibid.*
[61] *New York Times*, Sunday, January 6, 1991.

If we look back over 20th Century music, which we are now in a position to do, one fact stands out: severely atonal composition, once regarded as the wave of the future, is leaving remarkably few ripples.

And then, with passing reference to Schoenberg's *Violin Concerto* (1936), Henahan adds that "Purely instrumental works can leave a reasonably experienced listener to modern music untouched and shamefully eager for intermission."[62]

A similar air of discontent surfaces in a painful tale with an ironic twist. It is in Hugh Thomson's review of Glenn Gould's local Toronto performance in 1958. After noting that just before playing the Schoenberg *Piano Concerto*, Gould had cut one of his fingers playing Bach's *D-Minor Concerto*. Thomson observes that "when he began to play this Schoenberg Concerto, blood kept spreading over the keys. This was probably all to the good, because if there ever was a work that needed some blood, it's Schoenberg's piano concerto." [63]

Thomson's and Henahan's observations are not musically nor geographically unique. As recently as 2003, British musicologist Ben Earle published a remarkable disclosure[64] of earnest attempts over the previous half century by respected figures in his country—even with help from the venerable BBC—to implant 12-tone music more securely into the public repertoire. The final score of accomplishment? Zilch. That lingering English highbrow malaise re serial music had been mourned back in 1961 by musicologist Hugh Wood, who blamed it not on the music but on listeners. In his judgment, [65]

we lack in this country a 'Schoenberg-generation'—not merely of composers, but of teachers, theorists, and above all, of listeners, for whom the hearing and appreciation for the masterworks of the Second Viennese School, written so long ago, is a familiar experience.

---

[62] Let us note, however, that Essa Pekka Salonen recently recorded this *Concerto*.

[63] Quoted from the *Toronto Star* by Otto Friedrich in *Glenn Gould: A Life and Variations*, 75-76.

[64] Earle, "Taste, Power, and Trying to Understand Op. 36: British Attempts to Popularize Schoenberg."

[65] "English Contemporary Music," 156.

A possible explanation for that shortage bemoaned by Wood is suggested on a worldwide basis by musicologist Rose Rosengard Subotnik. She doubts the efficacy predicated for what serial advocates have called "structural listening," seeing it as a misdirected approach to the musical experience. For most listeners, she notes, "the barriers of Schoenberg's style, which in many ways seems to stimulate a condition of great cultural distance, are simply too formidable to be penetrated and discounted as secondary by a focus on structure." [66] She then amplifies her discontent with this imposed obligation for the "structural" approach, observing that even in its "replete" version, it "seems the least useful for entering the semiotic domain of sound and style. . . [it] is not in a position to define much of a positive role for society, style, or ultimately even sound in the reception of music." [67]

Let us close this discussion with a simple "moral of the tale." It is that when style assumes a greater significance than substance in the creative process, results are likely to suffer. Problems loom large when artists of any medium let ideologies blur sight of their craft's fundamental bases, leading them to veer into regions that—*creative* though they may be—cannot accommodate the *human* basis for their invocation. Artifacts that demand time-consuming study and descriptive overlay to unlock their aesthetic secrets are dubious works of art. They are best known as *MetaArt*.

As for Serialism's flaws, less colorful causes than untrained cognition are not hard to find. The denial of a central and consuming musical property, pitch contexts, was at the base of this collapse of perceptual identity. The 12-tone system introduced *negative* consequences more grave than imagined; it did not just forfeit tonality in music: it abandoned *Pitch* itself as a principal coagulating source. That denial culminated in an approach that bears questionable relevance to the projection of *perceived* musical unity. As we shall confirm in Chapter 6, there

---

[66] "Toward a Deconstruction of Structural Listening," 114.
[67] *Ibid.*, 115.

is no empirical support for the *Grundgestalt* power of a 12-tone row, as claimed by the champions of Serialism. If that be true, then pitch, as a property of the musical fabric, has become a secondary player. Music must now depend upon its other contextualizing properties for its meaning.

This fact was not totally lost on some who would be least expected to confirm it. Henri Pousseur was by no means of the Moldy Fig school of his era; indeed, he was a recognized member of the so-called "Darmstadt School," one of the most prestigious avant-garde groups of the 1950s that boasted such members as Boulez, Stockhausen, and Berio. But an ironic—and wholly unintentional—denial of those touted structuring powers for serial procedures is embedded in opening sentences of an article he wrote in 1966.[68] He first observes that "Serial music is often thought of as the fruit of excessive speculation and the result of an exclusive mustering of the powers of reason." Then he follows by noting a surprising conclusion: with truly careful listening—"concrete listening"—hearing such music can lead to "the impression of finding oneself in the presence of consequences of an aleatory free play."

And there is a far-reaching implication in this discovery. It is that the most carefully wrought pre-fabrications can lead to anything but order perceived to be analogous with those pre-fabs.

Our subsequent discussions will confirm such a conclusion, offering reliable evidence that confidence in the serialists' syllogism was misplaced. Motivated by a flawed ideology and reinforced by a narrow view of music's history, it developed from misunderstood musical conditions and their causes. That flawed perspective derived from nothing more solid than (1) a skewed conception of the pitch context and the kinematics of music and (2) a naïve conviction about a rapidly "evolving" humanity. It was a basis as uninformed and misleading as the Ptolmaic view of the cosmos was for 16th-century thinkers.

---

[68] "The Question of Order in New Music," 93. He was teaching that year at the State University of New York in Buffalo

Schoenberg's error was the same made earlier by playwright Ibsen in assuming his power to divine the way of all flesh. It was a perspective philosopher Paul Johnson brands "typically Victorian,"[69] a view based on the assumption that a member of the "...enlightened minority would always progress in a desirable direction." And in a relevant historical apercu, Johnson adds that "it is a curious delusion of intellectuals, from Rousseau onwards, that they can solve the perennial difficulties of human education at a stroke, by setting up a new system." [70]

It's a cozy notion that the anointed can make reliable predictions of future generations' behaviors, but it is less than a reliable guide, regardless of the genius of the artist. Philosopher Wittgenstein wisely voiced no optimism for those who, with impassioned assurance, laid foundations for the future. The fulfillment of human dreams about where science, art, or philosophy might be headed in the future could only be accidental. The dreams of the most ardent genius are but "an extension of his own world, PERHAPS what he wishes (and perhaps not), but not reality."[71]

Even if music is that purest art of abstraction claimed, it's not the malleable stuff required to meet any and all ideological goals. I have found no more forceful denial for such naiveté than that of psychologist Steven Pinker. Discussing the down-to-earth epistemic facts of life (in a way deconstructionists and poststructuralists *et al.* would find reprehensible) he avers that

> The laws of physics dictate that objects denser than water are found on the bottom of the lake, not on the surface. Laws of natural selection and physics dictate that objects that move swiftly through fluid have streamlined shapes. The laws of genetics make offspring resemble their parents. Laws of anatomy, physics and human intentions force chairs to have shapes and materials that make them stable supports.

---

[69] *Intellectuals*, 99.
[70] Johnson, *Loc. cit.*, 123.
[71] *Culture and Value*, 57e.

Pinker goes on to observe a further troubling fact, one more directly relevant to our tale:

> The denial of human nature has spread beyond the academy and has led to a disconnect between intellectual life and common sense . . . This is the mentality of a cult, in which fantastical beliefs are flaunted as proof of one's piety. [72]

That element of "human nature" is implicit in the conclusion reached by composer Rochberg about serialist shortcomings, that "the 12-tone method seeks salvation in methodology—and the rational controls methodology demands." And then the music it produces "can then only be explained or justified by references to the operation of that system." [73]

Our next four chapters confirm that the denial of "human nature" may obscure some elemental—and inescapable—elements of any art, music included. Coherence is a minimal condition of aesthetic satisfaction. Musical coherence may happily cohabit with numerical approaches to the creative process, but eternal bliss for a monogamous marriage of mathematics and music is pure fiction. It is nonetheless a fiction long accepted as fact by some highly intelligent people.

Serialism wasn't the first case in human history of fancied successes expected from flawed premises. We humans have a way of latching on to imposing ideas and holding them as incontrovertible, despite mounting evidence they are fictive. It's a virus as contagious and deadly in the arts as in politics or religion. Weston LaBarre frames it in basic terms of regret when he observes that we humans "know" many things that are not so, and the folklores of the world are filled with such "knowledge." Indeed, "perhaps the bulk of all human belief is in things that are not only not so but cannot possibly be so." [74]

---

[72] Both quotes are from *How the Mind Works*, 308.
[73] *The Aesthetics of Survival*, 51.
[74] LaBarre, *Op. Cit.*, 234.

It's hard to read justifications for Serialism or rehashings of its heavy computational goodies without realizing that the system—the *how*—has indeed come to overshadow the product—the *what*.[75] With an ironic twist of fate, an oddball kind of notoriety began to supersede the method as a composer's tool; the accompanying folklore fulfilled a systemic desire beyond the music it produced. For historians it meant yet another venerated "period" to enlarge the style succession of *Medieval-Renaissance-Classical-Romantic-Impressionist.* Now *Serialist* could be added at the end. For musicologists and theorists that meant an insider's new way of tinkering with the flora and fauna of music's very being. It was a fresh approach that even sported a provocative new vocabulary, the basis for the most fascinating case of *MetaMusic* to come along since Pythagoreanism.

In that context it's hard to forget Lord Byron's fetching conclusion: "When a man talks of his system, it is like a woman's talk of her virtue. I let them talk on." And yet there often comes a time when the headiest of talk must be faced with simple facts.

---

[75] I say this despite Schoenberg's insistence in several contexts that for him the sound is all that really counts.

Chapter 3

THOSE KINDRED FRUITS OF 'REVOLUTION'

How could this happen? Here were certifiably brilliant people working hard to create objects destined for human adoration, yet their products motivate indifference—or even antagonism—among a targeted audience. Was the Schoenbergian epiphany a solo flight within the arts? By no means. As we observed in opening discussions, it was a time of change in the world at large, as deep and broad in the Arts as in other fields of human activity. Within those changes the old *Schizo Syndrome* took its toll on a broad front, although the most eccentric shifts for painters and writers were a bit different from those in music.

They shared much of music's ideological roots, but their histories of representational images were not that of composers, who had dealt with more "abstract" things, a condition many of the visual and lexical Arts admired and envied. Painters and writers shared that heightened awareness of the creative self mentioned earlier, a sense that begat struggles to "express" images other than characteristics of an external object, events of an ordered life. Their approaches and results place those of Serialism into a perspective otherwise limited.

Means chosen to affect such changes were easier to understand than those of music, although their goals were similarly expressed in the loftiest of abstract terms. Painters and writers nonetheless had their unique banners of togetherness, one of which especially stood out, tersely encapsulated in the term *Secessionist*. Its real meaning was simple: only what was new was legitimate. The chiaroscuro of depictive painting, the blow-by-blow reportage of human life, were now passé.

The Painted Word [1]

Painter Wassily Kandinsky [2] was a leader, early in that revolutionary time. For him it was an essence suspected of lying somewhere deep within "true art." He found a most willing and able compatriot in composer Schoenberg, who for Kandinsky represented a human connection with music's innate condition of abstraction. The painter's *Composition VII* and *Klänge* of 1913 had reached a shocking level of departure from the past, a state derived from his will to "abstract." Both works succeeded, perhaps excessively: nothing is visible in their picture planes to suggest that anything of the real world has been *abstracted*. That apparent lack of a "There there," in the Gertrude Stein tradition, gives ever greater poignancy to the painter's later statement that "I want people to see finally what lies *behind* my paintings."[3]

Kandinsky's motivating convictions echoed philosopher Wittgenstein's ruling that things of real value can only be demonstrated, not described in words. A similar testament to the ineffable resides in painter Paul Klee's conclusion that his task as a painter was to "make the invisible visible." But sayable or not, visible or not, criteria of legitimacy were formulated as ethereal platitudes neither individuals nor institutions could hope to realize—except perhaps as *MetaArt*. It was a time for singing lyrics of longing for altered states of being, hymns to an imaginary perfection. Typical hokum was the state of "Vitalism" that favored feeling over thought. With a tinge of irony, it was the kind of mindset that enabled Hitler to become an earthly menace in the 1930s and 40s.

With ideals "as simple (and often as simple-minded) as they are abstract, those lyrics of longing led to the kinds of self-deluding convictions humanity finds hard to deny." And as Roger Kimball further observes, setting up unreachable criteria of legitimacy enables one "to indulge in credulousness as a

---

[1] Tom Wolfe's coinage of 1975 is too good to miss here.

[2] He was joined in this by counterpart Mark Rothko toward the middle of the century. Anticipating later discussions, note that composers Schoenberg and his younger contemporary Morton Feldman represent in different ways artistic soul mates of Kandinsky and Rothko.

[3] Reported in *Kandinsky*, Vol. I, 5.

deliberate policy, undistracted by any contact with the less edifying realities of human nature." [4]

As irony would have it, replacement solutions soon became cramping new orthodoxies. But that didn't' keep despised bourgeois traditions from yielding to whatever might ease the birthing of a dual ideology, the Siamese Twins of Self-Expression and Abstraction. They initially were compatible motivators. In hands of the less talented their results proved to be more suicide than salvation.

The Visual Progression of –isms

A useful convention lumps the three-decade departure, 1880-1910, say from the paintings of such as John Constable and Francisco Goya, into four canonic states: *Impressionism, Expressionism, Abstractionism, and Non-Objectivism.* [5]

The first of those states can be traced at least to the light-bathed visions of William Turner (1775-1851). [6] By three decades after his death a rather simple yet vital shift became apparent when painters began to "adjust" images, "having their way" with canvas or stone, in that way condensing representations to bare essentials. It was in part a condition magnified by reaction to the photographic processes developed by Daguerre from 1839. If the camera could record objects with unmatched accuracy (within its black and white limits), painting and sculpting were obsolete—unless they could develop justifying roles of their own.[7] Evidence of this will to project one's personality onto objects nudged

---

[4] Roger Kimball, *The Long March*, 28

[5] The latter two represent what can accurately be called *revolutionary*; both blatantly thumbed their noses at representation of a real world. For some, however, like Austrian Gustav Klimt, the romance of classicism remained a fertile attraction, even though full-blooded modernists were reluctant to admit it,

Edward Lockspeiser rules that there was no painter of the 19th century whose "scope of expression" was more extensive than Turner's. See his *Music and Painting*, 49.

[7] Some painters—Picasso a prime example—were infatuated with the creative potential of the photographic print. And note that such photographic masters as Ansel Adams nudged the black and white photograph into the realm of Impressionism and Expressionism, shooting objects with filtered lenses under especially dramatic light conditions, then manipulating those images in the printing process.

representation into a new realm of being, that second state usually termed *Expressionism*. As Vincent van Gogh told his brother Theo, the main objective in painting his Arles bedroom (1889) was to project an aura of relaxation, to express a sense of hovering sleep.[8]

Pablo Picasso provides a handy mini-history of painting's development toward the ideal espoused by Kandinsky, but the Spaniard avoided a state of purest abstraction. From his *Woman's Head* or *Child with Pigeons* (1901), through darkly mysterious paintings like *Woman Dancing* and *Three Seated Figures*, his work shifted slightly to even less identifiable real-world origins. Or take the swaths of brown, black and ochre of his *Guitar* (1916). They add up to what *is*—and yet *is not*—a guitar. He has abstracted from what he and his viewer know to be the essence of "guitar," but it has become his own. Even the simulated nail and hanging wire at the painting's top confirm the object-within-object state, the individualized nature of the whole.

For some painters the three intersecting styles of *Impressionism*, *Expressionism* and *Abstractionism* progressed beyond the realm of mere "adjustment." After reaching the last stop on the line in this fooling around with the dynamics of object-artist-viewer, they reached *Non-Objectivism*. Kandinsky summed up the progression in 1925 as an evolving that hovered between the worlds of nature and art. He called it *Doppelklang;*[9] his hopes for its success were as fervent as they were abstract. If all went well, Art's values would emerge as a force equal to "the totality of life . . . a life-giving force, that our present doubts about its significance and justification will seem to us as the result of an inexplicable dazzlement."[10]

Heady stuff! It reverberates with historian Crane Brinton's observation that many of the early 20th century ideologues longed for "a state of immaterial

---

[8] Gombrich, *The Story of Art*, 438.
[9] See *"Abstrakte Kunst"* in Leipzig's Der Cicerone, Complete Works, Vol. I, 512. My best translation of *Doppelklang* in this context would be "dual basis," or "double intent."
[10] Kandinsky, *Op. cit.,* 512.

bliss."[11] It was an ideology seconded by Kandinsky's friend Schoenberg, with concurrence from colleagues Paul Klee and Piet Mondrian. It formed a sturdy base for a kind of theorizing and descriptive verbiage scholars and critics continue to pile on to the artifacts, a basis for *MetaArt*. But unlike music, no system was developed for painting, no methodology born for guiding the creative act.

Kandinsky observed that music used its resources "not to represent natural appearance, but to express inner life of the artist and to create a unique life of musical tone."[12] His direct model was Schoenberg, who at the time was toying with his revolutionary approaches to pitch fabrications. His painterly retrievals from an internally guided psyche led directly to images separated from real-world contexts. The term *Abstraction* no longer fit. One need not ponder for long what might be the "external meaning" or "source" of his *Composition with Red, Black, Blue, Yellow and Grey* of 1920. It lives a life of its own, radiating images of no designated (or even hinted) external world.

Under such conditions painting became a solitary world. It was inhabited only by the trio of Painter/Painting/Viewer, inching yet closer to the heralded peak state of "inner necessity," the *Grundfläche* championed by both Kandinsky and Schoenberg. Transcendent principles were assumed to hold things together. This move toward transcendence of all but the *unsayable* had one ironic result: volumes of justifying descriptives emerged to fill in the visual void. *MetaArt* was on a roll.

The touted Revolution began with a broad ideology of subjectivism and a separation of *how to* from *what is*. It loomed even larger as the century progressed. But once that goal of total abstraction is in sight, a homely old problem of communication rears its ugly head: Is the artist free to provide such limited *visual* guidance that any potential message is up for grabs? Must communication depend on such uncontrolled factors by the creator?

[11] *Ideas and Men*, 493.
[12] *The Spiritual in Art*, Vol. I, 154.

A brief glance into the current lives of two sub-categories of the visual arts, both bred during the Revolution, can yield perspective for such questions, even as they apply to music. One of those sub-categories followed the total abstraction route anointed by Kandinsky; the other opted for a quite different approach, one aligned with a passion for eccentric ploys that dismisses Art as a serious undertaking. I speak of *Dada*. It is a condition that boasts a few musical cousins.

The Arts of Minimal Intervention

The *Dada* of Marcel Duchamp, Tristan Tzara and Francis Picabia was an approach in which representation may be present yet wholly redirected. In its beginnings *Dada* sought to reveal the silliness of culture and traditional Art, to achieve "the destruction of the museum," to release Art from the "moldy vault of tradition." The genre thrives today in "found" or "altered" works that become *Art* by virtue of intrusion and interaction of a self-proclaimed *Artist*. The artifact itself is secondary to its conceptualization, its accompanying or implied verbiage. It demands no directly creative skills for its creation. It can amuse, but there are good reasons to believe that it fails to achieve the status of Art. One skeptic, critic Harold Rosenberg, aptly characterized it as "The Dadaist subversion of art."

Recent *Dada* sightings have reached esoteric heights of eccentricity (along with heavy press coverage). They enjoy a special prominence via critics who find *Showbiz* shock the merit badge of aesthetic value. Katsushige Nakahashi's *Zero Project* is a notable addition to the show. Art critic Leah Ollman's coverage in the *Los Angeles Times* [13] conveyed the key role played by explanatory prose in the genre's status qua Art. The story is not complex.

A 1/32 scale model of a Japanese Zero fighter is constructed from a plastic kit. Some 125,000 2-millimeter photographs of sections of the model are made.

---

[13] Sept. 15, 2005, E 22.

These are then taped together by "intentionally careless"[14] helper-volunteers into a full-scale visual representation of the original aircraft. On a date chosen for its historical relevance (like December 7) the ersatz plane is taken to a location pertinent to the life story of the original aircraft, then ceremoniously set afire. Except for photographs made of the ritual itself and its ash residue, end of art work.

It's copy-ready *Dada*. Critic Ollman comes through with a straight–faced review, a model of *MetaArt* palaver matched only by descriptions of a new Napa Valley Beaujolais.

> Images of the burning planes evoke a visceral unease, akin to witnessing the wreckage of a crash landing. Yet the fire has intentionality. It's sacrificial, purifying. It releases the spirits of the dead. It clears the ground of myth and legend, allowing for more immediate perspectives on the experience of war and its aftermath.

There necessarily is an element of eccentricity in any creative act, but it cannot define the product. It is hard not to agree with Henri Laboit's conclusion that "a holdup or a violent assault on accepted mores does not necessarily make a person an artist."[15] Except, we must note, through ardent descriptive coverage by the media. But let us head off lofty discussions of impenetrability, opting instead for simple guidance from one of those two no-nonsense rubrics we outlined in our opening chapter. It holds that Art works—Chauvet cave paintings to a Gene Kelly dance routine—necessarily reveal artistry. And artistry is a noun that denotes a person of insight, control, technical skill of high order, a grasp of the whole and the ability to assemble it. The product is a rendering that could not have happened *except* via the exceedingly gifted and practiced talents of a maker.

The Nakahashi production fulfills the first, the contextual, of our "to-be-Art" criteria only obliquely: a ritual of separate acts is created, providing an

---

[14] Let us assume that the "careless" approach bore profound *Dada* overtones.
[15] *Op. cit.*, 210.

enclosing whole. There is no trace of our second criterion's demand for artistry (especially in the "intentionally careless" fabrications).

We need not be puzzled that the *Dada* hobbyhorse continues to prosper, accompanied by its reams of justifying theory. It prospers in part because its ground rules are fully democratic, highly forgiving of the untalented. Those rules embrace anything preserved in perceivable form, allowing rank amateurs an equal shot at artistic fame—graffiti enthusiasts included.[16] Like Britney Spears chanteuses who replace engaging vocal chords with naked navels, *Dada* confuses categories, mistakes style for substance. And there is a distinct downside: As anthropologist Ellen Dessanayake comments, such works "add to the impression of art world chicanery and further compound public distrust."[17]

Originally conceived in the visual world, music nonetheless has its *Dada* remnants in everything from John Cage's chic offspring to the improv fancies of Pauline Oliveros. With a judgmental frown in that direction, Pierre Boulez opined many years ago that "in music, Dadaism still retains the prestige (and naiveté) which it has long since lost everywhere else; its flimsy veils hide the sweet sickness of rosy dilettantism."[18]

Abstraction Beyond Abstraction

And then to that second potholed sidetrack of our story. It is wholly different in both intent and substance from the seductions of *Dada*. It's a dark back alley entered only by the most tenacious, echoing those ideals argued by Kandinsky a century ago. It is more relevant to matters of *MetaMusic*, for in that medium it dramatically resurrects the rock-bottom problem of parts adding up to wholes, an enigma especially prominent today among artists who practice to excess what Harold Rosenberg once designated "Reductive Painting." Depending

---

[16] A few graffiti graduates possess talents exceeding those of the typical billboard bandit. Some products of Jean-Michael Basquat are compatible with real artistry.

[17] *Art and Intimacy*, 171.

[18] *On Music Today*, 24.

upon the critic, it goes by other tags today, like *Reductivism, Minimalism* (or *Neo-Minimalism*), or even *Abstract-Expressionism*. There are documentable instances in which such ideologically-driven motivations push beyond the borders of *Abstraction* into *Nothingness*!

Many believe such works represent the most *avant* of our day. History provides a different story. The genre can be traced back to the black square on white background "Voids" of Kasimir Malevich, whose *minimalisms* were personal gifts to *Suprematism*. His favorite wish was expressed as "I want you to plunge into whiteness . . . and to swim in its infinity." It eerily resounds in many recent manifestoes for seeing with "eyes of the soul." [19]

The result today can be found in what are best known as super-minimalist creations, works intent upon achieving a simplistic precision derived from the least possible outlay of images. The late Agnes Martin (1912-2004) excelled in the genre. Her fastidious linear grids reflect a puritanical thrust that at times faintly reminds us of Mondrian's grids. One is a format of 45 elegantly drawn red ink verticals laid out in a square with 34 horizontals. Presented as a work due serious pondering, the resultant box of grids leaves everything to the imagination of the viewer—if one wishes to reach beyond the image of what rational people call "red-lined graph paper."

Martin claimed that her works "may stimulate yearning, helplessness, belligerence or remorse." This may in some *Ungesagt* and mystical way be true. Who knows? We are assured by critic Leah Ollman that the principal value of Martin's abstractions is their "interiority" (a characteristic they share with Nakahashi's *Zero Project*). Elaborating that judgment, she goes on to say that "it's less about external form than about internal processes and invisible forces—emotional, physical, spiritual, cosmic." Such works "symbolically convey movement toward transcendence." [20]

---

[19] And don't forget Thomson's *Silent Southern California Rectangle in Black and White* illustrated in our *Prologue*.

[20] *Los Angeles Times*, July 2, 2005, E 22.

Kandinsky would have loved such powerfully painted *MetaArt*—especially the transcendence part.

We may be accused of trusting our sensory powers excessively, mainly in our demand for part/whole dynamics. One refuge might be found in sermons preached by social gurus of the 1960s decade, invoking such conclusions as Herbert Marcuse's that "True knowledge and reason demand domination over—if not liberation from—the senses."[21] Such wisdom could help us escape the conclusion that part/whole absences represent flawed images—if not artistic dead ends. But that seems a cowardly hole for hiding. It furthermore is logically impossible: Any experiential beginning—just to witness an existence—demands that we *see* the marks made on paper by Martin, if only to confirm their being. So "liberation from the senses" becomes a hallow cry.

As visual treats, Martin's grids are not alone. Some Donald Judd sculptures of the 1960s share their part-whole barrenness, nonetheless motivating volumes of glorifying praise.[22] Four large canvases shown recently in a Los Angeles gallery share this condition of visual emptiness. They nonetheless led one exuberant critic to claim that they possess "authoritative power and hypnotic grace," attributes bordering on the "ritualistic." What the innocent viewer actually sees is nothing but four large rectangles of around 7' X 5'. One is black, one white, one yellow, and one of very dark green. *Contexts* we might be kind enough to call the assemblage as a whole, but consisting of mighty skimpy *Parts*.

Reductio absurdum longings extend from the less well known red-ink grids of Agnes Martin to highly touted (and expensive!) works by celebrated contemporary artists like Barnet Newman, Jo Bayer, and Yves Klein. Newman's "Thirteenth Station" from his *Thirteen Stations of the Cross* (1966) is a classic of the genre. His rectangle of 6 ½' by 5' is slashed, some 2/3 to the right side of the canvas, by a vertical white shaft. And that's it. In terms of figure/ground, it is one

---

[21] *One Dimensional Man*, 147.
[22] A prime example is the visual paucity of Judd's 10 ft. construction of Plexiglass and galvanized iron (untitled, 1969) in the Albright-Knox Gallery of Buffalo, NY.

barren step beyond a totally black rectangle. It provides an especially jarring image in the context of a title that suggests profoundly sacred meanings. [23] With Kandinsky's more searching creations of 1913 they represent peaks of visual solipsism.

Let us play on a famous coinage to describe a simple conclusion. It pertains to architectural revolutionary Mies van der Rohe's hallowed maxim "Less is more." Those words bear a unique truth in one very special way, but taken as generalized gospel they pose grave dangers. Applied to conventions of human diet such a rule can lead to anorexia—if not starvation. The condition is no more desirable in works of Art than for the maintenance human bodies.

Those uncontextualized creations of the past half-century continue to elicit yards of copy from critics and scholars. Their inherent vacuity opens up a free universe of verbal gymnastics, so the critic can become a major part of the act. The less there is to see, the more tedious the chore of unraveling meaning, the more there is to say. Tom Wolfe sized up the situation admirably many years ago: "It is art that "has become completely literary: the paintings and other works exist only to illustrate the text."[24]

Charles Demuth was a simple man, a figure far removed from any edge of the avant-garde. But he was a painter's painter. Like Ruskin, he thought art had something to do with how things looked. A note posted in his studio-apartment in Lancaster, PA, provides a more reasonable, a more productive and artful way of going about seeing what may be there to be seen. In his humble judgment, "Paintings must be looked at and looked at and looked at—they (the good ones) like it . . . No writing, no singing, no dancing will explain them. They are the final, the nth whoopee of sight."

---

[23] The painting can be seen in the 1966 volume of *Art News*. Newman revealed that the idea for his profound title for the series didn't occur to him until after he had completed the first three of the thirteen paintings.

[24] *The Painted Word*, 3.

Leaving Us With What?

Let's face it. The larger story of that 'Revolution' suggests that music was just another one of the boys in developing some early detours, some of them heavily freighted with obstacles for the beholder. For painting the drive was to impose an individual consciousness, rendering any work a uniquely personal object, whatever route might be taken. But as with many human pursuits, some guests at the abstraction table overate, replacing visual delight with conceptual play, more concern for *How* than for *What*. Although highly touted, they forged forks that veered too far astray from our human experiential mores. Like much of *Showbiz* and crossword puzzles, their excesses were victims of confused categories: *words* replaced *things*.

It's an irony of history that an Art consisting of spaceless voids had been promised by Piotr Ouspensky in one of his many melodramatic proclamations of 1913.[25] As a result of those zealous lurches toward a transformed world, he mde a prediction of things to come.

> The day is not far off when the vanquished phantoms of three-dimensional Space, of seemingly drop-like time, of melancholy causality . . . will prove to be for all of us exactly what they are: the annoying bars of a cage in which the human spirit is imprisoned.

And yet, here we are, still in jail!

Verbal Thrusts at Total Abstraction

Literature's NewAge flexings were no less venturesome, but they were less successful in the long run if one gauges success in terms of continuing practice. Closer ties are easier to find in lexical efforts of the 1910➔ era with the serialist scenario of music. Baffling complexity rather than less-is-more anorexia resides there in shocking abundance. *MetaLit* nonetheless thrives as a part of

---

[25] Cited in Susan Compton, *The World Backwards: Russian Futurist Books, 1912-1916*. The image of "escape" from "barred cages" achieved cliché status in the early 20th century. .

today's scholarship; whatever may have died an early death as stylistic triumph can survive decades of heavy theorizing. Reasons for comparative failure of the most eccentric paths in prose and poetry are not arcane. They are worth reviewing because their kinship with those of music and painting reveal even more starkly how ideological misfires can lead the best of intentions astray.

Our needs demand only a limited sampling, touching mainly upon some stars of the trade who, although highly acclaimed, at times fell short of comprehensibility. Jean Nicolas Rimbaud's huge corpus continued to haunt the serious writer into the 20th-Century, consciously or not, deserved or not. [26] With Gustave Flaubert, Charles Baudelaire, and Stéphane Mallarmé, he was one of the most influential writers when the Revolution got under way, especially for those who sought an idiosyncratic kind of indeterminacy in their narratives.

A handful of writers succumbed to a climate similar to that among some painters, a sense of serving otherworldly powers—if not just one's inner superpower. Germany's Rainier Maria Rilke, for instance, hinted of a quasi-religious calling; Irishman James Joyce centralized the artist's servitude to "higher forces; and American Ezra Pound conjured forth ancient worlds. The most extreme ventures proved to be elitist paths with nowhere to go, proving once again that the most exemplary ideals can lead to the lamest results.

Deepest 20th century roots for literary brushes with destiny were grounded in a split of Realism and Romanticism that can be traced back into the mid-19th century. The poetry of Robert Browning and Rudyard Kipling, the prose of Joseph Conrad, Alexandre Dumas *pere* and the Bronte sisters, sought more heightened emotional atmospheres than the down-to-earth action prose of George Meredith, Jane Austen, Herman Melville or Mark Twain—or F. Scott Fitzgerald and Thomas Mann of later years. Hindsight suggests the tempting over-simplification that writers of the times made a conscious choice between mastering prose (Realist) or poetry (Romanticist). Over-generalized though it be,

---

[26] One must take pause in making encompassing judgments about a highly vaunted writer who, to this day, poses insuperable demands on those who translate his work.

from that milieu grew a formidable shift in perspective, poets leading the way. It was a path that at times clouded the difference between the two.

One favored NewAge ploy, passed on especially by Gertrude Stein and James Joyce, aimed to draw the reader into the writer's momentary stream of thought. Words of no apparent story relevance are flaunted, sometimes even repeated to further deny expectations of normal discourse. To amplify the effect, supports for rational inference might be removed by discarding the serial introduction of characters, along with a randomized chronology of events.

These were tricks later used with success in modern cinematic productions. But film versions were less problematic for the viewer; they could more immediately be unraveled because dialogue was supported by visual images, making random chronology easier to grasp. In literature the results were often easer celebrated as chic than as comprehensible, but there was a silver lining to the condition: interpreting the most advanced case of the foggy genre became a discipline of its own, a cheap *MetaLit* ticket to fame for a struggling critic, even tenure for an Assistant Professor. A fitting designation for such heavy doses of applied verbiage was that of "torturous analyses of meaning."

Lexical Fun and Games

American expatriates Gertrude Stein (1874-1946) and Ezra Pound (1885-1972) both approached language as the fodder of personal creativity rather than as mere transmitter of ideas and events of the real world. Esoteric, gifted, pioneering and masterful as some critics have designated them to have been, many of their passages are untranslatable; words don't readily shape up into contexts. Both writers are models of what Donald Kuspit had in mind when he spoke of avant-garde artists who revolt against their audiences like adolescents against their families. In ways similar to Schoenberg in music and Kandinsky in painting, Stein and Pound represent strange phenomena in the public world. Both pose barriers of comprehension; they nonetheless continue to be analyzed and praised in impressive circles as "famous literary figures." As early as 1913 one flamboyant champion of modernism, Mabel Dodge, exclaimed that the name of Gertrude Stein was better known by sophisticates of New York than the name of God. Widely known or not, she was arguably the most rambunctious of all.

At times she wrote as if habits of direct communication were obsolete. As esoteric—as revolutionary—as some critics considered her work to be, many passages are untranslatable with any public assurance.[27] They cannot be parsed; words don't shape up into contexts. Is our ruling of "difficult to comprehend" fair and just? Or is it merely an uninformed evaluation by an insensitive prig, who like those who fail to succumb to the aural thorns of Schoenberg's music lack the required preparation? Let us keep in mind that our long term goal is to separate pure bullshit [28] from *perceivable* reality in the land of literary Oz.

A classic example of Steinian impenetrability is her "short story" *As a Wife Has a Cow A Love Story*. First published in Eugene Jolas's *transition*, [29] the adjective *idiosyncratic* is perhaps the kindest one might apply, although critics have squandered gallons of ink in teasing esoteric meanings from its disjointed word-manipulations. Its first paragraph of two sentences suffices in revealing the "story's" unique qualities. I'll reproduce here only a few initial sentences from following paragraphs. (The "style" remains consistent throughout.)

As a Wife Has a Cow A Love Story

"Nearly all of it to be as a wife has a cow, a love story. All of it to be as a wife has a cow, all of it to be as a wife has a cow, a love story.

[¶ 2] As to be all of it as to be a wife as a wife has a cow, a love story . .

[¶ 3] has made, as it has made as it has made, has made has to be as a wife has a cow, a love story . . .

---

[27] She produced a wide range of work, including novels, plays, critiques, one opera libretto, memoirs, and poetry.

[28] I use the term in the sense established by Harry Frankfurt in his classic *On Bullshit* (Princeton U. Press, 2005)

[29] In Volume III, three years after her more famous *Tender Buttons*.

[¶ 4] When he can, and for that when he can, for that. When he can. For that when he can. For that. And when he can and for that. Or that, and when he can. For that and when he can . . ."

Engaging? Well, maybe for some, but only in a fleeting and weird way, and even then not for reasons of narration. A first thought is sheer wonderment: was author or editor (or both) hopelessly drunk? Or were they just playing a game of lexical hide-and-seek? Any engagement enjoyed within has more to do with one's hunch that meaning must be hiding somewhere in those flashing verbal clues. But the flashes never add up to fires. We are impressed that any presumably sane—much less "famous"—author would have the temerity to write such repetitious anti-mimetic nonsense. In the spirit of *Art pour l'Art*, Jolas printed it in his periodical *transition*.

Stein's repetition-as-obsession cliché wasn't wholly lost on posterity. It survived to crop up in strange places—even Eldridge Cleaver's vaunted *Soul on Ice* of the infamous 1960s. Expressing his passion to find a worthy leader for his own revolution, Cleaver's taste tended toward ". . . an American Lenin, Fidel, a Mao-Mao, A MAO MAO, A MAO MAO, A MAO MAO, A MAO MAO, A MAO MAO." [30] The "technique" seems to have accumulated no further literary power—unless we recognize in it the womb of current Rap. [31]

Even Stein's less obtuse prose revels in word-fetishism and erratic punctuation, both bearing the stamp of forced eccentricity. Her description of the nature of World War I, within a vignette she wrote about Picasso a decade after her *Love Story*, is at least decipherable, though still classic Stein.

> Really the composition of this war was not the composition of all previous wars, the composition was not a composition in which there was one man at the centre surrounded by a lot of other men but a composition that had neither a beginning or an end, a

---

[30] *Soul on Ice*, 19. *The New York Times* picked this book as one of the ten best for 1968.
[31] But Rap enjoys the contexts formed by a simplistic musical background.

composition In which one corner was as important as another corner, in fact the composition of cubism.[32]

This bulging sentence leaves us with two irrepressible images: the word *composition* and the forced metaphor of cubism as the causes of a war. And therein resides the big problem: the *massage* is more compelling than the *message*.

Stein's stretched limits are more accurately blamed on overdeveloped ego than premonitions of divine calling. It was a trait she shared with her contemporary D.H. Lawrence. Outrageous though her results may be, they were lauded by some highly respected people, in addition to immediate fans on the *Rue de Fleurs*. Novelist Sherwood Anderson admired her wild frolics with what he called "the little housekeeping words." With them she uplifted the English language from its genteel ruts of the past. [33]

Anderson's enthusiasm was not shared by all esteemed critics of the time. Eugene Jolas published her, but his admiration was severely limited. "I am obliged to say," he recalled in later years, "that I saw, and see today, little inventiveness in her writing." In his view her problem was elemental: "not only did she seem to be quite devoid of a metaphysical awareness but I also found her aesthetic approach both gratuitous and lacking in substance." [34] Even Windham Lewis, who was one of the most provocative of NewAge enthusiasts, described the Stein approach in 1927 as one big ego trip, "a thick, monotonous prose-song." In his judgment she had sacrificed real prose for a ritualization of language mistakenly lauded as representative "of the masses." [35]

Others in those times worked hard to stretch the bounds of communication, to overcome the past, whether in prose or poetry. Irishman James Joyce remains an icon of English literature, yet some of his work suffered the same fits for

---

[32] *Gertrude on Picasso*, 18-19.

[33] Anderson, "Introduction" to the Stein collection *Geography and Plays of 1922*.

[34] *Man From Babel*, 116-117.

[35] In *Time and Western Man*. Let us note, however, that Lewis also found the prose of both Ernest Hemingway and Aldous Huxley less than rewarding.

achieving a uniquely personal delivery, in his case a penchant for recreating the campy speech of his beloved Irish.[36] His dialectical idiosyncrasies such as "had a kidscad buttened a bland old isaac" and "socie sethers wroth with twone nathanjoe"[37] cause more headaches than flashes of fulfillment. The beginning paragraph of his "Opening Pages of a Work in Progress," serialized in Jolas's first volume of *transition*, is a milestone worth reconsidering.

> Reversion brings us back to Howth Castle & Environs. Sir Tristram, violer d'mores, fr' over the short sea, had passencore rearrived from North Amorica on this side the scraggy isthmus of Europe Minor to wielderfight his penisolate war: nor had topsawyer's rocks by the stream Oconee exaggerated themselves to Laurens County's gorgeos, while they went doubling their number all the time, nor avoice from afire bellowsed mishe to tauftauf thurart peatrick; not yet, though all's fair in vanessy were sosie sethers wroth with twone nathanjoe. Rot a peck of pa's malt had Jhem or Shen brewed by arcchlight and rory end to the regginbrow was to be seen ringsome on the waterface.

Heavy massage, light message. But Joyce was at least a real story teller; even his more outrageous flings didn't measure up to the in-your-face blatherings of Stein, nor did they achieve the density reached by his American pal Ezra Pound.

Pound's expressed goal may sound hackneyed by now: rid English literature of its bondage, especially its "stifling" metrics, restore a "living flow" to language. [38] He clearly harmonized with Kandinsky's mantra that "There is no 'must' in art, which is forever free," yet his detour was the opposite of the painter's, more in the direction of Schoenberg's highly-calculated complexity. In fact, many of his products bear cryptographic densities that can remind us of the "study hard" regimen widely advised for appreciating the music of Serialism. He

---

[36] There's an irony here: Irish writer immortalizing the beloved local speech of hometowners while he lived his life everywhere except in Ireland.

[37] From his "Work in Progress" that later would become *Finegan's Wake. transition* I, April, 1927, p. 9.

[38] See F.S. Flint, "Contemporary French Poetry" in *Poetry Review* August, 1912. Reprinted in Cyrena Pondron's *Road From Paris* (see pages 89-92), 86-145.

overloaded the message with esoterica rather than reduce it to a state of contextual anorexia.

His gems can be as baffling as Stein's. Their jam-packed deliveries allude to monumentally esoteric sources—ancient history, medieval or ancient Chinese poetry, Confucian philosophy, Provençal song, *et al*, all mixed into a flood of bits that lack evident connections. Lines from the middle of his *Canto XLIII* reveals Pound at his most esoteric in 1930.[39]

> ACTUM SENIS in Parochjia S. Giovnnis
> blank leaves at end up to the index
> hoc die decim' octavo from the Incarnation
> year 1623. Celso had a wheat scheme
> July to December, July to November
> Grass nowhere out of place.
>   Pine cuts the sky into three
> Thus BANK of the grassland was raised into Seignory
> stati fatti Signoria, being present Paris Bolgarini
> credit of the Commune of Siena
> 12 of the Bailey present…went into committee
> I cancellarius wrote to His Highness
> A New Mount that shall receive from all sorts of persons
> From Luoghi public and private, privileged and non-privileged
> A base, a fondo, a deep, a sure and a certain
> the City having '*entrate*'
>   the customs and public income
> 150 to M scudi
>   200
> To guarantee which . . . . . .

And the result is?

Maybe you can tell me. Snatches of inclusive meaning *may* be there, but only for those willing and able to unravel the sources. And even if that goal is reached, the product as poetic image may prove to be less than delightful. Pound's succession of built-in roadblocks was his way of achieving that state of complex

---

[39] *The Cantos of Ezra Pound*, 219.

"simultaneity," the stream-of-consciousness [40] celebrated by the most *avant* of the times.

Like Kandinsky and Schoenberg, Pound reveled in theory-spinning. He produced seven volumes of *MetaLit* between 1918 and 1938, attempting to define both his cause and *modus operandi*. Most evident is an addictive concern for style, a set of classics of the "How-to-and-Why" genre. They swim in coldly abstract waters yet spare no words in defending his approach. He first referred to his stylistic uniqueness as *Imagism*, [41] later opting for the more chic *Vorticism* coined by Wyndham Lewis. [42] And, continuing the "clarification," he tells us that the image is not an idea. "It is a radiant node or cluster; it is what I can, and must perforce, call a VORTEX, from which, and through which, and into which, Ideas are constantly rushing."[43] He would have been better off devoting more time to writing poetry.

Also like serialist composers, Pound has enjoyed fervent supporters, defenders who have added tons of words to the meta-corpus yet little help in elucidating his poetic cause. One latter day champion, Eva Hesse [44] tackled the problem with typical results: entangled in her own esoteric contradictions. Pound's vorticist words, she explains, project a certain "sensual knowledge" rather than mere ideas. The successful reader must learn to differentiate *ideation* from "having ideas," sensual knowledge from plain old everyday knowledge. Such enlightenment is eminently designed to achieve goals of interpretation

---

[40] The term "stream of consciousness" was coined by psychologist William James, who died in 1910.

[41] For Pound's contemporary Alice Henderson, "Imagism" had come to mean "almost any kind of poetry written in unrhymed irregular verse" that contained "some sort of pictorial impression." (*Poetry*, March, 1918, 340.)

[42] Amy Lowell's collection of "Imagist Poetry" infuriated Pound, who demanded that she no longer use the term to designate what she had in mind. (This was Pound's source of the strange term, *Amygism*.) Wyndham Lewis had coined the term *Vorticism* to distinguish his art from *Cubism* and *Futurism*. See Reed Dasenbrock's *The Literary Vorticism of Ezra Pund and Wyndham Lewis* for a thorough rundown on the subject.

[43] In *Gaudier-Brzeska: A Memoir*, 92. Pound's mulling over images and vortices probably came from his acquaintance with the work of Ferdinand de Saussure, father of modern linguistics.

[44] *New Approaches to Ezra Pound*.

espoused by Morris Zap in David Lodge's *Small World*. For Zap it is a ritual well-calculated to uphold "the institution of academic literary studies." (He came before coinage of the term *MetaLit*.)

Most critics of today resolve the meaning issue by concluding that Pound's "images" were "clusters of signs." Just how both differ from his "vortexes" is best left as one of Wittgenstein's *Ungesagt*. The remaining—the overarching question— is a simple one: "Why bother?" That's a conclusion reached by some of our more astute critics like poet Randall Jarrell. In a 1940 review of Pound's *The Fifth Decad of Cantos* he decides that his poetry is

> "an extremely eccentric, slangy, illogical sentence-fragment note-taking sort of prose but prose; the constant quotations from letters or documents or diaries are no different from the verse that frames them." [45]

As mentioned earlier, Pound shared his histrionics of ancient times with English contemporary D.H. Lawrence, but his drive was more overpowering, more complex and overloaded. As Diana Trilling once observed, his poetry "too often got lost in the sticky mire of his endless philosophizing." We need not muddy that pond further with fuss today over the political and sociological misfires that at times rendered his poetry more propaganda than poetry. After WW I he frothed with intense political ideologies which he did not hesitate to inject into his writing. [46] That's a different problem.

My point here is that one must work hard to derive meaning—not to mention fulfillment—from much of Pound's work. Like the labor and extra information demanded for "appreciating" the more recondite products of Serialism, perceiving anything demands extra-sensory help. One must be prepared to work overtime to ferret out the noble qualities, to fill in the voids. Critic Peter Wilson's

---

[45] In "Poets: Old, New and Aging," 9.
[46] He was an avid fan of Benito Mussolini and Adolf Hitler.

recommendation for those who wish to struggle through Pound's more tangled works provides options, but it is straightforward: [47]

> One approach is to look up and absorb the significance of every reference. Its polar opposite is an unsupported reading: if an allusion means nothing, the reader infers whatever the verbal ambiance of the text allows and moves on.

So one can bravely go it alone, accepting the consequences in good faith, or one can follow a more studious path. The latter demands a *Thesaurus*, a *Dictionary of Greek Mythology*, an *Encyclopedia of Ancient Chinese*, and a *Greek History*, thumb moistened for assured page turnings. Those guides are found in bookstores today. [48] They are literary counterparts of the lore that counts and explains the notes of Serialism and fastidiously describes its row operations. It is remarkably akin to the Hard Work regimen Charles Wuorinen prescribes for understanding the music of Schoenberg.

Scientist-philosopher Peter Medawar may never have read a word of Stein or Pound, yet he aptly defined their sins in describing what he calls "the literary syndrome in science." [49] It is a style that "deliberately exploits the voluptuary and rhetorical uses of obscurity, a style which at first intrigues and dazzles, but in the end bewilders and disgusts."

I mention these foibles of other arts only because they match the disarming cases of music for which sonic essence assumes a secondary role. It's a profound curiosity that the title "master" is applied when an author's written word, a painter's canvas, a composer's score must be regarded only as co-players, only as

---

[47] Wilson, *Op.cit.,* 149.

[48] Like William Cookson's *A Guide to the Cantos of Ezra Pound* (Croom Helm, 1985), and Carroll F. Terrell's *A Companion to the Cantos of Ezra Pound* (University of California Press, 1993).

[49] *Pluto's Republic*, 59.

fuses that ignite the real creative fires, the interpretive toil that may lead to meaning. [50]

The basic materials of the different arts are fundamentally different. Words can't match the manipulative potential enjoyed by pigments or tones; it's a deep and long-term limitation dedicated to survival, a cognitive set of expectations that begins in infancy. When parts don't add up to wholes we console with poor Phoebe Zeitgeist, [51] who could understand only the phonetics of language without deriving accumulated meanings. There's no question that lexical masturbation can be fun, but, like its sexual counterpart, it suffers as communication.

Visual and sonic creations also connect with "reality" in quite different ways, but they possess at least one central likeness: if they are intended to possess referential meaning, both are understood *pre-facto* to be but reminders of something else, whether object or emotion.[52] This is no recent discovery. Radicalist Windham Lewis opined early in the revolutionary century that the visual image has an immediate primacy unavailable to writer or composer. Language, on the other hand, motivates ideation, perhaps even a word-picture, an image of dual eye/ear appeal. [53]

And there is yet another critical difference. Although shared with music, it separates literature from visual arts. It has to do with that dirty thing called *money* and the markets that enable its transmission. Individuals and museums buy paintings and sculptures as property in a way they don't buy novels and poems or sonatas. Those visual delights enjoy an owners' market, a kind of consumer value foreign to the sister arts. In music only reproductions are marketable; one cannot buy and possess a Beethoven symphony: only reproductions are marketable. But one must—if one is the sucker it takes—pay up to $2200 for a "painting" by the

---

[50] LitCrits today might call it "close readings." Impressed by Pound's inherent talent, Eric Hornberger regretted that he didn't persist longer under the influence of Robert Browning's poetry.

[51] In Werner Fassbinder's dark comedy *Blood on the Cat's Neck*.

[52] For music the "representational" power is especially narrow and fuzzy.

[53] *Wyndham Lewis on Art: Collected Writings*, 218.

Brooklyn terrier named Tilly, whose "art works" have adorned the walls of museums from Amsterdam to Bermuda.[54] This market issue may at first blush seem irrelevant as well as trivial. In fact it is critical to our culture's value system, a major determinant of what gets talked about in the Art world, what survives, what dies away fast, what garners big bucks.

By now we have seen compelling evidences of 'revolutionary' artifacts that manage only to confuse, works flaunting egregious sins as communicators yet immortalized in yards of explanatory copy. Another profound curiosity when the title "Master" is applied only by those who judge an author's written word, the painter's canvas, or the composer's score as but co-players, those fuses that ignite the real creative fire: compilation of a thorough explanation and interpretation of the whole.

What I'm trying to get across is the basic notion that Stein, Pound, Kandinsky, and Schoenberg all shared their driving ideological motives. But painters and writers spawned changes during those early 20th-Century flexes without that extra something unique to the music arsenal: an objective system, a calculated prefab method for going about it. They lacked that "something crucial" that could justify what Tom Wolfe jokingly referred to in painting as "a persuasive theory."[55] For many it seemed to be music's NewAge answer to progress. Seen with the hindsight of some eight decades, it suffered flawed conceptual premises that continue to haunt it. Those embedded flaws are the substance of our following three chapters.

Let us close this discussion with a simple "moral of the tale." It is that problems loom large when artists allow ideologies to blur sight of their craft's fundamental bases, when they veer into regions that cannot accommodate the human basis for their invocation. In light of the most rambunctiously devious specimens, it's fascinating that a surviving literary giant of the previous century

---

[54] As reported on the CBS *Sunday Morning Show*, 13 July, 2008.
[55] *The Painted Word*, 2.

offered a most rational tip for his coeval colleagues. It came too late to help Stein or Pound, Kandinsky or Schoenberg, but in 1935 T.S. Eliot advised that [56]

> We cannot affect intelligent change, unless we hold fast to the permanent Essentials; and a clear understanding of what we should hold fast to, and what abandon, should make us all the better prepared to carry out the changes that are needed.

Even more to the point for talented literati—or composers or painters—seeking uniqueness is the wisdom passed on in Strunk and White's classic text *The Elements of Style*.[57] Again much too late for those 1910 revolutionaries, it bore infallible advice: "To achieve style, begin by affecting none."

---

[56] "Literature and the Modern World," 574.
[57] This classic text also dates from 1935.

Chapter 4

DASHES OF SONIC REALITY –
MIDST HEAVY THEORY-SPINNING

Any system, any plan of execution, is best founded in a soil that ensures continued health. Several basic presumptions were crucial to dodecaphonism; they have not been examined to the extent they deserve. Like Kandinsky's ultimate abstractions, Gertrude Stein's narcissistic rants and Ezra Pound's preening in ancient mirrors, enforced atonality—with or without a 12-tone row—was a risky soap for post-Romantic cleansing.

If public acclaim-by-the-numbers is our sole criterion, we need not fret mindlessly over the grandstand demerits of serial composition; music is for people. J.S. Bach's *Well-Tempered Clavier* is heard less often today than Toni Braxton's *Time of Our Lives*. *Showbiz* always carries the majority. *QED*. But the *Showbiz* criterion is a too easy option. It ignores what we humans fancy as dependable, long-term paths to knowing, distinctions between the profound and the trivial artifacts that enter our lives, long term bases for testing the truth of any conceptualization. Clues continue to mount by the decades that the musical utility of serialized atonality was narrowly limited, that it would not become the NewAge turnpike to artistic fulfillment it was professed to be.

Since that heralded musical makeover bears signs of a lost battle, the fervor of remaining apologists demands that we seek causes of failure. There are commanding signs from history, from anthropology, and from modern studies of human perception that clinch a more profound conclusion. Fatal flaws can be found in (1) the conceptual argument for creating the 12-tone system, (2) its systemic protocols, and (3) its claimed perceptual powers . The ideologies blinded the idealists. And—most ironic of all—a few hardheaded reality checks along the way could have reduced ardor for the dream. It was an imaginative way for a composer to order the pitch domain when no other way seemed appropriate (or forthcoming). But as a commanding method for organizing pitches into contexts, it was impotent. It is an unfortunate fact that revolutionaries don't always examine the non-ideological tenets of their revolts.

Let us first bare flaws in conceptual roots that ultimately led to missteps. I have discussed several of them at length elsewhere,[1] showing a flimsy basis for the conviction that by 1910 music's pitch basis was ripe for total overhaul. I now wish to caste in more direct and non-jargon terms why both the *nature* and the *history* of tonality, as it was championed by atonalists, were misconceived. In Chapter 5 our focus will move to our enormous knowledge of music from both ancient and primitive cultures, observing common properties that underlie the music of our species. And then in Chapter 6 we'll move on to formal studies of human cognition and perception that defy any fantasies about "evolving" and "improving" human aural capacities over the past few centuries. Such claims were but bayings at a cloudy moon by highly sophisticated people.

First to those flawed claims about nuts and bolts.

Replacing Old Scales and Chords With New Rows

Early 20th century thinkers drew a defining conclusion about the pitch scenario: that star player called *tonality*, or *key*,[2] had been a property only since the late Renaissance, and it had barely hung on through the Chopin-to-Mahler years. That conclusion continues to be widely nourished by some musicologists.

And what was the basis of tonality, its source or cause? The basic explanation went like this: The roots of this condition reside in a signature

---

[1] Principally in *Schoenberg's Error, Tonality in Music,* and "From Sounds to Music."
[2] Schoenberg made a logical distinction: Tonality (*Tonalität*) was a broader, more inclusive property of pitch play in time, while key (*Tonart*) referred to specific conditions of tonality, such as the major and minor keys.

collection of seven notes, known to us as (1) the major or minor scale and/or (2) three fundamental chords I, IV, and V (*Tonic, Subdominant,* and *Dominant*). Both collections contain the same notes. [3] Both claims, whether invoked together or separately, derive from a naïve conception of the pitch/time kinetics that form the musical perception. Both invoke these pitch prototypes as causes—and thus evidence of the presence—of tonality. This limited perspective also persists today among many music theorists and historians.

But designating either or both as *causes* rather than *products* puts the cart before the horse. It is reminiscent of pre-Einsteinian cosmologies in which the planets of a constellation are thought to be responsible for their own orbits rather than *results* of external/internal dynamics. [4] Applied to our own solar system, the sun of that conception was not a causal (nor even central) force in guiding planet earth's orbitings in predictable patterns.

Schoenberg's version of this erroneous idea, a special collection of notes as irreducible catalyst for pitch cohesion, came primarily from fellow Austrian Simon Sechter. [5] It is readily documentable within Schoenberg's writings. [6] In 1922 he spoke of how there had been a "decline of the church medieval modes" and how they had been replaced by major and minor scales. [7] He then identifies those same modes as carriers of properties strangely beyond their acknowledged "modal" attributes, fully missing the central aural meanings of those historic modes. In his judgment they all actually "belong" to a major or minor scale. [8] In one of the most curious explanatory passages of music's history, he conceptualizes the *Dorian Mode* as in fact something else. Since it contains the

---

[3] For Schoenberg, as for his contemporaries, the minor scale demanded some heavier explaining. Although a useful "replacement" for the major scale, it was regarded as inferior. We'll touch upon this curiosity later.

[4] One fanciful "system," exposed in the *Archéomètric* of Saint-Yves d'Alveydre (1907), related notes of the major scale to the planetary order of Jupiter (1) Mars (2), Sun (3), Venus (4), Mercury (5), Moon (6), and Saturn (7). (See Godwin, *Music and the Occult*, 188-191.) Most revelations relied on more earthly bases!

[5] *Grundsätz der mujsikalische Komposition*, (3 vols.) Leipzig, 1853-54.

[6] See *Schoenberg's Error*, 54-59.

[7] *Theory of Harmony*, 1922 ed., 118.

[8] *Style and Idea*, 276.

notes *d e f g a b c* ("with leading tones *E-F* and *B-C*") it is "without a doubt in the key of C major tonality." This conception means that note *D* was in fact not a principal ingredient in a Gregorian Chant of Modes I and II in the medieval system, nor did note *A* play a crucial role in such chants' *ambitus* (or melodic range). And that is a momentous error, an error that wholly misses the point of the medieval classifications of modes. Most importantly, it ignores the shared bases of what were called "tonal" scales and what earlier were called "modes."[9]

Several of Schoenberg's champions have come to admit his ill-based conception of the pitch palette. Music historian Bryan Simms, for example, observes that Schoenberg's perspective on tonal harmony "was not always adequate to explain extended tonal structures" He also erred in his interpretation of what he called the weakening of tonality in some 19th century music. The condition he described "was often the product of a defective theory faced with an enriched harmonic language." [10]

Our theorizing ancestors, as well as Schoenberg, would have profited from an ancient hint of Aristoxenus when he observed that a scale is a *product*: "A scale . . . is to be regarded as the compound of two or more intervals."[11] And scales remain residues rather than causes over 2,000 years later. That a scale is a "*C*-major scale" demands the prior *musical* projection, in any note mix, of *C* as a central factor. The 7-note major/minor scales of 1600-1900 were not the *structural* linchpins of tonal music, nor were the pitch kinetics of "modality" inherently different from those of "tonality," although descriptions and names differed. As we shall note in greater detail in Chapter 5, the world's music consistently reveals more elemental sources than scales as their sources of pitch context.

---

[9] Robert Wienpahl's definition is favored by some historians: "Tonality is a vertical concept; modality is horizontal." (And never the twain shall meet!) *Journal of Music Theory* IV:2 (Nov. 1960), 131-152.
[10] *The Atonal Music of Arnold Schoenberg*, 12-13.
[11] *The Harmonics*, 176.

Both conditions, modal and tonal, depended upon the rock-bottom musical basis, the kinetics of tones-in-time. The idea that they were both worn out by around 1900, that they must be replaced by a newly "evolved" collection (like a 12-note row), was but a classic case of a desired end justifying a fancied means: pure hogwash. The postulated evolving chain itself, of Modes →Scales→12-Tone Sets, was one of the more unfortunate mismemes of our past. Surface appearances gave it a certain allure; best of all, it fit the pop ideology of that 1900-1920 era.

Even ancient documentation confirms that the chromatic gamut is no modern invention; it can't be lumped into a 19th-20th-century singularity. The content of such scales occurs in a multiplicity of forms in much earlier music. For the moment let us observe that Classic Greek music of Plato's time turned to "exotic" pitch content for much the same reasons Wagner did: when the scenario's emotional tone demanded it. Scholar M.L. West cites a passage from "an impassioned tragic supplication," a fragment of Zeno's papyrus from c. 250 B.C. In West's notation the tune's basic notes are *f g a b-flat*, c-double-flat, and they are centered on note *a*. In some parts it is embellished with semitones wholly foreign to the "more diatonic" content previously established, even with a quarter-tone thrown in (as between *g*-flat and *f*, *c-double-flat* and *b*, *b* and *b-flat*.).

Ex. 4.1: Fragment from Zeno papyrus[12]

go- na- ton   e - pi - ka - tas - ki - on

West also describes choice passages in which pitches exceeding established diatonic content perform melodically decorative functions. These "chromatics" occur as embellishments of basic pitch content, what he calls "underlying melodic progression." A choice instance occurs when

---

[12] From M.L. West, *Ancient Greek Music*, 196.

the three-note basis

He also recognized instances of "true modulation" and "mode change" within that ancient repertoire,[13] when "either the focus shifts to a different note. . . or it remains on the same note but the interval pattern made by the other notes changes." There are other Greek instances of non-diatonics as well, like "slides" that move in a single direction by semitones. They are no different from those heard in contemporary Indian sitar performance or in down-home American blues.

But even today the notion of scale as result rather than as cause isn't widely acknowledged. Its fate is reminiscent of some 20th century physical scientists who found the Watson/Krick penetration of DNA structure and genetic function hard to accept, despite its clear and decisive proof. The new conceptualization was unwelcome mainly because it seemed too simple and straightforward when compared to the previous conception.[14] The primacy of intervals in music's play of pitches-in-time is of similar direct simplicity—and equally hard for some moderns to acknowledge.

The cause/result duplicity mirrors a mix-up between perceptual *datum* and theoretical *construct* that trails back into ancient history.[15] It's a confusion that can mislead anyone seeking to unravel the ultimate core of melodic structuring. As Hans Reichenbach once admitted about his personal development of ethnomusical skills "I had first of all to rid myself of the notion that the scale is to be regarded as the fundamental shape of melodic forms."[16]

---

[13] *Ibid.*, 187.

[14] See Medawar, *Pluto's Republic*, 271.

[15] Especially relevant are Stefan Mengozzi's discussions of *ductio* as opposed to *propietas*, in "Virtual Segments: The Hexachordal System in the Late Middle Ages," 440-447.

[16] "The Tonality of English and Gaelic Folksong," 269.

Simple Facts to the Contrary

The tune *Scarborough Fair* of Example 4.2 contains the same *c-d-e-f-g-a-b*-set of notes Schoenberg used in his discussion. We have compelling reasons to ask why it need be linked in any definitive way with "*C* major." Such a tie is tantamount to saying that the sentence "Have you been to the mall?" means the same as "You have been to the mall!" because it contains the same words. Indeed, the "C-Major" designation would hide a fetching part of *Scarborough Fair's* charm, its unique pitch coloring, its *tonality*.[17] Among pitches, *D* prevails. It is the residue "tonic" listeners refer to as the "pitch of resolution," the "note that has the most relaxed feeling." Some would call it the "keynote." It is the *vectorial pitch* of the context.

Example 4.2: *Scarborough Fair*

But let us go further. The fact is that I can compose five other tunes using the same pitch collection of *C – c* and produce five *different* pitch hierarchies, or "keys." Note in these ersatz gems how interactions of time and pitch location[18]— melodic kinetics—co-opt to establish pecking orders, unique pitch hierarchies. But especially note that not one of these tunes boasts *C* as its hierarchical crown. Each projects its own unique residual pitch, or tonic, and for simple, demonstrable reasons.

---

[17] Readers may recall its scene-setting role in the 1960s film *The Graduate*.
[18] As first or last of a pattern, metric accent, location as highest/lowest, *et al.*

Ex. 4.3: Five Tunes, One pitch collection, five tonalities,[19]

A telltale binding agent inhabits each of those five. It is something more basic than a total note collection, a scale. It's a factor of pitch distribution evident in virtually all melodies of history. I call it the *Tonality Frame*.[20] It plays a leading role in the most elemental music-making we know, folk tunes and pop hits to symphonic marvels. Historian Curt Sachs recognized the essential nature of the tonality frame over sixty years ago in his discussion of pitch outlines in ancient music. In his words they represented a "presystematic trend," a basic element in the pitch organization of any national or period style. Those pitch outlines utilized

---

[19] That any pitch of the set could act as tonic was pointed out many years ago by R. Wilding-White; it didn't soak into the music-theoretic consciousness. See Wilding-White, "Observations re Tonality and Scale Theory."

[20] I introduced this concept of tonality frame in 1965 in Christ, *et al.*, *Materials and Structure of Music,* Vol I (1st Ed.), Pp. 24-31, then later in *Introduction to Music Reading.* For a more thorough discussion of the Tonality Frame, see chapters 13, 14, and 15 of my *Tonality in Music.*

the three most consonant intervals known in our hearing, 4th, 5th, and Octave. In Sach's words, these outlines "give the melody a solid skeleton, they stress certain notes for rest or suspension and, in short, prevent the melody from getting lost in anarchy." [21] Sachs was ahead of his time.

The same kind of framing action plays a basal role in the improvised music–making of small children; as with the melodies created by adults, it is a principal source of pitch context. Psychologist Lyle Davidson concludes that such frames result from "the size of the interval that a child can use to organize off-the-cuff musical performances." [22] As we shall demonstrate in detail later, the same kind of framing occurs as a grouping property for melodies from over the world. It is a fundament of our hearing, so it requires some explanation, both in terms of its universal presence and its causes.

The Pitch Contexts of Melody

The notation of *God Save the Queen* shown here is "in the key of C."

Ex. 4.4: *God Save the Queen*

Why *C*? Not just because that note occurs most often. In fact, both *e* and *f* occur nine times to its eight. As ethnomusicologist Mantle Hood once observed in describing pitch hierarchy in Javanese music, "the number of *times* pitch 1 occurs

---

[21] Sachs, *The Rise of Music in the Ancient World*, 64.
[22] "Tonal Structures of Children's Early Songs," 363.

. . . may have little significance compared to *where* it occurs,"[23] and *C*'s primacy in *God Save the Queen* is not different. As with real estate, location is everything! In music it's a matter both of *where, how,* and for *how long* things happen. First are the time/form properties mentioned earlier.

1. The tune begins with *C*;

2. subsequent patterns bear *C* as rhythmically important;

3. the first phrase ends (m. 4) with *C*, after orbitings above and below have confirmed it as pitch fulcrum.

So far, *C* is *contextually* important. Then *G* comes along in measure 7; it is metrically accented and begins a new phrase, so with *C* it plays a formative role.

In fact, that *G* is a defining pitch factor, bearing a special fealty with the *C* already enshrined rhythmically. The enclosing *C< G* span (interval of a "5th") provides a frame with a unique property: we humans tend to "favor" the lower pitch *C* as vectorial center, [24] as pitch focus. Every time we rehear the first six or seven pitches of *God Save the Queen* we are induced to image what has preceded and what follows in just that way—with *C* as vectorial focus. Why is that *C<G* relation so prominent for us? Because of its primal role in the *harmonic series*.[25] It is a crucial item in our cognitive arsenal, part of almost every sound we hear.

Ex. 4.5: The Harmonic Series

(Only 1 through 8 partials shown)

---

[23] *The Ethnomusicologist*, 334.

[24] A *vector* is a directional force. Perhaps my reader has heard an airline pilot announce to passengers that "We are now vectoring in on O'Hare."

[25] Also known as the "overtone series."

There is nothing rare, nothing mysterious, nothing theoretically profound about this pitch hierarchy, this auditory matrix.[26] It is one of those enduring properties of "human nature" celebrated by psychologist Pinker. Or let us think of it as a *sonic tropism*, to borrow philosopher John Searle's coinage.[27] It's a cognitive inhibition, an auditory prop comparable to those of visual dynamics, like lines projecting a directional "force," as in Example 4.6, where lines "point to" a non-existent point of focus, a vectorial focus that is the context's nucleus. [28]

Ex. 4.6: Visual vectors

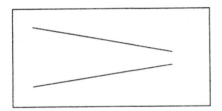

In case you don't know what it might sound like, the 3-4-5 partials of the series are made explicit every time a bugler plays his "calls."[29] The one known as *Taps*, played in military posts for funerals and marking the onset of evening, begins on partial #3. It then moves up through #4,[30] finally peaking toward the end on #6, as shown in Example 4.7, finally ending on #4. And that #4, which is a pitch-class duplicate of #1. They contribute the *root*, or vectorial focus, of the series.

---

[26] It is anathema to PostMods who prefer to think that the principles of music are products solely of artistic development. It nonetheless is a factor readily confirmable by the most rigorous empirical standards.

[27] *The Rediscovery of Mind*, 173

[28] The relative lightness/darkness, obscurity/clarity of visual experience can produce the same kinds of background/foreground vectoring.

[29] The bugle is called a "natural" horn because it has no pitch-altering valves like cornets and trumpets, nor a slide like the trombone. It can produce the pitches of only one harmonic series.

[30] Note that the opening (on #3) is a metrically unaccented pitch, while the #4 is accented.

Ex. 4.7: Bugle Call Taps and its partials

Partials: 3   4   5   6

And let us note another, a seemingly arcane yet paramount feature of the harmonic series. A violinist plays a note; we say we hear a single tone. But in fact our ear/brain processing is feeding us a simplified product from the web of pitches to which our inner ear's hair cells are responding. In this way the totality—the entirety of the series—forms the tone quality, or *timbre*, of that single pitch we say we hear. This recognition is crucial: the word *tonality* refers to "tone" as a broader aspect of experience, a larger context. In that context *Time/Space* assumes the kind of contextual *harmonic* condition formed by the single complex tone.

Whatever we might choose to call it, this ordering of the pitch realm is a part of our experiential makeup, an imposed cognitive inhibition. Philosopher Andrew Ushenko long ago elaborated on the same condition John Searle called a *tropism*, but he preferred to call it *vectorial*, a "dynamic directedness, or bearing upon others . . . an agency of influence of control."[31] And as Ushenko later elaborates, as "a contextual quality" it combines the function of "a property and a relation." [32]

Pitch vectoring is just one condition of our hearing, one part of the dynamics that enable pitch contexts to emerge from pitch parts. Poetic and musical meter, the measuring off of time, is another vectorial condition. A simple example occurs when we hear a series of equally–spaced taps on a drum in a soft-**loud**/soft/**loud** succession. The high-probability perception—the imposed

---

[31] *Dynamics of Art*, 6.
[32] *Ibid*, 37.

context—is of duple meter: 2-**ONE**, 2-**ONE**, etc. There is a vectorial prominence—the "downbeat"—in each louder tap of the series.[33]

So we are talking about elemental matters. The more prominent pitch relations found low in the harmonic series,[34] as between 1 and 2 (octave), 2 and 3 (5th), 3 - 4 (4th), 4 - 5 (major 3rd), are especially powerful in their vectorial powers, in their strength to act as the pitch-poles of a context. Their prominence in the pitch realm has been confirmed and reconfirmed by empirical evidence. As acoustician Andrew Pikler averred a half-century ago, the unique role of the octave (1-2 of the series) is present unless the listener suffers pathological irregularities in the pitch sense (*Paeracusis qualitatis*). Denial of the psychophysical reality of this anchoring in the octave would, as Pikler continues, "contradict basic auditory experience."[35]

It is important to note that these properties of our pitch world are not all-powerful in initiating this "tending toward," this tropism of pitch hierarchy. They are unique to the pitch world, but they work, give-and-take, with other properties. It's a grave error to ignore the importance of the total *mix*, pitch, time, loudness, timbre and texture as co-determinants, to forget "the importance of *the manner* in which pitches provide context for one another as the music unfolds before the listener."[36]

Music's vectorial properties were conveniently ignored by those who fantasized about gaining total freedom for their art. Theirs was a curious refusal to acknowledge behavioral realities, a syndrome not unlike embarrassment produced during the Victorian Age by public discussions of sex—except, as psychologist Pinker notes, it is even worse: "it distorts our science and scholarship, our public discourse, and our day-to-day lives." [37] And as Pinker adds, we can no more turn

---

[33] Given an extended series of taps of equal loudness, we take our pick of metric pattern.
[34] Prominent because of greater energy.
[35] "The Diatonic Foundation of Hearing," *Acta Musicologica* 11 (1955), 440.
[36] Butler and Brown, 193. (My italics.)
[37] *The Blank Slate*, ix.

off our elaborate system of cognitive inhibitions "than we can override our stomachs and tell them when to release their digestive enzymes."[38]

In view of the harmonic series and its role in our hearing, can we really believe that our perceived inequities of pitch intervals are products of cultural conditioning? Are they, as Schoenberg once claimed, products of "art" rather than of native cognitive forces? Evidence suggests the latter, the less malleable cause. There is nothing new nor arcane about these undemocratic pitch conditions; even infants display their presence from early on. Studying responses of 6-yr old children to pitch patterns, psychologists Schellenberg and Trehub concluded that "listeners form relatively stable memory representations for octaves, fifths, and fourths."[39] Other studies reveal that infants find certain intervals, like 5[ths], 4[ths], and 3[rds], easier to encode and remember than those of more complex ratios.[40] In their cribs they differentiate Mama's voice by *harmonic* content, separating its sound from voices of a different timbre. The discrimination of consonance from dissonance and the ability to differentiate one timbre from another are in place by the age of 2-to-4 months.[41] So the pitch hierarchy plays a decisive role in our sound worlds even before birth. By no means is it a habit internalized after hearing all of those nursery rhymes and kindergarten songs and TV commercials.[42]

Evangelists of atonalism and dodecaphonism knew the harmonic series, but mainly as a curiosity of history, a quaint remnant of Pythagorean number–

---

[38] *Ibid.*, 412. Physical causes for the harmonic series are measurable on an eardrum or the hair cells within the human cochlea. H. Fletcher helped to initiate our understanding of auditory processing as early as the 1930s, positing a theory in which hearing content begins on the basilar membrane and in the auditory nerve, thus both mechanical and "electrical." See his "A Space-time Pattern of Hearing," *Journal of the Acoustical Society of America* 1930, 311-343.

[39] "Childrens' discrimination of melodic intervals," 1048.

[40] See Schellenberg and Trehub 96a and 96b, as well as Trainor and Heinmiller, 1998.

[41] See Trainor, Tsang, and Cheung, 2002; Schellenberg and Trehub, 1996; Trehub and Trainor, 1998; Zentner and Kagan, 1998; and Deliège and Sloboda, 1996.

[42] Empirical studies indicate highly developed neonate pitch and timbre discrimination three to four months before birth. The fetus responds to environmental sounds by the sixth prenatal month. See Lecanuet, pp. 23-25; Trehub, Endman, and Thorpe, 308; Fassbender, 67 and 80. Extensive reports are to be found in Werner and Marean, *Human Auditory Development*, as well as Lecanuet, Granier-Deferre, and Bushnel, "Human Fetal Auditory Perception."

play. a purely mathematical construct. Or more practically, it represented the way a violin's string can be divided to produce higher pitches. There was no inkling that such a fixed relational condition might be an inescapable component of all audible worlds. And thus it was rejected—and still is—by a number of thinkers, from Schoenberg to dodecaphonic gurus Milton Babbitt and Allen Forte. It is a condition blindly ignored by those who find credible Milton Babbitt's coinage "Overtone Follies." [43]

Enthusiasm was strong late in the last century for establishing controllable—even dispensable—causes as a base for what we hear. One reigning argument was the irrelevance of pitch hierarchy, ignoring neuro-physiological roots for the experience of consonance and dissonance at the same time. [44] The real world presents a different picture. Those who prefer to deny such biologically-imposed conditions of "human nature" would profit from attention to philosopher John Searle's reminder that "mental events and processes are as much part of our biological history as digestion, mitosis, meiosis, or enzyme secretion." [45] I repeat: We can't turn off our cognitive "inhibitions." We can ignore them, but that's another game.

The same pitch intervals are mentioned as playing critical roles in ancient music treatises. Historian Stefano Mengozzi, for instance, makes clear that medieval theorist Guido d'Arezzo recognized how "the octave plays an all pervasive role as a regulative diatonic segment. . ." In Guido's vocabulary the tones of an octave are what they are for us today: they are "equal-sounding." Furthermore, the interval of the 5th (remember the pitch frame of *God Save the Queen*?) possesses "an *almost-perfect* affinity." [46] Even the most exotic note-systems, made of tunings wholly "eccentric" by standards of the West, include the

---

[43] For one recent example see Stephen Dembski, "The Structure of Construction," Pp. 17-34, *In Theory Only*, Vol. 13, June, 2007.

[44] Paul Hindemith's explanation of over a half-century ago (*The Craft of Musical Composition*) has been criticized as too deterministic, too anti-dodecaphonic. His explanations contain systemic flaws, but none to negate his fundamental premises.

[45] Searle, *Loc. cit.*, 1.

[46] "Virtual Segments: The Hexachordal System in the Late Middle Ages," 430, 432, 436.

octave as the basic divider of their pitch ranges. In Chapter 5 we'll encounter the same pervasive roles of pitch dominance in the musics of other cultures.

Looking back at the tunes of Ex.4.3, notice that their frames utilize lower (and thus more intrusive) intervals of the harmonic series in commanding ways:

Ex. 4.8: Tonality Frames for the Five Tunes of Ex. 4.3

Serialist protocol is explicitly aware of the dangers octaves and 5ths and major or minor triads pose for a 12-tone stew. They are "dangerous" intervals; they can negate a desired absence of tonal sense. One icon of mid-century Serialism, Pierre Boulez, observed the basic problem and the need for aware composers to circumvent it. Sparing no words, he outlined the prevailing perspective of preference, ways to ensure that 12-tone rows enact their intended roles. One rule is to establish "a universe where consonance and dissonance are abolished." In such a context music's "horizontal and vertical oppositions" [47] are diluted; octaves and triads are contaminated fuels for the desired serial fire. When octaves are too evident within a texture, they

> have a tendency to reinstate a functional principle of identity—of structural identification—in the dialectic of sound relationships: strongly gravitational intervals, combinations of intervals already assimilated into an established function. The octave and the triad are simply the most striking examples. [48]

And Boulez later adds:

---

[47] *Boulez on Music Today*, 132. He makes a fuzzy distinction between what he calls *actual* and *virtual* octaves. In his judgment the actual kind are the more dangerous. See page 46, *Loc. cit.*
[48] *Ibid.*, 49.

Those forbidden intervals, like octaves, create a weakening, a hole, in the succession of sound relationships by way of provisionally reinstating a principle of identity denied by the other sounds, so that they are at variance with the principal [sic] of structural organisation [sic].[49]

Note well that those elements listed by Boulez are undesirables in such neighborhoods for a simple reason: they contain 5^{ths} and 4^{ths} and 3^{rds}, those infectious intervals from low in the harmonic series.

The Boulez diagnosis and proffered cure make explicit a perplexing set of circumstances for any thoughtful musician. Here are brilliant people telling us that there is this pernicious aspect of the audible world, a kind of gravitational pull so basic to the psyche that one must work hard to banish it from politically-correct products. [50] It's hard to imagine a more blatant admission of a music system gone astray, an ideology contradicting—or at best negating—a fundamental reality that feeds perceptual dynamics.

Inequities of our pitch system, like those represented by the harmonic series, have been as much a source of confusion as enlightenment within music's history. When viewed from a superficial vantage point they have motivated some hilarious theorizing among the incautious. Early champions of the scale as pitch base were delighted to note one particular condition: four of the major scale's seven notes (1-2-3-5) are "found" in the lowest nine partials of the harmonic series. This added a reassuring delight, further proof of the major scale's sanctity. But their joy was tempered by another realization: the vaunted subdominant (fourth note, or F in a C scale) was encased as a significant component of much tonal music. Imagine the *Amen* cadence of any Protestant hymn without it! But its root pitch, IV, can't be found in the series.[51] What an annoying roadblock to theory-making!

---

[49] *Ibid.*, 132.

[50] Alban Berg didn't let this power of consonant sounds and suggestions of tonal centers bridle his creativity in serialized passages of his *Violin Concerto*.

[51] The 11th partial of the C series is closer to $F\#$ than to F, so ineligible for the role.

No problem!

Absence of that relation of the 4th degree led to an immaculate conception: it was christened *The Undertone Series*. A product of pure navel-gazing, it "yielded" that coveted element, supplying the missing note for the five lower notes of the doctrinal major scale. And it provided even more! It also gave "natural" proof of the minor triad (the *Unterklang!*) as a primary chord.

Ex. 4.9: Pitch Prototypes (both real and fictive)

This fantasized symmetry, *overtone* series balanced by *undertone* replica, continues to color some of the more fanciful thinking about music's pitch structure today—pure hogwash though it be. For those who are unwilling to separate fact from fable, it also provides circumstantial proof of the harmonic series' irrelevance. Milton Babbitt's early denial of its relevance defies all known empirical studies of sonance, yet his quaint conclusion is as emphatic as it is unfounded: "the succession of intervals in the overtone series does not correspond to the categorizations of 'consonant' and 'dissonant', even in relative terms. . ."[52]

Theorist Allen Forte had proclaimed the official—the less frolicsome—position even earlier than Babbitt, in his *Contemporary Tone Structures* of 1955. He there denies the cognitive powers of the harmonic series (or of any pitch hierarchy) *even as it might relate to tonal music*. Couched in one of the prize misstatements of music history, Forte informs the world that "The pure overtone series as it exists in nature is unknown to modern ears. Fine adjustments have been made to conform to equal temperament." [53] He later confirms this naïve claim in his fiery response to a negative review of that book. The reviewer, according to Forte, "seems to equate the overtone series with 'nature,' not realizing that the overtone series is itself a construct which conceivably may one day be replaced by a different construct."[54]

As Forte may have learned subsequently, replacement is yet to come. He may have had equal-temperament in mind, but that tuning is only a man-made compromise.[55] Unnoticed by listeners, it has no power over how our ears process sound, nor does it influence the timbre we hear for any single tone. Audition is the singular evidence of what music is, what it can or cannot be. Evolution has not released us from the harmonic series prison, nor is it likely to do so in the near future. Serialist theory spinners like Forte would have profited from heeding that old Latin proverb *Natura non facit saltum*: "Nature does not make leaps." The fact is, it sometimes moves not at all.[56]

---

[52] To my knowledge first made in his defining thrust "The Structure and Function of Music Theory," 18-19. His claim extends further than we need repeat, lamely (and inexplicably)finding contradiction in the traditional regard of the 4th (3-4) as more consonant than major 3rd (4-5), minor 6th (5-8) more consonant than the tritone (3-7).

[53] Linguistic curiosity makes us wonder how this condition can "exist in nature" yet be "unknown to modern ears."

[54] *Journal of Music Theory*, November, 1957, 204.

[55] Simply put, it divides the octave (2:1) into twelve equal semitones (1.04956:1.0). This enables fixed-pitch instruments like pianos to play in tune in any key.

[56] A revealing look into the powers of "nature" in our responses to sonic things is a 1997 study by William Forde Thompson and Richard Parncutt: "Perceptual Judgments of Triads and Dyads: Assessment of a Psychoacoustic Model."

Our literature brims over with assurances that the 19th century's rich chromaticism, abrupt melodic angularity, and avoidance of traditional cadences "undermined" the tonal tradition, paving the road to 12-tone chromaticism. Musicologist Lawrence Kramer paints a more insightful picture: music of Romanticism's masters didn't lack the harmonic directedness typical of Bach, Haydn, and Mozart. [57] Furthermore, as I might add, generalizing grandly about *Tristan's* "high chromaticism" ignores its wealth of blandly diatonic passages. Like any good opera composer, Wagner chose his pitches to match dramatic needs. Indeed, most works of the Wagnerian era cited as "tonally unstable" are heavily freighted with sections of simple, straightforward diatonicism, tonic chords frequent and unmistakable, traditional cadences abundant.

Let us make explicit just one evident conclusion: conceptual evidence doesn't tally well with the myth of creeping chromaticism, especially when posited as a decisive clue to evolutionary inevitability, "a vision of musical entropy." As current repertories, from the high-artiest to the pits-of-Pop, continue to convince us, tonality turned out to be a durable basis for 20th- and 21st-century music. Musicologist Joseph Strauss has confirmed that most composers (50 to 90% of them) during Serialism's most alluring times (1950s and 60s) ". . . in all corners of the musical marketplace, wrote in a relatively conservative idiom, with a style that maintained strong ties to a traditional tonality." And, adding a point crucial for our broader story, Strauss observes that "Serialism . . . commanded an intellectual interest out of proportion to its actual measurable presence on the musical scene."[58]

Music harbors some of the same instinctive behaviors encountered in language. As Noam Chomsky reminded us long ago, a child enters this world primed to acquire a language. That child's linguistic "deep structure" is nothing more than the essential functions, the *universals*, which all languages share.

---

[57] See Kramer's discussion, *Op. cit.*, 192.
[58] "The Myth of Serial Tyranny," 302-303.

Contexts are crucial and the sonic art is not different. A musical phrase, like a sentence, is more like a tree, certainly not a chain of undifferentiated links. It's a tree whose roots, like those of its horticultural counterpart, are configured in ways that are largely predetermined. It's a tree whose meaning can be fathomed only as a set of parts within a dynamic whole. In music those parts are aided and abetted by certain perceptual tropisms—like that of the harmonic series—that affect our perception of pitch.

Let us recall the reference to psychologist Steven Pinker's credible summary of such conditions in our *Prologue*, his reminder that the mind enjoys drives and faculties derived from information in the human genome, common across cultures and difficult, if not impossible, to alter. The record shows that throughout history we have organized the sounds of music in ways that accommodate the processing predilections of our auditory/neural equipment, just as we have designed our tools to fit the processing predilections of two hands with ten digits dominated by a finger/thumb operational capability.

As a humorous historical aside for closure, observe that the "information in the genome," as it might relate to pitch particles, didn't dampen enthusiasm for the "progressive change" canon, the naïve ideology of a continuing evolution for tones. After all, if $3 + 2$ = the 5 of music's ancient pentatonicism; and if $5 + 2$ = the 7 of major/minor diatonicism; and if $7 + 5$ = the 12 of dodecaphonism; then why not $12 + 7 = 19$. And behold the virgin birth in 1932 of the "19-tone System" attended by Russian-born Joseph Yasser (*A Theory of Evolving Tonality*). It was yet another path taken in the revolutionary quest for ever greater abundance of "official" notes to fill the octave. Fabrications of quarter-tone systems were popular too, fulfilling a potential forecast by Busoni in 1907.[59] Those creations still haven't caught on with the human race a century later—except as occasional decorative overlay for more basic properties.

---

[59] In his *Entwerf einer neuen Aesthetik der Tonkunst*. By 1923, A. Förster of Prague had devised a keyboard capable of producing quarter-tones, thus able to perform pieces composed by brothers Alois and Karl Haba as well as Ernest Bloch.

Chapter 5

MEANWHILE: BEYOND OUR
WEST-EUROPEAN ORBIT

There are further compelling reasons for questioning that revolutionary tenet about atonality and twelve-tone sets as scheduled stops on the evolutionary train. One source inheres in the actual music and explanatory documents left to us from the riches of modern ethnomusicology. Hard evidence tells a more unified story of humanity's music; the "evolving chain" turns out to be made more of surface impressions than of elemental ingredients.

We can't know with certainty how ancient peoples—especially those from remote lands—perceptualized the music they heard. This should surprise no one: I can only guess how my next-door neighbors respond to the music they hear. Musicians aren't alone in this limitation of knowing, although their task may involve more abstract matters than those of other fields. As psychologist Morton Hunt traces the ontological byways of history,[1] paths reveal stark contrasts as well as similarities. Geologists find their prime evidence in the sedimentary layers of our planet; for cosmologists hard evidence begins with those ancient lights emitted by remote galaxies; physicists assemble their evidence from atomic particles and tracks made in cloud chambers of emulsion; and for biologists the developmental path runs all the way from the fossils of prehistory to humanity.

We are equally limited in studies of the mind and its operations. We can't quite penetrate its interior, although we can track images from which to infer processes that preceded them. Musicologists have at least one opening: we possess some actual tracks, artifacts from remote sources. We also treasure a few explanatory documents left to us by coeval thinkers in more advanced societies,

---

[1] In his monumental *The Story of Psychology*.

as well as tightly reasoned explanations by living scholars. We even have recordings of songs passed on intact over many generations, often as the sacred possessions of a people, thus facsimiles of the original substance.

Cross-cultural samplings show the gist of evidence. They demonstrate that standardized pitch hierarchies were a decisive property of music long before the 18th and 19th centuries; they were not limited to Caucasian ethnic strains, nor were they radically different from what we find in our own pop, folk, and art musics. As ethnomusicology pioneer Mantle Hood once suggested to me, "We have all paid too much attention to scales and intervals without attending to what is really important: tonality." [2]

Those basic pitch bricks and their defining mortar play major roles in the most prosaic of tribal tunes, just as they do in the musics of Palestrina, Mozart, and Ellington.

Exotic Melodies, Conventional Frames

Classical Greece is the bastion of the West-European claim to culture, so we'll start there before looking in on more exotic sources, both earlier and later. An authentic melody from no later than the 1st century A.D. found on a Grecian tombstone is a prized classic. It spins a jaunty tune, its lyric an ancient admonition to "Have a nice day." [3]

5.1: *Hymn to Seikilos* (100 B.C.-100 A.D.)

Pitch Frame

---

[2] In a private conversation at the University of Hawaii in 1968.
[3] "As long as you live, be cheerful; let nothing grieve you. For life is short, and time claims its tribute."

Like *God Save the Queen*, its pitches play within a straightforward plot; it even stars the same interval of a 5th. Its first pitch is A; its line plays around with a peak of E; its second phrase (m. 5) begins with the opening A, a pitch that returns five times within the closing phrase. Our summary illustrates the tune's simple framing, its context of pitch.

What do we call that distillation? We could pick from several historical nomenclatures of our fractured musicology, from Greek *Phrygian* to medieval *Hypo-Mixolydian* to 19th century "altered A-major." But names are secondary to the genetic kinship this melody shares with songs by Schubert or Gershwin or Led Zepplin—or *God Save the Queen*. Let us favor a path of wise reductionism and call the condition by its most accurate generic name: *Tonality*. Its evidence resides in that "solid skeleton" mentioned many years ago by musicologist Curt Sachs. It is the pitch outline that keeps the melody from "getting lost in anarchy." [4]

The same conditions prevail in songs from over the globe, confirming that the pitch patterning of *Seikilos* is no rare phenomenon. When the pitches of a music-maker transcend the level of ritual chant, or mere background rhythms for a dance, they cross the great divide to become *Melody*; they have grown into a thing-in-itself. They reach this status in part by virtue of the contextualizing pitch potentials, the musical kinetics we discussed in Chapter 4. A 20th century specialist in African music, Eric von Hornbostel, long ago confirmed such framing actions in the most primitive of tunes, through use of certain intervals such as 4^{ths} and 5^{ths}.

> They are . . . used as constructive elements determining the distance between predominant notes, the compass of melodic phrases, and the rise or fall of a melody when its position is changed (transposed). In this way they mark off the field where melody is at play. [5]

It's a simple and demonstrable fact: most melodies of this world cut obvious paths through standardized pitch frames. All do not; some reflect the

---

[4] *The Rise of Music in the Ancient World*, 64.
[5] "African Negro Music," 35-36.

fleeting kinds of ambiguities we sometimes (but rarely) encounter in the tunes of our own folk and pop cultures.[6] Some melodies defy an assured interpretation of overall pitch context, as it may have been conceived by members of that melody's culture. But most are immediately evident. Melody 5.2a resembles the ancient Greek Seikelos hymn in this respect. It could not be more direct in its framing of the 5th *a – e*. Melody 2b, on the other hand, vacillates between *a -e* and *c - g - c* frames.

Does this shift of framing in the second tune, *La Mintso*, suggest that its creators didn't hear music the way we do? That's unlikely. Such vacillations reveal nothing more than a richness of pitch play that makes the music all the more engaging. In this respect it is not different from melody 2c, *Crawdad Song*, that comes from the American South tradition. The same kind of mixing, with pitches *d* and *f* vying for vectorial prominence, occurs in the Paiute song (2d). As with the "Crawdad Song," it provides much of the tune's unique charm.

5.2a *Kuro'I Nye*, African folksong (Nketia, *Music in Ghana*)

---

[6] Think of the opening phrase of Hoagy Carmichael's *Stardust*. Without its accompanying chords it offers a baffling pitch-context problem for anyone hearing it for the first time.

5.2b: *La Mintso*, African folk duet (Niketia, *Music in Ghana*, 127)

2c: *Crawdad Song* (East Texas folksong)

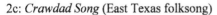

You get a line and I'll get a pole honey

Pitch Frame

5.2d: Paiute Song (G.Herzog, "Speech-Melody and Primitive Music "

Tonality Frame

112

On the other hand, melodies 2e and 2f suggest nothing less than shifting frames, or modulation. In the first, *Ta Avo*, it's a simple shift from the *a* tonic of mm 1-4 to the *d* tonic that emerges by mm. 8-9. In *Halo Nelo* the shifts contribute to the tune's overall phrase form of A^{1-2} and B^{1-2}.

5.2e: *Ta Avo na Legra*, African folksong (Nketia, *The Musical Languages of Sub-Saharan Africa*)

pitch synopsis by sections

Overall potential frame

2f: *Halo Nelo*, Rumanian Children's Song (Kacarova-Kuludova, *Studia Memoriae Belae Bartók Sacra*)

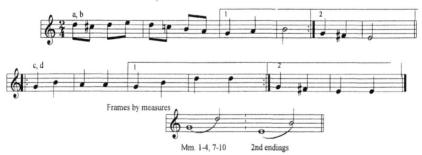

Frames by measures

Mm. 1-4, 7-10   2nd endings

The next melody is more typical of the world's repertoires, more uniform in positing focal points. In traditional nomenclature it is in the Dorian mode, but most relevant to us is the way it projects dominating pitches within the neatly prescribed frame of *D –d*.

5.2g: *The Crafty Lover*, English folksong

The next three melodies are unique in their separate ways. The African Women's Song (2h) suggests an *F* tonic in the beginning, yet its continuation establishes C as unquestionable vectorial focus. On the other hand, the Vedic melody (2i) is of such limited pitch content and rhythmic uniformity that it is closer to chant than to true melody. Its brief *e* and *a* both function as decoratives for the *G* that dominates. By contrast, the Hungarian tune of 2j is full blown melody of unquestionable pitch dominance, despite some hint of *C* in its first phrase.

Ex. 5.2h: African Women's Duet (von Hornbostel, "African Music")

2i: Vedic melody (E. Felber, 1912)

114

2j: *Jánoshidi vársártéren*, Hungarian Folksong (*Studia Memoriae Belae Bartók Sacra*)

Ja-nos-hi - di   va sar te ren,

Tonality Frame

I have reservations about the rhythmic monotony as notated in the medieval Chinese song of 2l, although its cultural function was ritualistic. The pitch complement, an f - f ambitus, however, is probably authentic. Its pitch orientation is as clear as those of 2m and 2n, although they are from wholly different milieus and cultures.

2k: "Here We are Gathering Duckweed," Chinese melody, Tang Dynasty

Tonality Frame

And melodies 2l and 2m are too straightforward to require explanation

21: Byzantine Christmas Hymn

E - so-se la-orthauma-tur-gon   ,

Tonality Frame

2m: "Hymn to John the Baptist" (*Liber Usualis* 1504)

Ut que-ant lax - is

Tonality Frame

Ancient Textual Confirmations of Pitch Hierarchy

Should these congealing correspondences, circling the globe from ancient to modern, surprise us? Has human perception not changed in its most elemental characteristics over the centuries? Not if these melodies and descriptive texts can be trusted. As early as Aristoxenus (born in Tarentum, 354 B.C.) [7] melodies were known as tapestries woven from unequal threads. In his historic *The Harmonics*

---

[7] Aristoxenus is the most respected source of his times re music's structure and nature. He was a pupil of Aristotle.

he describes the formulated Greek scale's "middle note," the *mese*,[8] as a "foundation" for its associated pitches; other pitches share a unique dependence upon it. This binding "middle-note/dependent-notes" condition is that of *context*; Aristoxenus describes it as deriving from our two faculties of "hearing and intellect." He then adds a most insightful comment, observing that "by the latter [intellect] we contemplate the *functions* of the notes."[9]

So it seems that for 4th century B.C. music lovers—even before the *Seikilos* epitaph was chiseled into stone—the human apprehension of a melody depended, as Aristoxenus put it, on the ability to ". . . perceive the sound that is present, and remember that which is past."[10] In other words, apprehending the coagulation into a context demands the mixing of past and present pitch parts. So things haven't changed much in 4,000 years. The pitch dynamics fit admirably into one of those rubrics for any Art we set up in Chapter 1: parts add up into wholes to project meaning as a "thing." In this case, pitches are in the limelight.

Even more unequivocal Greek correspondences were voiced a couple of centuries after Aristoxenus in the *Problems* of Pseudo-Aristotle.[11] They describe a functioning pitch axis. The *mese* (or "middle tone") he describes in his *Problem XIX* could be the *Do* in a folksong of old Appalachia, the keynote of a Mozart *Minuet*, the *Sa* for a North Indian *Raga*.[12] As he puts it, "all the best tunes make frequent use of the *mese*, and all good musicians employ it frequently, and quickly revert to it, even if they leave it, but not to any other note to the same extent."[13]

---

[8] The theoretical Greek scale extended over an octave. The fourth note up from its bottom–its fundamental note–was called the "middle note" or *mese* (pronounced "messy"). For a discussion of the more encompassing classical Greek Greater Perfect System, see Thomson, *Tonality in Music*, 193-199.

[9] *The Harmonics*, 189, my italics.

[10] *Ibid.*, 193-194.

[11] We aren't certain who the author was, but it wasn't Aristotle. Greek music scholar Thomas Mathieson has assured me that whoever it was, he or she lived no later than the 2nd century B.C.

[12] See Walter Kaufmann, *The Ragas of North India*, especially page 5.

[13] *Problems*, Book I, Problem XIX, #20.

16th-century Italian Gioseffo Zarlino makes the same point many centuries later, warning composers to adequately project the intended pitch hierarchy (he called it *mode*) in their renascent music. To do this, they must "frequently sound the members of the *diapason* [octave] in which the mode is composed, namely the *diapente* [5th] *diatesseron* [4th]."[14] Recast into an updated lexical universe of tonality, Zarlino is passing on some basic wisdom to his colleagues: In the *D* modes (1 and 2), *A* and *D* must occur often to make evident the intended pitch structure.

5.3: Dorian octaves

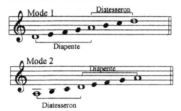

Or let us look back into appraisals of sonance. Have our perceptions of pitch intervals changed since Pseudo-Aristotle? His words force us to recall the harmonic series discussed in Chapter 4. He marvels at the striking likeness of octave-related pitches and asks rhetorically: "Why does the low note contain the sound of the high note? Is it because the low note is heavier? It is like an obtuse angle whereas the high note is like an acute angle." [15]

These are indicting words from ancient times. They confirm a binding uniformity between us and listeners of centuries past. They point to pitch kinetics derived from the same contextual values of sound that endure today. If Pseudo-Aristotle reflects the auditory mores of his fellow Athenians, then ancient Greeks heard the octave as the purest pitch interval—greatest consonance—followed by

---

[14] *On the Modes*, 48.
[15] *Loc. Cit.*, I, XIX, 13. Rome's Boethius of the 6th century extends the same query in his *Fundamentals of Music*, 169.

the 5th and 4th. Such stories are not rare in the annals of world cultures. Our ears don't disagree today.[16]

Nor need we assume that Pseudo-Aristotle and Aristoxenus were the first to mention pitch-interval purity. Musicologist Eric Werner convincingly argues that recognition of the octave's unique musical role (as well as its impressive 1:2 mathematical ratio) "took place many centuries before the division of the octave, as a scale, into 8 unequal steps."[17] Acknowledgment of that sonic reality in the near East probably influenced the Greeks in Werner's opinion, via that mythological giant we know as Pythagoras.

Reliable documentation drawn from more recent primitive peoples, data acquired empirically over the past century, is as informative and confirmative as revelations from ancient times. Such data reveal a uniformity that is not a product of cross-cultural borrowings, nor do they suggest evolved cognitive powers.

Ethnomusicologist John Blacking assures us there are shared elements "common to the human psyche" found in the most remote cultures. Although they may not be immediately apparent to outsiders, they are part of "the surface of structures." An authority in music of the Venda culture in the Transvaal area of South Africa, Blacking has observed deep common roots for many years, a persistence of conformities that "throws a light upon similitudes inherent in human nature and the fundament of music." [18]

Pitch hierarchy is evident in the most exotic of scale systems, even in performance practices whose documents claim quite different note-tunings from ours.[19] That's true of the "modal" scales of the Vietnamese *Dan Tranh*. In describing their nature, ethnomusicologists Keefe, Burns, and Nguyen observe

---

[16] Pseudo-Aristotle's denial of consonance for 3^{rds} was ideological, based on fealty to the Pythagorean mathematical ratios. That gave the octave (ratio of 2:1) highest mark, 5th (3:2) with the 4th (4:3) close behind. The 3 + 5 (= 8) of the Major 3rd exceeded the magic number 7.

[17] "The Oldest Sources of Octave and Octoechos," 1.

[18] Quotes are from *How Musical is Man*, 109.

[19] Performers don't fully agree with the "fixed" tuning of a piano; and thus they vary pitches slightly to suit their taste. Violinists, singers, and guitarists, naturally depart from "tempered tunings." We don't formulate these into "systems" and claim their primacy, although we have the means to do so.

that they actually possess a clear and simple tonal structure. Getting down to nuts and bolts, they attest that "such structures include at the least a tonic, but also a hierarchical [sic] of tonal relationships between the pitch classes." [20]

As we have observed, pitch hierarchy is evident in some of the most primitive melodies of history, and let us note that a great number of different pitches is not demanded to create that condition. Ethnomusicologists Bruno Nettl and Walter Wiora have both pointed out that the low pitch of such sparse collections usually acts as central pitch, or "tonic." [21] In an attempt to characterize the simplest dimensions of a universal melodic "style," Nettl observes that such a prototype is made of "a short phrase repeated several or many times, with minor variations, using three or four pitches within a range of a fifth."[22]

But we would be misled to believe that all primitive melodies are limited to such a narrow pitch field. Citing a 3,400 yr. old song, historian Robert Fink argues the presence of 5- and 7-pitch note collections in some of the very earliest known music.[23]

These widespread conformities of pitch are anything but peculiar. Our limited sampling reveals their widespread existence in time and space. They necessarily reflect a uniform human proclivity for structure that covers the tribal gamut. They further confirm Psychologist Pinker's astute summing up quoted in our *Prologue*: the conclusion seems unavoidable that the human species is pre-equipped with reasoning and facilities of communication that cut across cultures, innate talents traceable to information in the *homo sapiens* genome.

Even More Exotic Scale Sources

Whatever their pitch-count or their fancied origins, note collections were thought of as serious business by musicians of ancient worlds. Stories of royal or

---

[20] In "Vietnamese Modal Scales of the Dan Tranh," 452.

[21] See Nettl, "Music in Primitive Culture," 48, and Wiora, "Older Than Pentatony," 190.

[22] Nettl, "An Ethnomusicologist Contemplates Music Universals," 469.

[23] In *The Origin of Music*, 6.

divine origins abound in the annals of world cultures, and they usually tag certain notes with hierarchical functions. Their designations are as fascinating as they are informative. Even before their Egyptian and Babylonian successors, Sumerians (c. 3,000-2,000 B.C.) assigned grandiose names for pitch functions. One was the note *Anu*, or "Father of the Gods," that enacted the role of Unity (or *One*). It was principal pitch or reference point, that which "enclosed all things," a "do-nothing" deity. Ergo: Let us call it *Do*, or *Tonic*, or *Finalis*!

Fleshing out that same scale controlled by *Anu* was its fifth note, *Ea Enki*, formed by the ratio 2:3, and thus a 5th. It was known as "the busiest deity in Sumer." In addition to organizing the earth, it was "the most powerful shaping force in music after the octave." [24] Those are the same 8^{ves} and 5^{ths} and 4^{ths} we encountered in Chapter 4 as partials 1:2, 2:3 and 3:4 of the harmonic series, the same frames for tonality in everything from *God Save the Queen* to Ellington's *I've Got It Bad and That Ain't Good*. They've been controlling cultural novelties for many years.

Our knowledge of ancient Chinese pitch systems far exceeds what we know about those of Sumer. From before 3,000 B.C. and into the European Middle Ages, Chinese music-makers wove a fascinating tapestry of explanatory lore. Music was an honorable pastime. *The Ancient Book of Rites* from sometime before the 8th century B.C. attests to its honorable role by noting that "it is the province of the superior man alone to understand the principles of music."[25] That tapestry begins with nothing less than the "invention" of music by mythical Emperor Fu Hsi (c. 2953 B.C.), and it continues into the modernity of 13th and 14th centuries. It is a complex, at times uneven story. Most relevant for us are its less fanciful parts that share deep affinities with Western ways.

---

[24] Ernest McClain, "Musical Theory and Ancient Cosmology," 378-381.

[25] Quoted by Levis, *Foundation of Chinese Musical Art*, 7.

According to Chinese historian Hsu Wen Ying, pitches of his native culture's earliest scales were derived from phases of the moon.[26] Accounts grew less colorful, more earthy, over the years; by 240 B.C. musician Leu Buhwei explained the Chinese pitch universe—still a set of twelve notes—had been concocted by cutting twelve bamboo tubes of equal diameters to ratio-related lengths. The process then followed a procedure of alternating "5th up" and "4th down",[27] carried out to eleven places. Like Eve's derivation from Adam, the lowest pitch, "male" *F*, or *Yin*, begets "female" *C,* or *Yang*,[28] and on through the pitch family of twelve.[29]   And thus from antiquity the Chinese musician recognized a 12-pitch division of the octave.[30]

Ex. 5.4: *Liuh-leu* Stacked Fifths

As legend has it, that ancient Chinese scale's first note, "Yellow Bell," was named for the alleged founder of the Chinese Empire, *Hôang-tsong* [31] (c. 2697 B.C.). In the *Yin-Yang* tradition, it was said to "engender" (again like Adam of Christian myth) the remaining eleven. The first five of those offspring (*F C G D A*) formed the pentatonic (5-note) pitch pool. Along with a heptatonic (7-note) system, it reigned in ancient Chinese music.[32] Exactly the same kinds of scales,

---

[26] *Origins of Music in China,* 17. No less fanciful were some of the elaborate bonds between the major scale and planetary orders found by a few 20th century theorists.

[27] Which in pitch-classes is the analogue of a 5th above.

[28] See Leu Shyh Chuenchiou, Vol. *Inliuh* (63), quoted by Laurence Picken, in *The Oxford History of Music* I, 94. Also see Chao-Mei Pa, *The Yellow Bell,* 13-14.

[29] Music theorists know it as the "Pythagorean gamut."

[30] Levis, *Loc. Cit.,* 63.

[31] Also called Huang Ti by some writers. See Robert Marks, "The Music and Musical Instruments of Ancient China," 593.

[32] A version familiar to anyone who knows derivation of the Pythagorean scale.

derived by adding and subtracting 5^{ths}, were demonstrated in 2nd- millennium Babylon as the "Great Dragon" tuning.[33]

Carefully observe one fact: the pentatonic scale used in Chinese melody (at least into the Chou dynasty around 1122 B.C.) is not different from the pitch content of traditional folk songs of Eastern and Western cultures today. And there is a further structural affinity: "decorative" pitches called *pien tones* (or "side tones") for principal pitch *C* and *G* were recognized elements too. *Pien chih*, or "side *G*," and *Pien Kung*, or "side *C*" were acknowledged "passing tones" in relation to the more basic pentatonic $C - D - E - G - A$ set.[34]

And there is yet another element of familiarity.

Quoting from the ancient *Book of Chou Properties*, theorist Cheng Yi Chen informs us that each note of that 5-note scale could function as the *fundamental* tone of a melody.[35] Known as the *hsüan-kung* principle, this "adaptability" was pre-confirmation of what we demonstrated in Chapter 4, with our five tunes fabricated from the same seven notes but sporting different tonics. It also corresponds with medieval scale theory, in which all modes contain the same set of notes, the designation of each mode determined by a melody's enclosing pitch frame, its *ambitus*.

Whatever may have been the origin of the most ancient of Chinese scales (and let us doubt that they were put together in less than a century), historian Ying is confident that the background of Chinese music had been established by the time of Emperor Shun (2255 B.C.). The very recognition of those ancient 12-note collections as late as 240 B.C. further erodes any notion of a simple and predictable pitch evolution, a progressive growth that by the 20th century had blossomed into the 12 pitch-class world. A more realistic perspective realizes that

---

[33] The same system is symbolically imbedded in Plato's *Critias* dialogue (Book I. Jowett Ed. 77-78), with the earthly family of God Poseidon and maiden Cleito consisting of five sets of twins.

[34] Levis, *Loc.cit.*, 69.

[35] See Cheng-Yih Chen, *Science and Technology in Chinese Civilization*, 27, as well as "The Generation of Chromatic Scales," 182.

developments of musical instruments (notably harpsichord and piano in later times) had more to do with that growth—that "evolution"—than changes in human auditory capacities or the availability of scale notes.

Other official quarries of pitch collections don't end with the ancient worlds. Long after Chinese *Anu* and *Ea Enki*; similar origins crop up in various cultural guises through history. As late as the 13th century a 17-note scale sanctioned for Arabic music by Safi ad-Din al-Urnwai was cut from much the same cloth. Derived from earlier efforts of al-Farabi, who died in 950, this fabrication sought legitimacy by adding and subtracting 5[ths] and 4[ths] from a reference pitch, then reducing the total into a single octave.[36] You will remember it as the derivation process illustrated by the Chinese *Liuh-leu*.

Historian Flora Levin reminds us that "even the word used in ancient documents to denote the octave relationship [*diapason*] meant 'the interval which extends *through all the notes*'."[37] And more directly pertinent to our quest here, Levin tells of Greek linkage of the *Mese* ("middle note") with the Sun, *all other notes as planets nested around it.*[38] As we noted earlier, this dominance of the 8[ve] (1-8) and the perfect 5th (1-5) pervades the literature of medieval music theory from 9th to 15th century.[39] It was no product of "Art," not something hatched up by Bach, Mozart and Brahms.

Evidence From Later Primitive Musics

Ethnomusicologist Bruno Nettl has devoted his career to the study of non-Western musics. One of his most significant conclusions is that such repertories

---

[36] This accounting hasn't lacked skeptics. 20th Century musicologist Habib Hassan Touma admires the precision of the calculations but doubts relevancy of the results because made from "a purely abstract basis" (which is true). He observes (*The Music of the Arabs*, 18) that Arabic intervals *as performed* await precise measurement.

[37] In *The Manual of Harmonics of Nichomachus and the Pythagorean Tradition*. (My italics.)

[38] *Ibid.*, 6.

[39] The most convincing accountings of medieval theorizing I know are those of historian Stefan Mengozzi.

sport melodies in which 8^{ves}, 4^{ths}, and 5^{ths} are central to pitch structure. Even the tunings of those notes are special; "their intonation is more fixed and conforms more consistently with the simpler acoustical ratios than is true of most other intervals." [40]

Nettl refrains from using the term *tonality* for such musics. Why? Because no native informants had vocabularies for verbalizing such matters. Like those peoples studied by anthropologist Dessanayake who lacked a word for love (even though it flourished among them), Nettle's subjects lacked the lexical machinery for describing what is obviously present. He thus opts for the more generalized term "tonal organization," perhaps thinking that it avoids the loaded dice some might associate with traditional harmonic conceptions of "tonality." [41] But it is impossible to mask out the obvious: tonality, as pitch perspective, abounds in this music. Nettl does argue that adequate descriptions of tonal organization in such music should "indicate the tonic and show whether the tonic changes in the course of the piece (modulation) . . ."[42] And in our lexicon, the presence of a *tonic*—and its condescension to another tonic—is a central bit of evidence for the presence of a *tonality*.

I mentioned ethnomusicologist Blacking earlier. He is less reserved about names than Nettl; he prefers terms consistent with the reality of what they describe. Songs combed from the primitive culture of Venda bear evident identities with Western mores. Studied on the spot, the culture itself bears unique values and routines of living, but those routines and their products nonetheless confirm the same kind of "common logic across cultures" depicted by psychologist Pinker. Musicians of Venda described their music's sounds for Blacking in functional ways impressively akin to our own and to those of ancient China. Their central pitch, their *tonic* or *chief tone*, was called *phala*; an octave above it was *phalana*, or "little *phala*." The pitch just above *phala* was *thakula*, or

---

[40] *Music in Primitive Culture*, 59.
[41] I suspect that "tonal organization" would have worked no better than "tonality" in the vocabularies of most primitive cultures."
[42] *Ibid*.

"lifter," so-named because its function was to lead a melody back down into its *phala*. The *thakula* is said to perform *a defining relationship* with *phala*, bearing the designation "companion tone." [43]

And our clues of syncretism don't end there. Those functionally-named pitches of Venda share remarkable traits with Javanese nomenclature too. As ethnomusicologist Mantle Hood once noted about that culture's scalar system, "each principal pitch has a particular role, which governs not only the basic structure of a piece but also the various strata of the improvising parts."[44]

So let us add another check to our scoreboard: Like those august and elaborate Chinese and medieval precedents, the music of Venda doesn't support the simplistic fiction of a non-hierarchic pitch world, certainly not of a fewer-to-more evolution of pitches over the ages. As ethnomusicologist Blacking makes clear, a host of note collections prevailed for filling in the elemental frames.

> The melodies of songs may use anything from one to seven tones, selected from various heptatonic [7-tone] modes. Songs that use five tones may be based on a pentatonic scale or on selections of five tones from a heptatonic mode (like the "Ode to Joy" in Beethoven's Ninth Symphony!).[45]

Furthermore, Venda musicians played 7-pitch xylophones and reed pipes long before they adopted 5-pitch reed pipes, a fact that leads Blacking to observe that "according to evolutionary theories of music history, the Venda should be going backward—like the Chinese, who selected a pentatonic scale for their music although they knew and had used bigger and better scales!" [46]

And finally, there is yet another repertoire rich in cognate traits. One need only look and listen in order to find them in abundance in Hindu music. As rich and exotic as its surface may sound to Western ears, as esoteric as its explanatory

---

[43] Blacking, *Op. Cit.*, 85.

[44] *The Ethnomusicologist*, 326-27.

[45] Blacking, *Op. Cit.*, 57. Blacking is harsh with the conventional treatment by historians in their evolutionary conceptions of music history. In his opinion, they mistakenly "trace musical development in terms of more tones to the octave, more thirds to the chord, and more instruments to the orchestra."

[46] *Ibid.*

vocabulary may seem, it too shares a simple harmonic basis with the musics of Bach and Haydn as well as China and Venda. It boasts a postulated scale of no less than 22 quarter tones, as well as a staggering atlas of different *ragas* (or pitch matrices). But these imposing collections can be misleading; what they represent is more theoretical frostings on the cake than core reality of practice. Musical performances feature a limited sampling of the alleged possibilities of pitch collections. Explanatory theory far exceeds practice.[47]

As complex and exotic in pitch content as explanations of an Indian *raga* may seem to be, its tonal anchorage is hard to miss in the real world of performance. Its notes designated as tonic (*Sa*, or *Shadjah*) and dominant (*Pa*, or *Pañchama*) are by custom reiterated by the ensemble's Tambura player.[48] It's not unlike an extended pedal point in Brahms, the drone of a Highlander's bagpipe tune, or the background I – IV – V bass underpinning of an American Blues. This tonal convention[49] is the pitch stage on which the continuing *raga* improvisation is enacted. A seasoned modern student of that music, Prabhakar Phatak, describes the condition as he discovered it in learning to perform the traditional Indian repertoire. A basic condition demands that "the performer would concentrate on the tonic [*Sa*] and the dominant [*Pa*] and the wafting harmonics. In the context of the tonic, he would seek in the harmonics clues for the key notes in the raga he planned to present." [50]

Phatak's play-by-play description goes on to recall from his own experience that "a framework of sound" came before one could fuse voice with "anchor note. . . the tonic and dominant would literally become the anchors of the recital."

---

[47] I have never heard such in the music of India, nor can I find anyone who has. If actually attempted, such fine tunings would be difficult—not to say impossible—to measure.

[48] When a *raga* doesn't contain a pitch a 5th above its *Sa*, the tambura pedal point typically uses a leading tone (1/2 step below *Sa*) in conjunction with the *Sa*.

[49] Dating back at least to Bharata's *Natya Sastra* of c. 500 A.D.

[50] I am indebted to Earnest McClain, who shared with me his personal correspondence with Prabhakar Phatak.

The same kinds of anchors have been documented in the court music of Korea, which enjoys a tradition extending into pre-history. Extended study by Unyung Nam of that culture's instrument the *p'iri* [51] reveals pitch conditions taken for granted in songs of the West. Despite exotic "pitch bends" [52] and other idiosyncrasies of the genre, phrase endings in melodies most often possess a final pitch consistent with a "tonic." Nam's summary confirms a conventional yet often ignored wisdom:

> "the existence of analogous tonal hierarchies in a non-Western repertoire ... consistent with earlier cross-cultural studies carried out with North Indian music and Balinese music..."[53]

In Summary, Two Pressing Conclusions

It should be clear by now that fallout from these collective *Ur*-origins runs a broad gamut. They extend from the most ancient of Chinese prototypes to the Greek Greater Perfect System, through the Byzantine *Octoechos* to cataloguings from more exotic Eastern repertories—variously called *Sléndro, raga, grama, murrcchana, laksana, maqam, pelog*, and on and on. Like the note "systems" of our own culture's popular music, they can be complex in theory yet rooted in simple sonic foundations. As in our music of the West, central octaves, along with 5^{ths} and 4^{ths}, dominate their scenarios; the Indian lexicon designates the function of central note as the *Sa*; descriptions of Japanese music turn to words derived from one of their major instruments, the Shamisen, in which the instrument's three strings and their tunings "defined the *nuclear* tones forming the framework of its music." [54]

---

[51] The *p'iri* is an ancient double reed instrument still very much in use.
[52] Which in songs of the American South we call "blue notes."
[53] Nam, "Pitch distributions in Korean court music," 247.
[55] Allison McQueen Tokita, "Mode and Scale: Modulation and Tuning in *Japanese Shamisen Music: the Case of Kiyomoto Narrative*," 4.

128

Let us not be misled when people remote from our culture refer to esoteric numerical plottings, or "pitch bendings," implying real (or maybe just imagined) tuning systems of dazzling complexity. This need not blind us to a simple fact: their own explanations of their actual music and their descriptive nomenclatures took root in *what they heard*. And what they describe shares a basis with ours— especially in explicit recognition that any scale note may act as fundament, or tonic, for its collection. And it goes beyond that central point. No blues singer of the American tradition would find the idea of pitch bendings a novel idea. We don't bother to measure and enshrine those oscillatory products as primary issues, however, as some cultures have.

Greek Scholar M.L. West seems to have spoken for the music of all times and peoples when he described the pitch content of ancient Greek scales. The collection itself is of no significance "until we identify its tonic note. Only when we determine how the pattern of tones and semitones relates to the tonic do we know something about the modality of the piece." [55] And that *modality*, let us remember, is just another word for the music's tonality, its *pitch context*.

Before closing this discussion, let us address just one aspect of serialists' claim about music's evolution, how the pitch body was so inflated by 1900 that a richer matrix was demanded—if music were to progress. The additive concept seems so simple, so right. But it enjoys no support from the records of humanity's past. As we have seen, there was no one-to-many crawl, no $1 + 2 = 3, 3 + 2 = 5, 5 + 2 = 7, 7 + 5 = 12, 12 + 7 = 19$ "progress" in the evolution of pitch resources. Nor have any of the so-called "quarter-tone" systems codified from late in the 19th century into the 20th survived as standardized commodities, despite their avid promotion by enthusiasts.

We can learn a basic lesson from the world's note-theorizing. It is that pitch contents from early on were usually codified as collections—as *scales, ladders, gamuts, sléndros, modes, et al.* And thus was engrained over the

---

[55] *Ancient Greek Music*, 186.

centuries the idea that *the collection* itself, the note family, served as catalyst for pitch coherence. Its definitive form for the 19th and 20th centuries was enunciated in 1844 by French theorist François Joseph Fétis, whose simple explanation was that "Tonality resides in the melodic and harmonic affinities *of the sounds of the scale*, which determine the successions and aggregations of these sounds."[56]

Fétis' relegation of powers overlooked the fact those "affinities of sounds" rather than the note collection *per se*—the scale—are the conditions that bind it all together. Deeper properties were present in the pitch dynamics of those successions and aggregations. Fétis put the cart before the horse; for the most part, music theorists since his time have retained his flip-flop interpretation.

Cultures of this world have consistently recognized in some glorious yet defining way the primacy of octaves and 5[ths] as womb and sperm of pitch coalitions. Even the intervallic roots noted for major and minor scales were not an *evolved* product of late Renaissance theorizing, nor were they, as Schoenberg claimed, products "of Art." Those roots cannot be jokingly dismissed as outmoded products of an "Overtone Follies." They were, and they remain, a crucial part of what veteran ethnomusicologist Mieczyslaw Kolinski knew as basic principles of making music. They are matters of music's structure in any cultural context, rooted as they are in the structure of the human nervous system. And as Kolinsky aptly rules, "Biology and culture cannot be divorced from each other."[57]

---

[56] François-Joesf Fétis, *Traité* , 249 (my italics). The term *tonalité* originated with Alexandre-Étienne Choron. Fétis (1784-1871) was one of the first to apply it methodically. For him it described the central element in the music he knew. It was an ingenious coinage, linking as it did the contextual property of pitches-in-time with the centrality of a single tone.

[57] *Recent Trends in Ethnomusicology*, 1-2.

Chapter 6

EMPIRICAL PSYCHOLOGY'S VERDICT

Our attention now focuses on central canons of Serialism, especially that a 12-tone row, as an imaged *whole*, provides perceptual glue for the musical experience. "The main advantage" of his method, in Schoenberg's words, was "its unifying effect." Put into historical context, the assumption was—and remains— that the unique 12-note row takes over the contextualizing function for pitch that the scale—or more accurately, tonality—provided in earlier music. We have witnessed the folly of scales as *causes* of pitch unity in tonal music. Let us now observe a similar fate for 12-tone rows.

Theorist Fred Lerdahl manages to clarify such matters in a brilliant examination of this issue. He leaves a trail of ambiguity, however, in so far as just what might be the perceptual powers of a row. Observing that Schoenberg himself denied listeners' ability to "identify" rows when hearing such music,[1] he then adds his own confirmation: "there is no reason to suppose that listeners identify rows when hearing twelve-tone works." And most of us could voice only an "Amen!" to that conclusion. But there seems to be more than simple *identity-as-recognition* to Lerdahl's (as well as to Schoenberg's) conception of 12-tone powers. The waters begin to cloud with the rejoinder that "This is not to say that the row structure for *Op. 33a* has no effect on how the piece is grasped aurally. Rather, its effect is indirect."

---

[1] The crux of this ambiguity revolves around what is meant by "identify." He's probably referring to the recognition and retention of a *particular* row rather than the retention of an elemental unifying presence, and in this he is correct. For his basis he cites Schoenberg's well known letter to Rudolf Kolisch of 27 July, 1931. The core of Lerdahl's discussion is in *Tonal Pitch Space*, 375-380.

So, "identifiable" or not, the implication seems to be clear: the row somehow replaces the prolongational powers [2] inherent to tonal music. It does that through its "emphasis on surface intervallic patternings and with associations among subsets of the row." But that proposed "indirect effect" of a row on auralization becomes hopelessly obscured when Lerdahl further confides that the very organization of tone rows "makes them difficult to cognize. This cognitive opacity provides potent evidence that the musical mind inclines toward other ways of structuring musical materials."[3]

The upshot of all this is less than clear. We are left with the vague sense that some kind of indescribable synthesis, an "indirect effect," enables a composer, via a 12-note set, to posit holistic powers within the musical experience. Perhaps it's another one of those *Ungesagt* conditions championed by Wittgenstein—although a number of writers have joined Lerdahl in trying to "say it." A notable example is Professor David Lewin, who speaks at length about row-based textures that exhibit pitch "centrality," about such lofty properties as "elemental tonal residues," "pitch-class axes," "antipodal centers," "harmonic bondings of pitch-classes," "pitch centers," and "centers of inversion." [4] All imply the kinds of pitch clottings we know as blood relatives of tonality. We shall discuss those ideas in depth in Chapter 7.

Lewin's perspective seems to align with Schoenberg's, for whom there was no ambiguity about such matters. As we noted in Chapter 2, Schoenberg claimed in 1949 that a row actually replaces "permanent reference to tonal centers." Since every pitch is derived from a basic set of twelve in his view, "the *Grundgestalt* is coherent because of this permanent reference to the basic set." [5] It would be hard to find a more resolute statement, and theorist David Epstein later

---

[2] A *prolongation*, for Lerdahl, demands some form of hierarchical connections. I prefer *contextualization* to avoid any semblance of meaning related to the theories of Heinrich Schenker.

[3] Lerdahl, 375.

[4] Lewin, "Inversional balance as an organizing force."

[5] Schoenberg further claims that references to the row *justify* "dissonant sounds."("My Evolution," *Style and Idea*, 91.)

seconds the motion. In his extensive discussion of the idea and its basal role in Schoenberg's thinking, he tells us that *Grundgestalten* were "basic shapes," and such were regarded "by Schoenberg as a unifying force of great magnitude . . . It was fundamental, furthermore, to twelve-tone music; for a basic shape was a work's elemental basis."[6]

Princeton's Edward T. Cone further lauded the permutational effectiveness of rows, noting results in Schoenberg's music similar to those described by Lewin. In Cone's words, "these transpositions, in connection with the hexachordal make-up of his rows,[7] produce the effect in his later works of a kind of super-tonality, perceptible even when not precisely definable." [8] Composer George Perle then takes the bouncing ball from Cone, pitching it to the nth degree by coining the designation "Twelve-tone Tonality." It signifies a potential of cohesion that has remained as an underground assumption among some very learned people—like many dogmas believed, even if not explicable, much less justifiable.

Let us not miss the conceptual duality of the doctrine. It holds (1) that the 12-tone collection in some way coheres in the listening experience, as a context-yielding *Gestalt*. And (2) that collection acts—if indirectly—as a bonding agent for extended musical rhetoric in which it forms the pitch base. It's the amalgamating property for tones, the pitch *Grund*; it replaces tonality as a source of pitch context.

Supporting arguments for this notion have been implicit in systemic elaborations by serialists over the past half-century. Truth of the claim is central to the recondite classifications and designations assembled over the years by two

---

[6] *Beyond Orpheus*, 17.

[7] This hexachordal makeup refers to a row whose first six notes bear some special relation to its second six. For example, the second hexachord of the row might be a mutant *(R, T, I, et al.)* of the first hexachord.

[8] "Music: A View from Delft," 68. I vividly recall a discusion with Cone during a flight from Bloomington, IN, to Chicago, one day back in the 1960s. His position: the ordering of the row is crucial; it determines the unique character of the composition. Mine was that it makes little difference, since the product is pitch–context neutral.

134

of Serialism's most esteemed proponents, Milton Babbitt and Allen Forte. Its enunciations usually suffer the same ambiguity implicit in Lerdahl's discussion. Classic is that of a serialist primer of 1975: "the twelve-note set serves as an unobtrusive unifying agent whose organizing role is more felt than directly perceived. . ."[9]

Lacking discussions of just how a *felt* experience differs from a *perceived* or *identified* (or identifiable) one, we are left with an ontological unease. All wavelengths seem to carry further shadings of Lerdahl's misty "indirect effect." And thus it remains an accepted postulate of human experience for many music theorists—whatever it *really* means, however it might be confirmed.

In a detailed report of 1979 in the *avant-garde* music journal-of-the-day, Robert Morris establishes unquestionable sonic credibility for these abstract collections, 12 pitch-classes all lined up in a Row. Successions of notes derived from an original row by transposition or inversion (*Tn* or *I* or both), as shown in Ex. 6.1, necessarily share the same intervals, and Morris draws a critical conclusion from this condition. He avers that "presumably, sets that are so related will be aurally as well as logically related, independently of their compositional realization." And, given this aural relatedness, he concludes that "it is therefore rational to assume that compositions will derive sonic and syntactic unity from the use of sets selected from the same SC [Set Class]."[10]

Example 6.1: 6-note Collections Related by Inversion and Interval contents

[9] Gary Wittlich, 391.
[10] Morris, "A similarity index for pitch-class sets," 445.

On the surface it all seems pretty reasonable and straightforward. But we are left to ponder Morris's use of such terms as "presumable" and "rational to assume." Perhaps deep inference—or maybe *faith* would be the more appropriate word—must rule the day.

There are more ramifications of this professed unifying power. They are significant. A seminal text of post-Schoenbergian theory, John Rahn's *Basic Atonal Theory*, vouches for pitch congealings and similarities unimagined before the age of the 12-tone row. We are assured that serial procedures meet our perceptual demands for music: the members of a set are "qualified or colored by their membership in a pitch class." [11] In other words, the attribute of pitch (or exact "height") isn't the whole story; it can be a high *B*–flat or a low *B*-flat and still bear a unique identity, within the set, with all other pitches of the same denomination (same "pitch-class"). This identity is common to the perception of tonality, but Rahn isn't talking about the well known recognition of octave relationships. For this reason we have cause for puzzlement: Could this be a latter day form of absolute pitch recognition, perhaps best referred to as "perfect pitch-class?" It is hard to postulate any other source for this alleged pitch bonding, this through-the-octave identity.

To my knowledge, no empirical study exists that supports a claim of pitch-class "color," except as that term might apply loosely to absolute pitch or to the function of a pitch-class in an established tonality. And rare are those among the population who possess "perfect pitch." For some, assured enunciations of this condition are nonetheless compelling; its alleged truth adds further luster to all previous assumptions for 12-tone rows within the music they inhabit. But strong faith often shades unfounded premises. Trustworthy skeptics have found such claims unconvincing, critically in need of objective proof, proof beyond convictions held by converts to the faith. Seeking auditory pitch consolidation of some kind, we are left with Gertrude Stein's "There's no there there!" Others

---

[11] Rahn, *Basic Atonal Theory*, p. 43.

have sought information of the most elemental kind by turning to the objective proving grounds of empirical psychology. Most such studies bear the sheen of disinterested research, hard science. All do not. Let us examine some of both.

Disturbing Reports to the Contrary

French psychologist Robert Francès arrived at conclusions in conflict with dodecaphonists' claims as early as 1954. [12] Controlled studies led him to conclude that serialized orderings provided no more perceptual memorability than random orderings. Indeed, when subjects tried to identify similarities between melodies and corresponding (or non-corresponding) parent rows, errors averaged 61.2%.

Francès then studied the coagulating potentials of 12-tone melodies accompanied by chords of the same basis. He reached further bleak conclusions: such textures present listeners "with inevitable non-meaning, in so far as the harmonic parameter is concerned. . . everything is unconnected; nothing can be counted on." [13] The capping conclusion from the whole of his studies is as profound as it is concise: "Serial unity lies more on the conceptual than on the perceptual level. . ."[14]

Those conclusions have been fiercely doubted and aggressively questioned by anyone still longing for empirical vindication of the dodecaphonic canon. Christian De Lannoy, for example, vigorously attacked the Francès studies in 1972, charging an excessively narrow conceptual basis. We'll discuss De Lannoy's motivating dissatisfactions and his own study presently.

Following in Francès's footsteps, listeners' ability to recognize fragments (or *subsets*) of 12-tone rows were tested by W.J. Dowling in 1972. His results suggested that recognition was slightly above chance for *I* (inverted) row forms, more difficult for *R* (retrograde) and *RI* (retrograde-inversion). But there is a

---

[12] "Recherches expérimentales sur le perception des strictures musicales." *The Perception of Music*, translation by Dowling.
[13] *Loc. Cit.,* 191.
[14] *Ibid.,* 116.

serious drawback in Dowling's study. The brevity and nature of his musical examples reduces their hard relevance to real-time dodecaphonic conditions. They consisted of successions of only five pitches, each related by a small interval and set in neutral rhythms (all pitches of equal duration). Indeed, his data may reveal only the ability of listeners to memorize short, temporally-neutral pitch successions, then recognize them (or not) in their inverted forms.

The De Lannoy study mentioned earlier was motivated specifically to correct flaws he found in the Francès studies. The opening sentence of his report not only sets the stage for what follows: it also provides one of the funniest bloopers of all PostMod discussions of music psychology. [15] In its entirety: "In the trial of dodecaphony were often put forward arguments that made the aesthetic value of dodecaphonic music dependent on its perceptibility."

Accepting the sentence as written, we are left wondering what any artifact's aesthetic value might depend upon, if not its perceptibility.

In De Lannoy's judgment the Francès studies erred in two main ways: (1) samples for prompters were excessively complex (too much to remember in the brief time allowed), thus leaving ". . . the memory of the listener . . . too heavily charged. . ." [16] And (2), Francès failed to compare discriminations of atonal samples with tonal, leaving his study without any "external criterion."

But De Lannoy's own study lacks the force of credible argument. One reason—which has nothing to do with the potential truth of his conclusions—is the sloppy editing that mars his report, leaving one unsure that the author's intentions (as in his opening sentence) are understood, his findings accurately reported. Even his charge that the Francès 12-note prompters were too complex, overtaxing for the subjects' memories, suggests a naïve grasp of what it's all about. Regardless of what may be his study's ultimate knowledge value and his charge that the Francès studies were flawed, their conclusions remain unproved

---

[15] To be fair, De Lannoy's more defensible meaning—that the row, *qua series*, be recognized—was probably intended, although not said.

[16] "Detection and discrimination of dodecaphonic series," 14. De Lannoy seems to have ignored the inherent complexities of 12-tone rows themselves.

by De Lannoy's own admission. Interpreting his total results, he backs off from earlier surety, observing that there are some kinds of series that ". . . will always be confused by both groups." And then his concluding opinion leaves little room for doubt: "There is no final sentence possible on the discriminability of 12-phonic music." But this conclusion doesn't dampen his ultimate optimism, wrapping it all up with the claim that "Dodecaphonic music is not fundamentally more or less discriminable than tonal music." [17] So we are left not with empirically verified conclusions but with lofty pronouncements grounded in opinion.

A more carefully controlled study in 1980 by psychologist Diana Deutsch approached much the same problems studied earlier by Francès, Dowling, and De Lannoy. As foil for 12-tone examples she incorporated some of the "tonal" prompters De Lannoy found missing in Francès's work. Using pitch recall strategies as proof of pattern apprehension and recognition, she concludes that a listener's ability to perceive a context is of ultimate utility.

> Sequences whose tonal structure could be parsimoniously encoded in hierarchical fashion were recalled with a high level of accuracy. Sequences that could not . . . produced substantially more errors in recall.[18]

Of greatest import in the Deutsch study are the numerous subject errors made in response to dodecaphonic samples. One of its significant products is direct confirmation of a fundamental precept of Gestalt theory: "we encode tonal materials by inferring sequence structures and alphabets at different hierarchical levels, together with their rules of combination." [19] Her studies suggest that encoding at those hierarchical levels demands more elaborate representation when a democratic set of twelve different pitches is involved.[20]

---

[17] *Ibid.*, 23.
[18] "The Processing of Structured and Unstructured Tonal Sequences," 381.
[19] *Ibid.*, 381.
[20] *Ibid.*, 388.

And there is more.

A 1981 study by W.R. Balch sought to learn whether listeners could identify 8-pitch melodic segments as rearrangements of a model pattern. As with Dowling's studies, the pitch sparseness and rhythmic simplicity of the examples Balch used reduce their relevance to our consuming question: "Can a 12-note set—a construct of *pitch classes* rather than specific *pitches*—be established as a unifying pattern within a musical context?" The prompters of Balch's study employed no 12-tone rows, yet its motivation is related since it used *I*, *R*, and *RI* transforms of diatonic patterns. The study's controlling question was somewhat vague and value-laden, asking subjects how well the second pitch sequence "followed" the first. Results were less than decisive. Several subjects recognized as related some inverted or retrograded segments, but retrograde-inversions were impossible. Those sonic and syntactic unities of pitch-classes promised by Morris seem to have evaporated.

The question of unifying power also got a negative conclusion from a 1994 study by Nicola Dibben. [21] Using two early serial works by Schoenberg as prompters, subjects yielded no evidence to suggest the kinds of hierarchical clumping readily demonstrated by tonal examples. For the atonal pieces, "underlying structure from the musical surface. . ." was not projected. And this again leaves us with less than optimism for dodecaphonic *Gestalten*. Indeed, the conviction of such powers for the row recalls popular belief in the cosmic powers of prayer.

But let us dig deeper.

Harmonic Recognitions

Related but different paths were taken by yet later empirical studies. Prompted by the question of *harmonic* potency in both atonal and 12-tone music, they tested auditory similarity or dissimilarity of complex chords, sonorities

---

[21] "The Cognitive Reality of Hierarchic Structure in Tonal and Atonal Music."

unfamiliar in traditional music. After all, Schoenberg had claimed [22] that "the set offers also the justification of dissonant sounds," so it is incumbent that we discover if and how this comes about. What congealing influence of a row can be projected by complex chords? Can a listener recognize such collections as more alike or unlike when their pitch/interval contents suggest one or the other?

Let us be specific. Is it reasonable to expect those first three chords of *Op. 33a* (Example 2.3). to be heard—even *felt*—as prototypes for the second three chords in measure 2?.[23] And will those first three chords echo later as a 12-part *Gestalt*, when strings of row-derived pitches occur arpeggiated, as in measures 32-33 (Ex. 6.2). Is this the sort of "effect on how the piece is grasped aurally" Lerdahl claims for a row? All would seem to be reasonable expectations (whether "felt" or "grasped" or "identified") if Serialist claims for 12-tone rows are more than wishful thinking. George Perle thought so: "Surely it is the . . . symmetrical relation between the first three and the last three of these chords that make sense to us as listeners and that we subsequently recall. [24]

Ex. **6.2** Later in Schoenberg, *Op 33a:*

I may be limited, but the only sense of symmetry I note when I listen to those opening chords are those of *texture* and *contour*, arpeggiations of equal numbers of tones in cascading high and low registers. I am aware of no *chordal* symmetry

---

[22] *Style and Idea*, 91.
[23] The second three chords are a product of retrograding the original 12 notes, then transposing them up a minor 3rd.
[24] *The Listening Composer*, 180.

induced by set parts.[25] But there are basic issues at stake here, especially in view of R.D. Morris's declaration noted earlier [26] that there will be "predictable degrees of aural similitude for chords of similar intervallic complexity."

How readily do we recognize similarities between highly complex chords? Such expectations as Morris's have not held up to the light of empirical research. Four relevant studies marked the 1984-1993 decade, their basic goal to test the validity of precisely those claims. Their overall motivating question: "Given complex chords *classified* as similar because of similar pitch content, what is their *heard* similarity?"

The first two studies were designed to check pitch-collection identities originally claimed by Allen Forte and later overhauled by C.H. Lord, identities relevant to any comparison of chordal content. The Forte/Lord ratings invoked objective indexes by interval content for any pitch collection, something long missing from the harmonic inventories of our tradition. The full complexity of such a system—which in its totality becomes tedious—need not be a part of our discussion. It nonetheless may be helpful for some readers to review briefly the system's basic features, making less cumbersome such terms as *interval-class* and *pitch-class*. They are critical in PostMod 12-tone theory.

As you may recall, the designation *pitch-class* refers to all pitches of the same name, all E-flats, all G-sharps, *et al.* And thus there are as many different Cs and As as the ear can detect (8-9 of each in the normal range of hearing). The designation *interval-class* is a bit testier. It derives from the fact that any pitch interval (a 5th, like $C\triangleleft G$), or a 3rd, like $C\triangleleft E$,) embodies its complement within an octave span. Note in Ex. 6.3 how each interval is complemented within its octave by its inverse. Note also that the result yields a total of only six "interval classes"

---

[25] Nachum Schoffman's thorough study of *33a* concludes that "the set structure consists of chords, and not the linear orders of the row." And those chords, in his judgment, " can hardly be distinguished from each other . . ." "Schoenberg Opus 33a Revisited," page 40.

[26] In "A similarity index for pitch-class sets," 466.

from the 12 pitch-class pot. (They apply over the pitch range, so that $C<G$ is the same *IC* as $C<g$ or g^1 or g^2.)

Ex. 6.3: Intervals and Their Inversions within the Octave

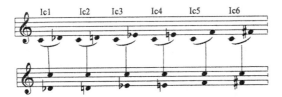

Allen Forte's identity system names any note collection according to its interval-class content. [27] The chords of Example 6.4 possess interval contents (what Forte called *vectors*[28]) based on the quantities named in their respective columns.

Ex. 6.4: Content Comparisons for three chords:

I-C Size in semitones (Content)

I-C	Chord A	Chord B	Chord C
1	1	1	2
2	1	1	1
3	0	2	0
4	1	1	0
5	2	0	2
6	1	1	1

---

[27] For more extended explanations see Forte 1964, Lord 1981. Further elaborations of the basic system can be found in Rahn, 1980; Spencer. 1983, and White, 1984.

[28] There is no sense of "directional force" projected by a collection of isolated intervals, yet that meaning is central to the *perceptual* meaning of the term *vector*. Forte perhaps chose the term because mathematics allows the meaning of *magnitude* in some contexts.

These enumerations enable comparisons of chords by numerical differences, which for the A/B and A/C pairs are as follows:

Chord A: 1 1 0 1 2 1	Chord A: 1 1 0 1 2 1
Chord B: 1 1 2 1 0 1	Chord C: 2 1 0 0 2 1
Difference: 0 0 2 0 2 0	1 0 0 1 0 0

C.H. Lord concluded that the A/C chord pair is "more similar" than the A/B pair. His conclusion differs from Forte's, who found the 0/2 and 2/0 differences in chord pairs A/B as "self-canceling," [29] leading him to opt for a "more similar" rating.

So what's to be made of these attempts at precise harmonic measurement, especially when disagreements reign among the experts? Or, most important for us, do they harbor relevance for the *perception* of atonal and 12-tone music? Of any music? Does duplicated interval content correspond with perceived chord similarities throughout the range of hearing, regardless of complexity? Listeners over the ages have recognized similarities and differences of many different chords in tonal music, from major and minor triads to the seven note 13th-chords of tradition. For this reason the ebb and flow of dissonance/consonance—even the projection of "mood" potentials by various chord types—play structuring roles in the music of our past. But how far does this potential extend into more complex mixes, the kinds of chords heard in atonal contexts? And further, if a string of 12 different notes can cast its unifying shadow as a *Gestalt*, does a series of chords based on a 12-tone row (like those of Schoenberg's *Opus 33a*) harbor the same potential?

A 1984 study by C.L. Bruner[30] tackled these questions in two experiments. She asked subjects to assign numerical ratings to chord pairs that best represented degrees of difference or similarity. Her results contradict any claims that "aural

---

[29] Presumably because the two minor 3rds are "cancelled out" by the more consonant two 4ths.

[30] "The Perception of Contemporary Pitch Structures."

similitude" exists. Then a more probing study in 1986 by Don B. Gibson Jr. [31] used Forte's classification system, his motivating question essentially the same as Bruner's: "Will subjects judge as 'more similar' chords classified as such by their interval content?" He avoided traditional tonal allusions or implications in his tests, something Bruner earlier had conjectured may have influenced several of the judgments in her tests.

Using 39 experimental items, Gibson devised a simple procedure typical of such empirical tests: subjects responded by noting whether the chords of Pair *A* (*X/Y*) or those of Pair *B* (*X/Z*) "Sound more alike." He confirmed Bruner's results: no evidence that aural "recognition" of chord similarities corresponded with those theorized for such complex sonorities.

But Gibson didn't give up. A second study in 1988 sought related but slightly different information. [32] Now the relative presence in chords of duplicated *pitches*, as opposed to duplicated *pitch-classes*, was the object. Put simply, he wished to determine whether the presence of octave-related pitches, like the *B*-flats in chords *A* and *A*[1], would project identity powers, rendering such chords more similar than chords *A* and *B*.

Ex. 6.5: Gibson Chord Comparisons with common pitches

Items in this study covered a broad harmonic spectrum, chords containing from three to nine pitches. The aim was aural affirmation (or not) of the pitch-class designation so basic to 12-tone theory: Will listeners hear two chords as more

---

[31] "The aural perception of non-traditional chords in selected theoretical relationships: A computer-generated experiment," 12,

[32] "The Aural Perception of Similarity in Non-Traditional Chords Related by Octave Equivalence."

similar when they contain duplicate pitch-classes? And what happens to that kinship if fewer pitches are present? Furthermore, are chords of duplicated *pitch-classes* equal, in their projection of harmonic similarity, to chords that contain duplicated *pitches*?

This new and more direct attack produced results further eroding credibility for the Schoenberg/Rahn/Morris claims. Results for both Gibson studies were conclusive in simple ways, especially since they included participants of extensive musical training as well as amateurs. No *aural* correlate of theorized similarity of the Forte/Lord classifications was detected in either study. Nor was any clue left that we humans may learn over time how better to discriminate the kinds of identities touted for 12-tone sets. Indeed, subjects who were experienced in hearing atonal music made no fewer error responses than others, thus contradicting guestimates made by Gilbert (1974) and Rahn (1980).

Still probing, Gibson mounted yet a third study in 1993; [33] in many respects it was a further refined continuation of the other two. Using the same two-pair chord scheme, he now focused on the recognition powers of maximum *pitch-class* changes as opposed to changes of *pitch*. His test contained two basic sections. *A*-chord pairs X/Y in both sections contained wholly different pitches (thus were *pitch-class complements*). Additionally, in this test's first section chord pairs *X/Z* share from one to four *pitches*; in the second section they share from one to four *pitch-classes*. Question: Will *B*-chord pair X/Z sound more alike because of shared *pitch* content than pairs that share *pitch-classes*? Or put more generally, do duplicated *pitch-classes* in chords bear the same identity power as duplicated *pitches*?

This third series of tests failed to support a possibility raised earlier by Gibson in 1988, that aural similarity in moderately complex chords might result from shared pitch-class content. This final study's conclusion was simple and direct: duplicated pitch-classes don't project aural similarity—at least, not in

---

[33] "The Effects of Pitch and Pitch-Class Content on the Aural Perception of Dissimilarity In Complementary Hexachords."

chords of high complexity. In Gibson's words, ". . .membership in a pitch class does not 'color' a pitch strongly enough to associate it with other octave-related members of the same class." Such results do not support Rahn's claim of 1980, Morris's of 1979.

Gibson's studies were models of empirical research. The upshot of all three is an indication of distinct schism, a separation of note-theory from sonic reality. They pose a stark contrast to similar studies of perceptual judgments dealing with the pitch materials of tonal music. Especially notable is that of William Forde Thompson and Richard Parncutt of 1997, in which the perceptual powers of certain intervals and chords are made apparent. [34] I could not state the results of Gibson's studies more firmly than he, when he says that [35]

> fundamental theoretical assumptions and relationships widely used in the analysis of atonal music are not effective predictors of aural relatedness when represented by experimental stimuli devoid of a musical context.

In other words, Francés must have been right back there a half-century ago: these matters chewed and rechewed in the intervening decades are more *conceptual* than *perceptual*. And the bets on 12-note rows as providers of that coveted *Grundgestalt* function grow riskier than ever.

Is There Still Hope?

To this date, credible studies by perceptual psychologists have not confirmed that 12-note rows *might* live up to claims. One test, from a set of four related tests, published in 1988 by psychologists Krumhansl, Sandell, and Sergeant, [36] suggested detection of underlying row content by subjects who had experienced considerable "academic training in music." [37] This cautious cause for

---

[34] "Perceptual Judgments of Triads and Dyads: Assessment of a Psychoacoustic Model."
[35] Gibson, 1993, 69.
[36] "The perception of tone hierarchies and mirror forms in twelve-tone serial music."
[37] *Ibid.*, 65.

optimism led to a tempting inference on the part of the three psychologists: Further research might confirm perceptual coherences of the sort claimed in the serialist tradition. [38]

Procedures for these studies were carefully planned, yet several aspects were vague, some goals highly ambitious, even colored by an unfortunate slant the authors confess: they *wished* their study to produce "positive results." Their guarded optimism, as well as credibility for some of the studies' implications, demand careful discussion.

All of the four tests incorporated rhythmically neutral segments composed from sets of 3, 6, 9, and 12 pitches, as well as excerpts from two Schoenberg compositions. Procedure *A* (used in Experiments 1 and 4) was planned to determine how fitting and confirming might be a "probe tone" sounded after hearing an established pitch collection: how well does it "fit with the preceding context in the musical sense of the atonal idiom." (Observe that this key question suffers almost as much interpretational space as W.R. Balch's "how well it *followed*" response in his studies of 1981.)

Experiments 2 and 3 of the Krumhansl, Sandell, and Sargent series used a different procedure. Subjects were asked to differentiate between two rows, one from Schoenberg's *Wind Quintet*, the other from his *String Quartet No. 4*. They were asked to classify all four forms (*Original, Inversion, Retrograde,* and *Retrograde-inversion*) according to whether they sound more like the row of one work or the other. Objectives and contents of Tests 2 and 3 are most relevant for us now: whether (and how) listeners can perceive similarities of original and permuted row forms.

All said and done, what they viewed as limited "positive results" don't shine brightly. [39] Given the procedures of the tests, they could be expected, but their revelation need not lead to conclusions about hierarchical contexts.

---

[38] *Ibid.*, 71-72, 72-75.

[39] For a more thorough dismantling of the argument see my *Tonality in Music*, 239-241.

Something other than the perception of *wholes* can be expected here in beating the odds. And yet, that condition of wholes is the key ontological condition that must be met.

Tests and Levels of Meaning

For comparison, let us speculate about listeners realizing a string of words as a *Gestalt*, enabling them to recognize lexical permutations as related. As we observed earlier, words aren't as malleable as pitches (nor are they invertable!), but they can shed some light on the processes of transformal recognition. As singularities they are probably easier for most listeners to remember than pitches.

Let us play with the word string "I went to not ask but you for find help some could." Twelve readily recognizable and differentiable words, even if a bit low on the *context* empowerment scale. If we retrograde them we hear "Could some help find for you but ask not to went I."

We slowly read each "sentence" to a group of attentive subjects, after informing them that they will hear two separate sequences. Their job is to tell us what relation bears between the second "sentence" and the first.

Attentive listeners, despite the semantic claptrap, will follow the established customs of verbal chunking. Lexical "context" is but a dim possibility; other tricks must be tried. They will most likely recognize that the first two words of the second "sentence" are a reversal of the last two words of the first." And vice versa.

Voila! It must be a retrograde!

But have our subjects dealt with lexical wholes in arriving at their conclusions?

Hardly. They have followed an easy but tarnished path of pragmatism, an accounting of beginnings and endings without bothering about resultant wholes. If we made only minor changes within the second string's interior, such as "Could some find help ask but you for to not went I" we probably would get the same answer: "Retrograde of #1." But this time it's wrong. The ends and beginnings are retrogrades but the interiors don't conform—at least, in orders—to "Sentence" No. 1. [40]

And herein lies the key, the most likely reason musically educated listeners could higher on the Krumnahsl, Sandell, and Sargeant recognition tests. They were not responding to *Gestalts*. Their basic auditory talents aren't that much better than those of the academically unwashed, but a large part of their training has been learning to recognize pitch intervals. As experienced musicians know, the first and last pairs of intervals in 12-tone rows aren't hard to remember—especially not when they are strikingly different, as in the two Schoenberg excerpts. Note in Example 6.6 how readily the trained musicians can tell the two apart, in their *I, R.* or *RI* transforms.

Ex. 6.6: Rows of Schoenberg's *String Quartet*, Op. 37 and *Quintet,* Op. 26

Musical insiders find it hard to mistake the *Quintet's* first interval (major 3rd) for the *Quartet's* first (semitone); and the *Quintet's* final interval (minor 3rd) is not easily mistaken for the *Quartet's* final interval (4th). Even octave displacements don't necessarily jinx this little ploy. A row permutation with a major 7th or minor 9th separating its first two pitches is still, for the trained musician, the potential opening semitone of the *Quartet's* row. They have the same note names, they

---

[40] And note what happens if we reorder the words to "I went to ask for some help but could not find you." A context has been produced . . . not unlike the way pitch meaning (or tonality) can be achieved by the ordering of pitches according to established syntactic mores.

share a "dissonant" relationship. They are, in the lingo of dodecaphonism, of the same *interval-class*.

So our suspicions are piqued. Those dim lights in the tunnel of the Krumhansl-Sandell-Sargeant studies may be better understood as "informed" guesses. Based on partial evidence; they demanded no sense of holism, no *Gesamtqualität*. The same could be the misleading result of any similar testing of full rows that follows the same "hear and compare" procedures. Studies of this kind do nothing to confirm the central premise of music theorizing we discussed earlier, that a pre-existent pitch collection—mode, scale, *raga*, 12-tone row—*in and of itself* projects pitch cohesion. A more realistic story suggests that any pitch content must be projected in time in certain ways for it to be anointed with contextualizing powers.

And there is yet another conclusion these studies provide. They remind us that unyielding harmonic complexity in an extended musical passage, the enforced constancy of dissonance heralded by Schoenberg, precludes the tension-release attribute that can play a meaningful role in the pitch domain. The conditions of "tension" and "resolution" are drowned in a monosonic sea. Another loss.

Continued testings of such pitch potentials should be expected over the years, probably following the basic path set in the Krumhansl, Sargeant and Sandell study of 1987. British psychologists Zoltan Dienes and Christopher Longuet-Higgins completed just such an extensive study in 2004. Their objective was to determine whether subjects can internalize—experience what they prefer to call "implicit learning"— collections of pitches derived from strict serial principles. One base assumption to be proved (or not) was that such unconscious learning can go beyond the bit-by-bit assimilation of adjacent elements.

Recognizing in the "democracy of notes" of the 12-tone method a "well-specified musical grammar that goes beyond just specifying allowable *n*-grams," their approach is important; it displays yet another thorny path for revealing the full dynamics of perceiving 12-tone music. Their quest ends on a note of optimism; as we shall note, however, confirmations of *Grundgestalten* for 12-tone rows are not evident.

Subjects both experienced and inexperienced in 12-tone repertory were chosen for tests: A principal goal was to determine if listeners could differentiate 6-pitch patterns (hexachords) that were products of serial permutations (*T, I, R,* or *RI*) of a given hexachord, as in Example 6.7.

Example 6.7

a. Permuted second hexachord

b. Non-permuted second hexachord

Note from the outset that the objects of study—the "learned" elements—were pairings of two 6-pitch sets, not complete 12-pc sets and their permutes. One such permutation (they use the term "transform") might consist of a second hexachord derived by transposition from the first.

c. Hx1 and Hx 2 derived by transposition

d. Hx 1 and Hx 2 derived by retrogression

Desired results for the experiments were simple: confirmation that training sessions would empower listeners to internalize pitch sets produced by such means, recognizing them as of greater unity ("more pleasant") than sets whose hexachords possessed no permuted parts. Thus an overall plan of "Training Phase" followed by "Testing Phase" governed the study's progress. A total of three formal experiments took place, plus one test of an individual subject.

Experiment I used 50 items, half of which were permutes. Of the 50, 35 were confined to one octave, the remaining 15 using some pitches beyond that restriction. For the Training Phase subjects were asked to rate each set on a 1-to-10 basis of "how pleasant." For the Test Phase they were asked to decide whether a set was based on the "rules" governing items in the Training Phase, at the same time rating their sense of confidence in making each choice. Results of Test I confirmed that chance prevailed: A score of 50% was posted for the 35 octave items, 48% for the 15 that extended over a wider range.

But a single subject, known only as "PF" (tested separately because he had extensive experience with atonal music), contradicted those results for the subjects of Experiment I. His scores for octave-confined sets ranged from 91% (2nd hexachords derived by transposition (or Ts) to 74% (RI hexachords).[41] For sets extending over an octave his scores were less than confirming for Ts (47%) and RIs (60%), while inversions and retrogrades got better results (73% and 80%).[42]

---

[41] According to the authors, a score in this test above 64% for 8^{ve} sets and above 80% for those wider than an octave are better than chance.

[42] I find the difference in his score for Ts (47% and Is (73%) and Rs (80-%) mystifying. I would expect the first to be higher, and even then that there not be a wide difference in such scores.

A kind of experimental searching then separated Experiment I from IIa and IIb. [43] Noting that simpler contours of test items for transforms might prove to be easier to remember and process, new items were designed. One such as Example 6.8 might represent the kind of T hexachord that musically untrained subjects could deal with.

Example 6.8

But once again Chance seemed to have the edge. Twenty-eight musically uneducated subjects scored 49%, after going through a Training Phase. In yet another run, forty musically untrained subjects, who had not sustained a Training Phase, scored 53%. Curious—if not baffling—results!

Comforted, nonetheless, by that singular flush of success with subject "PF", a new set of experiments ensued, now using items whose sets had been composed by such composers as Webern and Krenek. It was their hunch that proven 12-tone composers might have a talent for assembling rows of greater perceptual potency than those put together by chance operations.

Two groups were assembled for Experiment II. For the first, 32 subjects of musical experience were added, 10 of them graduate students who had a special interest in serial music. Then a second group of 14 student and faculty composers of high serialist competency participated in IIb.

The first experiment's Training Phase used second hexachords derived by transposition; the second phase used retrograde inversions (RIs). In the Training Phase subjects were asked to focus on the *relation* between the two hexachords of each item, distinguishing between Ts and RIs. Results were no more convincing

---

[43] It is not easy to follow the overall experimental plan as it is describe in pp. 540-547 of the report.

than in Experiment I, with a 48.1% score for the majority, 56.3% for the more seasoned ten. At least one implication seemed evident: the Training Phase biased participants to endorse test items of the same permute types in the Testing Phase. In other words, subjects to some degree had "internalized" those of their Training Phase exposure. In one early Training Phase exploration, separate from the formal tests, participants took tapes home, listening to them once a day for five days. Their recognition scores were no better: 51.7%.

The IIB series with 14 highly experienced subjects followed the procedures of IIA, except that RI transforms prevailed. Compared with those of IIA its results are especially curious, in that the T permutes score was 48%, compared with 56.3% for the musically experienced of IIa. This seemed to be evidence that participants were biased to endorse test items of the same transforms as used in the Training Phase. Further comparisons are informative—if not mystifying: the T permutes of IIa got higher scores (56.3%) than the RIs of IIb (51.9%).

By this time an overarching implication seemed evident: some types of permutation were easier to internalize than others. For instance, Ts in Test IIa were more readily internalized (56.3%) than RIs (51.9%), even contradicting star subject PF's scores. (Neither score exceeded what could be expected from chance.)

Dienes and Longuet-Higgens drew several broad conclusions from these extensive investigations. First was their sense that the training phase "biased participants to endorse test items of the same transforms as appeared in the training phase."[44] It was a bias that suggested, in their judgment, implicit learning rather than memorization of successive pitches or intervals. In other words, something akin to a *Grundgestalt* was in evidence—although they never use that term; and then (2) hexachords derived by transposition were more readily internalized than those derived by R or I or RI (even though star subject PF's

---

[44] Page 546.

scores did not confirm that conclusion); and (3), hexachords in which transforms exceeded an 8^{ve} were more difficult to match than those confined to a single 8^{ve}; and (4) musicians of considerable experience in serial music are more competent in such recognitions than those without that experience.

Clearly, these tests were carefully tuned to seek exactly what was in question, then carried out with utmost care in all details, including the computation of results. They also were fastidiously reported (at times to the point that excessive words cloud the picture). But methodology isn't everything. They fail to achieve a principal goal: proof that the permutations of serial *music* can be internalized by listeners to project a unity for the pitch world. That failure resides in more basic matters than just the selection of subjects, test procedures or computations of data.

First of all, the tests items were so rarified that they cannot represent the real world they were assumed to reflect. Like the Dowling items of 1972, brevity escaped reality. The music of 12-tone serialism is based on sets of twelve pitch-classes; a hexachord consists of only half that number. If experienced musicians have trouble matching transformations of 6-note patterns (as they did in all of these tests), they would suffer gargantuan obstacles in dealing with sets of double that population.

Add to this factor of comparative set complexity that of overall context. Dienes and Longuet-Higgins used patterns recorded by electronic piano, each pitch lasting .5 of a second, a uniform brief silence separating items. Compare this set of dynamics with that of actual music: pitch ranges covering multiple octaves, textures varying from solos to lines accompanied by a contrapuntal pattern to sets of chords. Even single lines may celebrate their freedom by skyrocketing through a range of three or four octaves (especially in some of Schoenberg's works). Pitch contours in real music are not always simple; they may be smooth or they may be erratic. It is but another facet of music's allure. More realistic were the Francès tests reported earlier in which subjects tried to match actual melodies with rows.

And let us not forget the property of rhythm. On several contextual levels of large-to-small, section-to-phrase-to-rhythm pattern, music's norm is not that of constant periodicity. The norm, note-by-note, is little of the repetitious uniformity that can help listeners in pitch-set matching. By comparison to the items of these hexachordal tests, a variety of durations faces the listener. It's is a part of the fulfillment that makes multitudes of tones into music, that differentiates *melody* from *chant*.

Finally, one ghost in the implicit learning closet is hard to hide. Tests in all cases except the scores of "PF" suggested that hexachords derived by T were easier to internalize than those of other permutations. A probable hunch is that contour can play a major role in this little testing drama. For but one example, note how much easier hexachords a/b are to match than c/d.

Example 6.8. Contrasting Hexachords

All of Which Means What?

Assured though the champions of Serialism may be, it's hard to accept foundational premises upon which it depends. By no means has empirical psychology over the past three decades confirmed the essential claim of a *Grundgestalt* power in a 12-tone row. On its own, such a construct seems to be incapable of projecting a pitch context. So has the curtain slowly but surely fallen on that magnificent 12-tone detour, music's 'Revolution'?

Not in academic circles. The spoils are divided between the music itself and protracted commentaries about its technical wherewithal, extended tracts of

MetaMusic. This state exists even though some experts of the 12-tone repertoire continue to extol the prominence and significance for the music itself. Historian Bryan Simms is certain that Schoenberg's priming influence, an influence felt by such 20th century composers as Boulez, Babbitt, Messiaen, Carter, and Rihm, ensures his ideological immortality. And this prophetic power "will continue to speak as urgently to the twenty-first century as it did to the twentieth." [45] Perhaps more penetrating hindsight can some day assure us of just how much that voice was heeded by composers within the 20th. As we noted earlier, it appears to have been less than overwhelming.

Analyses explaining with great care every notated detail of dodecaphonic works continue to appear, every explicable note-derivation of small and large dimension fastidiously reported, not a tone left unsterned. Just as literary critics have explained with ardor the *raison-d'être* for every departure from narrative explored by Joyce, Stein, or Pound, serialist explications go on and on. One must pause to ask: "Why all the words? If such deep and delicate exhumings are required, is not the object itself—presumably created for human hearing—badly formed, excessively contrived?

Critics of yesteryear carefully detailed the brushstroke-to-totality of, say, a painting by Rembrandt or van Ruisdael, striving to tell us why we marvel at such representations, why we feel empathy for the depicted mood, why we may shudder at deeper meanings emergent from the scene. But note that motivations for those explications were different. Their goals were to explain reasons for the *predetermined* success of the painting, not to explain why one *should* or even *can* appreciate them. Let us recall painter Charles Demuth's simple injunction attached to the wall of his studio in Lancaster, Pennsylvania: "No writing, no singing, no dancing will explain them."

As irony would have it, music's "writers and singers and dancers"— historians and theorists for the most part—have, in these waning years of music's

---

[45] *The Atonal Music of Arnold Schoenberg*, 6.

'Revolution', gained more mileage from Schoenberg's radical detour than listeners. The explanatory words of *MetaMusic* are separated from the conspiring sonic image to become a thing on its own. And this leads to an observation of general relevance, one that applies across the board for all the arts. When the art materials themselves—along with how people experience them—become secondary to explanatory ideologies, trouble is imminent. Categories have been confused. The very basis of that art is in danger of severe contamination. The *Schizo Syndrome* has won another takeover.

But let us pose three covering conclusions that may be drawn from the failure of empirical psychology to support the Serialist canon. They are made in deference to the need to leave more than one road open for future travels. Two are more radical than the third and diametrically opposed to it, yet all three are at least plausible—depending upon who draws the conclusion. Only one can be true.

The first holds that music's value and function are rightfully metamorphosed, by whatever technical means, into something sonically akin to Kandinsky's total abstractions in paint. It is there ensconced with explanatory overlay as *MetaMusic*, cozily removed from the concerns and valuations of listening people. Such blissful states are implied obliquely in the opening sentence of Christiaan DeLannoy's study quoted earlier; it's eerily reminiscent of those opined by Federico Busoni, later by Mel Powell and John Cage, echoing that continuing itch to "free" music from the petty mores of humanity. It's a conclusion wholly conformal with the classic question posed in the 1958 title of Serialism's revered pioneer, Milton Babbitt: "Who Cares If You Listen?" [46] It involves a callous perspective, one that is light-years remote from Virginia Woolfe's or playwright Arthur Miller's convictions that the mission of any art is to remind humanity of a single controlling principle: the universe is, and must remain, human-centered.

---

[46] The title was not Babbitt's; it was added by a *High Fidelity Magazine* editor, who found it fitting.

This first option is suggested in aesthetician José Ortega de Gasset's conclusion many years ago, upon reviewing the pluses and minuses of that rare commodity "Pure Art." Although he concluded it to be nothing but the dream of misguided optimists, he nonetheless ventures that "there doubtless can prevail a tendency toward a purification of art . . . a progressive elimination of the human, all too human, elements predominant in romantic and naturalistic productions." [47]

It's at least an option that leaves careful empiricists wondering. In this rarified sense let us recall psychologist Francès's conclusion that serial unity "lies more on the conceptual level," observing that within this first option's perspective it becomes not just an acceptable premise but a hallowed canon. Furthermore, it painfully confirms a broad paraphrase of Tom Wolfe's ruling for the visual arts: for music it becomes "it's not the hearing that counts, you ninny, its the believing in the concept!"

The second—and less radical—conclusion backs off just slightly. It holds that music molded from 12-tone rows and their offspring requires more intense and improved listening habits. Like unveilings of Gertrude Stein or Ezra Pound's lexical mysteries, it demands processings by superior thinkers blessed with an unfettered perspective—plus loaded with time, curiosity, and a yen for complex supporting documents. Those fancy probings by psychologists into perceptual bits and pieces prove nothing about music as *High Art*.

This second potential conclusion is a comfy super-elitist position. It was anticipated by Milton Babbitt in 1960 when he argued for "new demands of perception and conception upon the composer and listener." [48] It's a perspective rooted in the very basic *permutational* vs. *combinational* ground that separates serial from tonal music. Perhaps it was the condition Hans Keller opted for when he recommended "contrapuntal ears," what Charles Wuorinen had in mind in his arguments for enduring music of "inner strength," despite its outer thorns. This second alternative involves at least one drawback: it depends largely on the

---

[47] *The Dehumanization of Art and Other Essays on Art, Culture, and Literature*, 12.
[48] "Twelve-Tone Invariants as Compositional Determinants," 108.

treasured *Tabula rasa* mind, a premise of formal psychology that died with Watsonian Behaviorism.

Conclusions 1 and 2 are not mutually exclusive; they differ only in degree as positions of the same holier-than-thou perspective. Number 2 is but a continuation of trust in a rapidly evolving humanity, a self-improvement regimen that enables some of us to attain "higher" plateaus of perceptual understanding unknown by our predecessors. It bows faintly toward the idealist position described by aesthetician William H. Gass, the final—and most problematic—of three "avant-garde vicissitudes" he describes. They consist of "works to which habit won't acclimate us to render them comfy." [49]

But there's still that third possible conclusion, the least radical yet maybe the most plausible. It holds that the kinds of empirical studies we have reviewed suggest with high probability that the loudest shot of music's 'Revolution' was a misfire, the product of an epistemology inherited from flawed Hegelian mores, one in which subjective idealism anchors an absolute certainty. (And as Hegel's critic Heidegger would later note, represents nothing more than an unfortunate solipsism.) It was another fetching but potholed NewAge detour off music's Main Street.

Within this third perspective Atonality and Serialism—clever though they might be as slogans, engaging as they have proved to be for armchair theorists—planted a poor crop for continued human cultivation. It can help a composer lay out pitch content for music in which pitch is banned as an agent of context. Such prefabs can help achieve pitch neutrality, but they *replace* nothing in the musical experience provided by the pitch context of tonality, certainly nothing merging on those coveted *Grundgestalten*. As a compositional tool it nullifies pitch as a structural agent.

There are ancillary sub-conclusions to be drawn with this third conclusion. One holds that the old argument about the evolving human psyche, enabling it to

---

[49] "Vicisitudes of the *Avant-Garde*," *Harper's Magazine*, October 1988, 64.

process ever more complex pitch collections, was but wishful thinking. It was like arguing that humans began improving their bodily speed after 1900, since by today one can go from Los Angeles to New York City in just a few hours. A more realistic appraisal notes that, like the transportation business, the music business has changed over the years, but not because of physiological nor psychological leaps by *homo sapiens*. Music's technical resources and performance potentials changed to a degree with mechanical enhancements, fostering the kind of enriched chromatic pitch play that underlies this facet of music-making, from J.S. Bach's *Das Wohl-Tempierte Klavier* of 1722 through Paul Hindemith's *Ludus Tonalis* of 1943. Electronic enrichments since the 1960s have nudged the process even further; in the meantime, our ears and their transducers have not changed.

This third conclusion need not imply that dodecaphonic music is *prima facie* doomed to failure. Meaningful atonal music has been composed, from the early atonal works of Schoenberg to strictest dodecaphonic fruits of the late 20th century. Some masterworks of that century boast partially atonal and serialized works such as Alban Berg's *Wozzeck* and *Violin Concerto*, two early classics of the genre. Effective composers can compose effective music however they choose to go about it. Jazz drummer Gene Krupa "composed" many an engaging stream of musical images with quite limited pitch resources. They were rigidly atonal.

But our conceptual bearings need not be clouded by the encompassing talents of competent composers. Without careful attention, rotten timbers yield insecure walls; 12-tone rows yield no *perceptual* underpinnings for the music they inhabit. That conclusion is not uniquely mine. Fred Lerdahl voices much the same opinion, despite his apparent vacillation about the role of a row in providing identity vs. *Gestalten*. He concludes that such constructs possess no potential for creating the kinds of hierarchical pitch contexts. Its "pitch space," when controlled by manipulations of those generalizations called "pitch classes," is wholly neutral, incapable of promoting wholes from parts. And let us realize that such designations as "extended tonality" have as much lexical credibility and precision as the condition described as "partially pregnant."

In the end, Lerdahl's demurrer is thorough. He lists seven reasons for twelve-tone impotence, what he calls the "cognitive opacity" of serial composition. [50] In my judgment two of his reasons overlap with the other five, but all project a single overarching argument: the tone-row cannot, on its own, project the kinds of tree-like hierarchies we humans demand for cognitive-perceptual input. Used in a fiercely democratic way, its twelve units make collections inherently more complex than listeners can accommodate with any sense of fulfillment. And as for Schoenberg's *Opus 33a*, Lerdahl finds no reason for perceptual rejoicing, no easy way to describe its pitch-structural wherewithal as heard; the work fails to yield any convincing prolongational attributes, any criteria of salience. That shortcoming, with the row's inaccessibility as perceived structure, "suggests that a somewhat different approach, perhaps incorporating aspects of pc-set theory, is needed for representing and deriving how listeners understand this idiom." [51]

In other words, answers are too remote for current retrieval, too *Ungesagt* for business-as-usual.

And finally, another simple yet probing question, this one of considerable historical import: If both evidence of human cultural history and cognitive disposition contradict the conceptual and experiential bases claimed for dodecaphony, how can they survive as a part of our culture, even if only as the fodder of scholarly pursuit? Our question would seem destined to entail the same response *Porgy and Bess's* Lawyer Frazier gives Bess in their discussion of the divorce she seeks without a prior marriage: "That's a complication." [52]

Opting for the opinion that the rules of the music game aren't up for grabs, that we humans possess built-in cognitive/perceptual habits, is a conclusion too

---

[50] *Tonal Pitch Space*, 375.

[51] *Ibid.*, 380.

[52] Act II, Scene 1.

tough, too outré, for some to accept. And that's unfortunate. Psychologist Pinker carries no credentials as a musician, but he knows our problem well enough to agree with Lerdahl that "Listeners to atonal music do not have at their disposal a consistent, psychologically relevant set of principles by which to organize pitches at the musical surface." [53]

I'll close this discussion with two observations. First, when atonality prevails, inducers of context must be provided by other musical properties. And second, replacements of basic cognitive expectations in the real world of communication, whether by writers, painters, or composers, takes more than exceptional talent and a strong will. There are experiential archetypes that nudge such actions in predictable directions.

This is not a new conception of our world. Jung spoke of such ideas long ago, even looking back to the Platonic *Ideas* in designating their function in thought. [54] In our own day philosopher Anthony Stevens has elaborated on the same tune. Archetypes have the capacity to

> initiate, control and mediate the common behavioral characteristics and typical experiences of our kind, even though we are, for the most part, unaware of them. As the basis of all the usual phenomena of life, the archetypes transcend culture, race, and time. [55]

Music's perceptual archetypes got lost in the dodecaphonic smog, and the smog continues to veil some skies. The tracts we shall review in Chapter 7 have been revered by those who accept the dodecaphonic canon. Those tracts represent some of the most fastidious theorizing of our time; they either assume their messages' relevance of their messages the sound of music or they regard that relevance as irrelevant. Most disturbing of all, they typify discussions of Serialism

---

[53] Lerdahl, *Ibid.*

[54] Reminding us further of John Searle's *tropism* introduced *infra*, Chapter 4.

[55] *Archetypes*, 39.

that have limned the halls of academe over the past five decades, keeping alive at least the explanatory half of the *MetaMusic* they represent.

Entr'acte

SERIALIST SEEDS IN BOUNTIFUL BLOOM

I sided with Virginia Woolfe in our early discussions, choosing 1910 as banner year of the Arts Revolution. Fast-forward a half century and we are treated to another explosive premier, this one in music and readily tabbed. It was 1961 when an extensive bibliography of serial music was published.[1] Bearing over 800 entries, it began on a note of bravura:

> Twelve-tone technique, once thought to be the private and unintelligible musical language of a small group of composers, is today one of the most important influences of European and American music."

This optimistic claim fails to mention a crucial fact that was becoming evident even in that decade: the heralded importance of serialism was more that of numerical and verbal description than of listener delight. A veritable NoteFlux had been born, a fetching new symbolic system of mathematical roots securing its gloss of power.

Another interesting side note attended this system's hold, a condition recognized by some of the more astute observers of the times: This growing reign of influence was narrowly confined to our country's campuses of higher education. Allusions to such a geographical Oz—harboring fear that some of the more avid followers might let system overtake sanity—began to crop up in respectable places. Some of the concerned, like *New York Times* critic and music historian Paul Henry Lang, went even further, suggesting potentially unfortunate circumstances. Since colleges, universities and conservatories now could serve as

---

[1] Ann Phillips Basart, *Serial Music: A Classified Bibliography of Writings on Twelve-Tone and Electronic Music.*

home for aspiring young composers, perhaps the music created by them must no longer be subjected to aesthetic judgment. It was not long before this potential became a reality.

In fact, *composing* music became secondary to *explaining* one of its properties; it was a pastime with tenancy in the most prestigious seats of learning, from Harvard and Yale to Cal Berkeley. It represented the captivation of a select population, launching one of the most fascinating Arts detours on record. It was a special new form of *MetaArt* created by experts who fit Roger Kimball's brilliant coinage "connoisseurs of cant." Its basis was a new canon, one alleged to replace old ones that for centuries were assumed to provide music's perceptual bonds. It was a treasury for armchair tinkering, exceeding anything Schoenberg—not to mention Pythagoras—could have imagined.

This retirement to academe was for some the answer to a mixture of creation and production problems. In retrospect it seems like a response to Milton Babbitt's warning that avant-garde music could find a home in modern culture only by abandoning its long residency in middle class concert halls, moving instead to the university campus. After all, musical composition was like pure science, its only safe haven could be within the academic milieu, where abstract thought can be protected. And we must recall Harold Rosenberg's musings about the same creative conditions in the visual arts: this new haven protected "art as an excrescence of a theory." [2]

Keeping alive that glow projected by the 1961 serialist Bibliography, few issues of learned journals in music by 1970 didn't bear at least one article sharing some new angle, some new computational trick down the impressive side road known as Set Theory. The ready availability of computers for crunching numbers eased the quest, as well as added a tonier excitement of scientism. It was Pythagoreanism reborn, its extended explanations and elaborate calculations replacing actual music as a center of concern. As we shall see presently, when a

---

[2] *The De-Definition of Art*, 60.

musical artifact was on the operating table, dissections harbored shady relevance between appearance and guts. Schoenberg's system was enjoying the kind of support academe's developing LitCrits were providing in their "close readings" of the New World words such as those of Stein and Pound.

A sampling of titles from journals spanning five decades reflects the doctrinal tone as well as rarefied content of this second-generation literature of note-tinkering. Observe that few titles imply a direct concern for sonic images. The operational mores call for "modelings," and "determinants" and "structural implications" and "complementations" of bits of abstract gold, as they might relate to pre-compositional ore. Here was a new language for talking about musical things. That was a central part of its glamour.

* "Twelve-tone invariants as compositional determinants" (Milton Babbitt, 1960)

* "The Source-Set and its Aggregate Formations" (Donald Martino, 1961)

* "Context and Continuity in Atonal Work: A Set-Theoretic Approach" (Allen Forte, 1963)

* *Grundlagen der Musikalischen Reihentechnik* (Herbert Eimert, 1964)

* "On Eleven-Interval Twelve-Tone Rows" (Stefan Bauer-Mengelberg and Melvin Ferentz, 1965)

* "Some Combinational Properties of Pitch Structures" (Herbert Howe, 1965)

* *Aspects of the Twelve-Tone System: Its Formation and Structural Implications* (Harold Lewin, 1965)

* "The Domain and Relations of Set-Complex Theory" (Allen Forte, 1965)

* "Polarity and Atonalism" (F.G. Asenjo, 1966)

168

* "Toward a Twelve-Tone Polyphony" (Peter Westergaard, 1966)

* "Composition With Arrays" (Godfrey Winham, 1970)

* "A Solution to the Problems of Vertical Serialization" (Edward Kobin and Theodore Ashford, 1968)

* "Webern's Twelve-Tone Sketches" (George Perle, 1971)

* "The structure of all-interval series" (Robert Morris and Daniel Starr, 1973)

* "An Explication of Some Recent Mathematical Approaches to Musical Analysis" (Charles Lord, 1978)

* "Some new Constructions Involving Abstract PcSets, and Probabilistic Applications" (David Lewin, 1980)

* "Intervallic Similarity Relations in Atonal Set Analysis" (C.H. Lord, 1981)

* "An Intervallic Definition of Set Class" (Christopher Hasty, 1987)

* "Set Class Aggregate Structuring, Graph Theory, and Some Compositional Strategies" (James Bennighof, 1987)

* *Similarity of Interval-class Content Between Pitch Class Sets: The IcSIM Relation and Its Application* (Eric Isaacson, 1992)

* The Seventy-Seven partitions of the Aggregate: Analytical and Theoretical Implications" (Bryan Alegant, 1993)

* *Arnold Schoenberg: Notes, Sets, Forms* (Silvana Milstein, 1994)

* *Relative Saturation of Subsets and Interval Cycles as a Means for Determining Set-Class Similarity* (Michael Buchler, 1998)

* "A Geometric Approach to Pcset Similarity" (David Rogers, 1999)

* "Broken and Unbroken Interval Cycles and Their Use in Determining Pitch-Class Set Resemblance" (Michael Buchler, 2000)

• "Special Cases of the Interval Function Between Pitch-Class Sets X and Y" (David Lewin, 2001)

- "Operator sets and their functioning in composite interval-cycle set relations" (Robert W. Peck, 2004)

- "Aspects of Depth in K-net Analysis with Special Reference to Webern's Op. 16/4" (Henry Klumpenhouwer, 2005)

- Interval-class and order of presentation affect interval discrimination"(Tuire Kuusi, 2007)

Launched in 1962, Princeton's fledgling journal *Perspectives of New Music*[3] led the way in fostering this new basis for thinking and talking. It was with some irony that a decade later—without the remotest complicity—principals in that journal's development obliquely confirmed Copland's earlier putdown.[4] Speaking of the more *avant* of current composers, Benjamin Boretz and Eward T. Cone observed that "The invention of musical systems itself seems to be a part of the creative resource of composition, rather than its invariant context."[5] Their words were definitive of a model theory sweeping through the ranks of some of the brightest young composers, but their revelation missed a deeper truth: the call of the day was more that of tinkering with systems than composing. It was the newest version of *MetaMusic*.

Ample documentation existed within less than two decades that Serialism, once regarded as a kind of insider code, had achieved more than just "a radical revision of musical thought;" it had achieved the status one theorist identified as "a new musical dialectic."[6] That dialectic formed the base for a steady outpour of articles, books, lectures, seminars and learned meetings, all plumbing the intricate depths of twelve abstract entities,[7] how they can be classified, how they are

---

[3] Begun at Brandeis in 1962 by Arthur Berger and Benjamin Boretz, its editorial seat later moved to Princeton.

[4] *Infra*, 39.

[5] In their *Perspectives on Contemporary Music Theory*, ix.

[6] Gary Wittlich, *Aspects of Twentieth-Century Music*, 388. Most graduate music curricula of today include courses that deal with Set theory as a required subject.

[7] Abstract in that the notes of 12-tone rows are by definition *pitch-classes* rather than tones of a particular vibration rate (or pitch).

transformable into formulae of systemic beauty, how such formulations underlie the compositions of those converted to the faith.

Rooted in formal operations of mathematics, the system's fixation led to a distinct shift from the sound world designated by the nomenclature of pitches, intervals, scales, rhythms, melodies, and chords. Now the note world of pitch-classes (*pc*), interval-classes *(ic)*, sets, rows, combinatorialities, arrays, aggregates, subsets, transformations, and permutations reign. [8] It's a language that in several instances makes possible more precise descriptions of note collections, in ways traditional music-talk couldn't muster. In this way it was a helpful contribution to discourse. [9] But in other respects it resembled some Ezra Pound verse: a jarring form of communication. As one exponent of this transformational music-talk opined, outside criticism and commentary of the system *per se* was in short supply. This shortage of critical backtalk was "inhibited in part perhaps by the language barrier posed by the theory's mathematics." [10] Inhibitions or not, by the final quarter of the 20th-century Serialism's flowering bouquet had grown into a snug fit for Charles Fair's classic description of "that body of contemporary ideas which, although widely discussed and taken by many with the utmost seriousness, either lack support from existing evidence or are clearly contradicted by it."[11]

For just one example, a crucial term of Serialism, *Pitch-Class,* defines an abstraction. We can hear a *pitch*. We cannot hear a *pitch-class*. And thus at its very lexical roots lies a potential for separation of symbol from sound. The

---

[8] As we shall note presently, these are rather simple, homespun terms of designation compared to the hardcore brand. Dependence on mathematical style and vocabulary was (and continues to be) a serious problem for an audience of musicians. David Lewin seems slightly regretful for his own commission of such sins in a footnote of 27 years later. "Its style," he confesses, "unfortunately makes few concessions to a non-mathematical reader." (note, p. 89, *Generalized Musical Intervals and Transformations*)

[9] The designation "pitch-class" is most helpful in describing all notes whose names (like *G* and *B*-flat) occur over a broad range of octaves.

[10] Ramon Satyendra, "An informal introduction to some formal concepts from Lewin's transformational theory," 99.

[11] Fair, *The New Nonsense*, 33.

produce of these masters of serialistic prose is reminiscent of Immanuel Kant's gift to philosophy. As Peter Medawar described it,

> the harm Kant unwittingly did to philosophy was to make obscurity seem respectable. From Kant on, any petty metaphysician might hope to be given credit for profundity, if what he said was almost impossible to follow." [12]

There are two principal dimensions to the allure of Dodecaphonism. First is the inherent romance of numerical computation and description. For musicians seeking certainties beyond the imponderables of mere aesthetics, the twelve-tone garden remains a bountiful source. And then for artsy non-mathematicians it exudes the veritable smell of science. In this it furnished the PostMod wing of musicology a new kind of sub-culture, one whose members could be celebrated as an elect group, the kind accurately described as "an elect whose mastery of a certain style of discourse confers an insight unobtainable elsewhere and authorizes a knowing (and often smug) attitude." [13] For musicians who might be mathematically inclined it was a paved new road to fulfillment, a guaranteed escape from vaunted dogmas of past doctrine. As Arthur Koestler once noted— with a dash of his wry humor— "the ecstatic contemplation of geometrical forms and mathematical laws is . . . the most effective means of purging the soul of earthly passion . . . the principal link between man and divinity. [14]

And then there was a second most seductive dimension of it all. That was the heady excitement endemic to all trail-blazing, of moving with a select pack, whatever path might be taken. Both forms of gratification, numerical sortings and going with the crowd, are derived from impulses basic to the human ego.

As our previous discussions stressed, some basic facts of history, of acoustics, and of human cognition and perception don't auger well with the

---

[12] *Pluto's Republic*, 22.
[13] Gross and Leavitt, *Higher Superstition: The Academic Left and Its Quarrels with Science*, 73.
[14] *The Sleepwalkers*, 28.

transformings of serial recipes. This makes the inherent ties between "representation" (or *narrative*) and "reality" (*demonstrable fact*) as fascinating as they are questionable. But one crucial fact must be kept in mind: most dodecaphonic theorizing is eminently traceable to the bits and pieces it depicts, the *notes*. In this sense it is empirically dependable, verifiably "scientific," readily confirmable. Fastidiously so! The real problem is more primal. Those elements so carefully described are *secondary*, if not irrelevant, to music's sonic reality. Implied "meanings" are often specious, perceptually unfounded. They are meanings that hark of the architectural critic who describes a building by counting its bricks, then sorting through their chemical composition.

'Good theory' in any art is presumed to bear demonstrable correspondence to practice, so it's our responsibility to ask again the questions implicit in earlier chapters: "What relationship bears between these deduced schema and music *as heard*?" Do they describe elements of the *musical* experience? Or, instead, are they nothing more than recipes for cooking up impressive numeric stews, esoteric shoptalk? Do they contribute something vital to our knowledge of music?

For those engaged in serialist deducing, such questions have been of negligible import—if ever asked. After all, they have reasoned with Schoenberg, *notes* are a principal ingredient of music. And thus, *Ergo*: Any operation bearing on the mixing of *notes* is a *musical* operation. *QED*. At best, it's a curious—not to say sad— ontological condition for any field of knowledge.

Chapter 7

MASTERS OF *METAMUSIC*

Princeton's Milton Babbitt was unquestionably the most imposing oracle of latter day Serialism. His role in the groundbreaking Princeton-Columbia Computer Center in NYC of the 1960s further solidified his prominence as a NewAge music guru. One of the principal figures in the periodical *Perspectives of New Music* expressed what slowly emerged as a basic truth for a limited segment of the population: Babbitt played a leading role in developing postwar musical thought and expression. His significance "for musical composition, theory, and pedagogy in the United States is beyond that of any other individual." [1] He is a Fellow of the American Academy of Arts and Sciences as well as the American Academy of Arts and Letters.

Yale's Allen Forte provided systemic support, adding conceptual and organizational insights that furthered the movement's scientific tone. Then Harvard's David Lewin began catching up in the Ivy League triumvirate by the late 1960s. Their theorizing developed a fascinating condition: here was a daunting "science" of a sort, but one whose real-world basis—in what it purported to describe—was at best questionable. It's easy to recognize the armchair delights available from a collection of permutable elements, whether they be numbers, playing cards, words, people, or notes. Just the nine elements of a *Sudoku* puzzle can tantalize for hours on end. And in 12-tone theorizing there were twelve for the playing.

Beyond the Ivy-league triumvirate of Babbitt, Forte, and Lewin, there were Pierre Boulez, George Perle, and George Rochberg. Of the total, Boulez,

---

[1] Benjamin Boretz, quoted in the book jacket "advance praise" of *The Collected Essays of Milton Babbitt.*

Babbitt, Perle, and Rochberg were also in the forefront of those who utilized such techniques in composing, although as mentioned earlier, Rochberg dramatically defected in the 1960s. [2] Whatever may or may not have been imagined as their musical import, their ideological trappings helped forge a major schism in how some people think about musical things. The efflorescence of their combined descriptives can easily subdue the innocent, so it's important that the unblessed have some inkling of their seductive irrelevance. We'll glance into the gist and partial substances of just a select number of such positings, enough to recognize their depth, their breadth, their esotericism, and their ragged relevance to music as sonic experience.

As a point of departure, Milton Babbitt's prose is unmatched. Seminal for those who followed his path, it is arguably the most provocative, in style as well as in substance, of any serialist tracts from mid-century on. He contended early in the game that an acceptable theory of music must supply a basis for understanding "unprecedented musical utterances," adding that such a theory also must provide a "model for determinate and testable statements about musical compositions." [3] They are worthy goals. Both are central to our concerns here. Indeed, our task will be to test how well his decipherings live up to his own stated goals.

An early and typical contribution of the Babbitt oeuvre is a detailed description of pitch components he finds important in the bulk of serial music. For his source he uses row elements from the third movement of Schoenberg's *Fourth String Quartet*. Forgive the quotation's length; that's a secondary part of my overarching point. (I have deleted the paragraph's first 39 words.)

> Even a cursory examination reveals a number of significant techniques of local continuity and association: the exploitation of ordered adjacencies (the repeated adjacencies C-B of bar 619 and G-flat-F of bar 617 cross-associate with the opening two notes of the movement and the G-flat - F of the first violin in bar 621 to effect the closure of a structural unit: the

---

[2] His public disclosure of what he regarded as the dead ends of Serialism appeared in 1973, in "Reflections on Schoenberg."

[3] "The Structure and Function of Music Theory," *Collected Essays*, 171.

three-note adjacency C -B -G of 619 also registrationally duplicates the first three notes of the movement); the delinearization (the dyads of the first violin line of 620-21 are distributed among the three instruments that immediately follow); intervallic preparation and association (the simultaneously stated fourths of 619, 620, and 621 prepare the predefined fourth of the cello and viola in 623; the repeated C -B states with regard to the G in 619 the intervallic succession continued by the relation of the D-sharp- E to the B in the same measure); motivic progression (the joining of forms of the set in 618 gives rise to the motive stated in the prime set itself by the last three notes, and the third, fourth, and fifth notes;[4] the distribution of the elements of the inverted set between second violin and viola in 623 results in a three-note motive in the second violin which is the retrograde inversion of notes five, six and seven of the simultaneously stated prime, at precisely the same total pitch level, and at the same time, the resultant viola line reveals two sixteenth-note groups of four notes each which symmetrically permute the minor second and major third); functional "orchestration" (the six-note unit of the first violin in 620-21 combines with the six-note unit of 622-23 to form a set); *et cetera*. [5]

Ex. 7.1: Schoenberg, *Fourth String Quartet*, mm. 614-623

---

[4] I feel certain that this phrase should end with the closing of parentheses, but the original copy does not.

[5] "Some Aspects of Twelve-Tone Composition," *Collected Essays*, 41.

Even those who read musical notation find this Faulknerian sentence of 285 words tough sledding. It reflects the substance and style of much serialist shoptalk, a fit for Roger Kimball's coinage "aggressive impenetrability."

Of immediate interest for us are the implied meanings of several key words. Our special concern is for the *musical* assumptions they imply—words like *local continuity, closure, preparation, association,* and *progression.* It is hard to accept their import, the real-world sonic implications they bear, in Babbitt's review. As a beginning, let us rummage separately through each of his claims to consider their perceptual relevance. It will be tedious, but a less thorough appraisal could not achieve our goal. I have italicized words whose implications are critical.

> "Even a cursory examination reveals a number of significant techniques of local *continuity* and *association*: [1a] the exploitation of ordered adjacencies (the repeated adjacencies C-B of bar 619 and G-flat-F of bar 617 cross-associate with the opening two notes of the movement and [1b] the G-flat - F of the first violin in bar 621 to *effect the closure* of a structural unit:"

Observe first that the quartet's row contains a large number (five) of semitones (pc 1).[6] For this reason alone, one might expect that interval and its displacements to play a prominent role in patterns assembled from the row. Recognizing that majority then leads the curious to wonder: Could the occurrence

---

[6] The total lineup of interval-class successions is: *IC* 1= 5; 2=1; 3=0; 4=3; 5=2; 6=0.

of a single interval, without reinforcing rhythmic, textural, dynamic, or contoural features, project a sense of "association" with a corresponding segment of a row, thus binding with that earlier segment to project a structural base?

Semitones do play a notable role in this 3rd movement. There nonetheless are good reasons for skepticism about the correspondences Babbitt finds crucial. Note first that [1a] the semitone *C—B* he singles out in the opening two tones is too fleeting to achieve motivic stature, to be remembered for later claims of "cross-association" with such as the *G-flat—F* found three measures later (m. 617). [7] The opening statement's principal pitches—its defining pitches as heard— are *C—E-flat—D-flat—D-natural —B-flat*, the latter forming a rhythmic closure. Potential semitonal flags are raised by the *C —D*-flat *—D*-natural presence; but a careful examination reveals, however, that interval's appearances most often in rhythmically secondary roles. In measures 619—624, for instance, semitones occur as auxiliaries to rhythmically more prominent pitches.

There is no evidence in these measures of contexts primed by "ordered adjacencies." As we mentioned, five semitones [8] in the row implies their probability of turning up often within the music. But lacking special circumstances, they are pitted against too many competing intervals of greater contextual prominence to achieve structural status. Furthermore, any claim [1b] of *closure* projected by the *G-flat—F* in m. 621 suggests something music's history has never disclosed: the "closure" power of a descending semitone. It's an especially risky forecast within a context lacking any projection of tonal hierarchy.

> 2. "the three-note adjacency *C—B—G* of 619 also registrationally duplicates the first three notes of the movement);"

---

[7] An intent listener might more readily recall the *Quartet's* first movement, with its opening semitone of motivic prominence.

[8] Or, more correctly, five *IC*1s.

Again, let us recall that Babbitt's *C—B—G* touchstone wasn't stated in the opening measure in a way that ascends to auditory prominence. Pitches *B—G—A-flat* in that location are but fleeting wisps between *C* and *E*-flat. Perhaps the same interval succession from the *Quartet's* first movement (in the form of *D—C-sharp—A*) might be recalled by a listener. But even in that movement it isn't repeated in ways that hark of motivic status. Further, the *chordal C—B—G* of Vln. II and viola in m. 619 are hard to associate with the opening's *linear* statement, especially in view of the dissonant environment they form with the cello's *D-flat*. That they are *registral* duplicates seems to be thematically beside the point.

> 3. "delinearization (the dyads of the first violin line of 620-21 are distributed among the three instruments that immediately follow);"

This "association" risks an especially broad leap from written *notes* to heard *music*. Indeed, the chordal *A—E—B-flat—D* of Vln. II and Vla., plus the cello's *F—G-flat*, do exhaust Vln I's *E—D—A—B*-flat—*G*-flat—*F* line. But jumping to the conclusion that even the most alert listener might distill these correspondences into an *association* (3-voice texture with earlier line) assumes an unlikely coalescing of bits and pieces; these are textures of highly disparate content. And last, the cello's retrograded *F —G-flat* offers an improbable association with the preceding *G-flat—F* of Vln. I—except as corresponding note names. It is one of those detectable affinities in notes unlikely to arouse memorable kinships in the ear.

> 4. "intervallic *preparation* and *association* (the simultaneously stated fourths of 619, 620, and 621 *prepare* the *predefined* fourth of the cello and viola in 623;"

Let us recall that the *G—C* 4th formed by Vln. II/Vla. in m. 619 is not, qua interval, sonically imposing, especially in its surrounding dissonant context. Assigning it a "preparation" and "association" role for the equally unimposing (and fleeting) *A—D* 4th of 623 is whimsical at best. Even prominence as a defining pitch of the viola's *D* is questionable, since it functions as but a neighbor (*appoggiatura*) for the *E-flat*. That the interval of a 4th has been "predefined" in some notable way, making it apparent as an intervallic leitmotif, is another broad leap of faith. Added to the already exposed M3 and semitone as intervals of prominence, it overloads the dice.

> 5. "the repeated *C-B* states with regard to the *G* in 619 the intervallic succession continued by the relation of the *D*-sharp- *E* to the *B* in the same measure;"

Pitch *B* occurs only in the viola part, so we must wonder where these designated trichord relations reside to justify the tie of Vln. I's *D#—E* to the lower texture. Since the *B* is only in the Vla., any linkage between lower texture and Vln. I fragment is risky. What Babbitt must have in mind is the trichord relation of

And note that Vln. I's entrance, with its imposing rhythm, contour, and registral contrast, further reduces any continuing sense of the *B*'s presence in the viola; it also nullifies chances that the Vln. II, Vla., Cello presence might be heard as more than accompanimental (and thus secondary) background.

> 6. "motivic progression (the joining of forms of the set in 618 gives rise to the motive stated in the prime set itself by the last three notes, and the third, fourth, and fifth notes);"

What Babbitt seems to claim here is that a three-note motive is established, derived from *F—E—A* and its *G—A-flat—E*-flat permutation (IT2). There is nothing present in mm. 618 or 619 that projects a *G—A-flat—E*-flat succession corresponding to the original row's 3 – 4 - 5 notes. The only interval of a 4th in m. 620 occurs between the Viola (eighth-note *B*) and the Violin *E*. In that setting it is less than rhythmically impressive. How this alleged "joining of forms" is projected in Schoenberg's music—even in notes—remains a mystery. Perhaps we must once again resurrect our riff on Tom Wolfe that, after all, "Believing is hearing!"

> 7. [a] "the distribution of the elements of the inverted set between second violin and viola in 623 results in a three-note motive in the second violin which is the retrograde inversion of notes five, six and seven of the simultaneously stated prime, at precisely the same total pitch level, and at the same time, [b] the resultant viola line reveals two sixteenth-note groups of four notes each which symmetrically permute the minor second and major third);"

[a]The references are to Vln. II's *B—C—B-flat*, which is the retrograde inversion of the Cello's *C—B-flat—B*. In other words,

And [b], the viola line permutations of the *C—B—G* pattern (alleged to have been established in m. 1) occur here in the form of

And finally,

> 8. "functional "orchestration" (the six-note unit of the first violin in 620-21 combines with the six-note unit of 622-23 to form a set); *et cetera.*"

This tells us that Vln. I's six notes of mm. 620-21

complete the row with the six sounded in 622-23:

Very interesting. But, once again, this note-fact bears weak relevance to sonic reality. I have no sense of pattern-fulfillment, of *row-completion*, when I hear Mm. 622-23. Indeed, rare would be the listener who encapsulates six-note row parts (and their permutations) for matching to subsequent patterns—unless they are embedded in highly memorable contexts. These 6 X 6 partitionings are fleeting bits; their "meanings" *as segments of a 12-note totality* are unlikely to be apprehended as such. There is no context within which contributing parts can be linked.

Professor Babbitt could well have added two other delights of serial lore to his "orchestration" revelation, facts equally irrelevant to "determinate and testable statements" about *musical* structures: the second pattern is a retrograde of the prime row's first six notes:

And further, the Vln. II, Viola, Cello content of mm. 621-22 is a chordal version of the line just sounded by Vln. I.

These fastidiously sought and precisely asserted row/note implants give us some perspective on how Schoenberg put together the pitches of his *Quartet*. On that score Professor Babbitt's analysis is insightful. But there remains that central imposing problem hidden within. It arises from the fact that such enumerations suggest matters of perceptual import, sonic cement that holds the music together for a listener. They fail in that regard. They fail by disregarding the actual kinetics, the pitches-in-time universe in which the musical experience is grounded, the interactions that project musical meaning. Babbitt's error is not a rare one. Its nature and source are typical baggage for some contemporary musicians. When we analyze music from its notated page we tend to emphasize only those things represented by notes. They are *objective* evidence. We can trust them. But music notation cannot fully reflect the whole of sonic reality.

An implicit conviction underlies these careful exhumations of note relations, a conviction basic to all serialist doctrine. It holds that pitch-class particles and pitch-class segments assume central roles in the *musical* process. It is a flawed belief. The implication that recurring semitones and replicated hexachords, like those detailed by Babbitt, provide a perceptual glue is no more confirmed in the listening process than it is by empirical studies of perception. In this sense, pitch segments are not different from alphabetic letters: they do not, in and of themselves, project meaning. Let us use language again to make this point clear, a single sentence providing a basis for clarity:

> "Maureen regretted very early that her daughter had inherited her Father's exaggerated style of laughter."

These fifteen words unite; they make a readily decipherable message, a meaningful context. Do they project additional meanings one must apprehend to fully understand their message? Are there structural cues beyond verbs, subjects, clauses, *et al*, that one must uncover in order to fully comprehend their full meaning? Only if one seeks hidden codes where others fear to tread, like John Nash of *A Beautiful Mind*. And even then, breaking a code may not yield a real addition to the message!

Going back to our model sentence, let us study the mini-details of those fifteen words. Careful analysis can reveal some repeated adjacencies, in this case forming an inherent property of dominance. The letter succession *er* and its retrograde *re* occurs more often than any other (eleven times); it is the most prominent letter coupling of the sentence—if one is interested in letter-couplings.

There is but one plausible response to this discovery of imbedded dominance:

"So What?"

This insider fact—readily confirmed by count—has nothing to do with the sentence's message. Those eleven *er/re* bits don't rise to the threshold of structure, where *linguistic* meaning resides. Unless consciously sought, they are not even noticed, whether read or spoken. [9] And so it is with the intervallic bits of "local continuity" and "cross association" Professor Babbitt isolates in those opening Schoenbergian "sentences." As models for "determinate and testable statements about musical compositions" they fall short of compelling. This focus on the "ordered adjacencies" of row segments *per se,* as carriers of "local continuity and association," are more armchair theorizing about notes than descriptions of music. A more accurate picture unfolds in psychologist Diana Deutsch's empirical confirmation of a Gestalt principle mentioned earlier in chapter 6: "We work with different hierarchical levels, together with their rules of combination." Or even more pertinent to Babbitt's analysis of Schoenberg,

> The human mind is not a video camera. We do not store and process countless sensory bits; rather, we construct our inner and outer worlds according to the organizing principle of meaning. [10]

Recognition of this condition governing pitch bits takes us back to the more encompassing *Gesamtqualität* claimed for rows: they are figments of hopeful imaginations prodded by a flawed ideology. They are stark reminders of Don Gibson's conclusions that the assumptions and relationships typical of the analyses of serial music are best treated with skepticism. They depend too heavily upon *written notes* rather than *heard pitches.* Notation provides a kind of recipe, but the taste of the finished dish is something else.

---

[9] And by all means note that the retrograde condition borne by *re* to *er* is wholly irrelevant.

[10] M.E. Martinez, "Cognitive representations: distinctions, implications, and elaborations," 18.

184

We wonder: Is audition even pertinent to such descriptive "analyses" and "explanations" made within the serial milieu? It's easy to interpolate "meanings" from written notes. Like claims of Pythagoras and gurus of the Joseph Schillinger ilk, [11] serialist claims are stated with a resolute precision that shades their feeble implications for perception.

Such discussions as Babbitt's are not rare in the hard core literature of music from over the past five decades. They bear a scholasticism that could endure only in academe, just as the more arcane products of scholasticism in ancient times could survive only in monasteries. The ultimate misfortune is that musicology is replaced by cryptology, a condition hauntingly reminiscent of Babbitt's prediction that music would "cease to evolve"—even die as an art—if left unprotected by the academic world, where it benefits from a mix of theorists, composers and mathematicians.[12] There's a good chance he was confusing his personal brand of positivism with verifiable conditions. Thomas Rejelski touched upon the overarching problem more than a decade ago as a product of a loss of perspective, an indifference to musical realities.

> In seeking the "exact observation and strict correlation of data" more suitable to the inanimate subject matter of the physical sciences, many music researchers have disintegrated the subject matter of music—its musical integrity, its human interest—to the degree that their results are irrelevant and of no theoretical interest or pragmatic use. [13]

Vital Word Meanings

Even the vocabulary of serialist *MetaMusic* is both cramped and stretched to fit fancied conditions, conditions that reinforce an aura of systemic certainty. Take the term *atonal*: it's a vital word of the music vocabulary, but it has been so

---

[11] *The Schillinger System of Musical Composition* (1946) was a hot mid-20th century by-the-numbers approach to composition. Gershwin studied it and band leader-arranger Glen Miller was alleged to have composed his dance band's theme song, *Moonlight Serenade*, using it.
[12] His prediction meshed with the perspective of Edgar Varese, who had complained that, that "science alone can infuse [music] with youthful vigor." Reported in Varese, "The Liberation of Sound."
[13] "Scientism in experimental music research," 12.

bandied about that its root word *tonal* becomes indefinable. Despite Schoenberg's fanciful side-stepping, it has been freely applied by authors from Allen Forte and George Perle to Ethan Haimo's "revisionist thesis." [14] The term has been used whenever the musical substance seemed to lack the kinds of pitch orientation prescribed for music of the Classical and Romantic eras. But should we not share a more basic meaning for the term? Should we not know what *aural* experience, what *musical* condition prevails when the word applies to the repertoire of any era, when something can be confirmed perceptually as *atonal*?

We discussed the basic conditions that prevail when tonality exists in Chapter 4. Do we have precise and encompassing ways for answering questions about when atonality prevails?

A volume entitled *The Structure of Atonal Music* could be expected to harbor a commune of tight definitions, at least one of which—if not all—might illuminate the issue. But this early classic of the serialist genre is shockingly devoid of orientation. [15] One must decide independently what the absence of a *tonal* condition—thus *atonal*—might be. And that's not easy when author Allen Forte claims that Stravinsky's *Rite of Spring* is atonal. I'll spare my reader a review of that historic music, with its plethora of indelible tonic pitches (beginning with the bassoon's opening filigree around *A*). A full disclosure of the flaw in Forte's definitive conclusion would demand such.

Even more damaging than lexical sloppiness is the absence in Forte's book of a defining discussion of the atonal condition discussed in the subsequent 220 pages. We are left to conclude, with Schoenberg's assenting nod, that any music unfounded in the I, IV, and V chords of major or minor scales, like the selections in church hymnals, is *atonal*. And as we have noted in earlier

---

[14] Forte in *The Structure of Atonal Music* (1973), Perle in *Serial Composition and Atonality* (1968), Haimo in *Schoenberg's Transformation of Musical Language* (2006). Especially note Forte's title for an article of 1981: "A Musical Kaleidoscope: Schoenberg's First Atonal Masterwork, Opus 11. No. 1."

[15] In George Perle's opinion ("Pitch-Class Analysis: An evaluation") the book suffered "ways of talking about and analyzing music that have nothing whatever to do with what I would call 'common sense' experience."

discussions, this is just another naïve conception that prevails in our world of fractured musicology.

A nimble skirting of the issue occurs when Forte notes in his Preface that "Many gifted composers contributed to the [atonal] repertory: Alexander Scriabin, Charles Ives, Carl Ruggles, Ferruccino Busoni, and Karol Szymonowski." And then we get down to bare facts: "Any composition that exhibits the structural characteristics that are discussed [in this book], and that exhibits them throughout, may be regarded as atonal."

Forte's guidance recalls an old intellectual saw prized from childhood by Bertand Russell:

> "What is mind?"
> "No matter!"
> And what is matter?"
> "Never mind!"

This problem of meaning has flourished over the past several decades, especially in struggles by scholars to elucidate music produced from heavy probings into chromaticism. Nathan Haimo's extensive study begins with a discussion of the "tis" and "taints" of atonal. His best conclusion is that the term's meaning is "dubious." [16]

The pre-12-tone, or "atonal," music of Schoenberg has provided a veritable workshop for contradictory demonstrations of meaning that would seem to confirm that dubious state. His *Opus 11* of 1909 is a classic of the genre. Reading accounts of the "true" nature of that work's pitch structure can be an education in the vagaries of academic music. A single issue of the Journal published by the old Arnold Schoenberg Institute is a primer for the course. It begins with an extended article by Forte, who posits the reigning canon that the work is unquestionably *atonal*. In his judgment it furthermore is "the first work without text that depends solely upon its atonal musical organization for its

---

[16] *Schoenberg's Transformation of Musical Language*, 3.

coherence and beauty."[17] This conclusion has been shared by many imposing scholars, Rudolph Reti, [18] Jan Maergaard, [19] George Perle, Bryan Simms, and Gary Wittlich, [20] to mention only those who have made the strong arguments.

As irony would have it, however, there have been as many who "hear a different song" in *Op. 11, No. 1*. Among those non-believers have been Hugo Leichtentritt ("no trace of tonality," but evidence of a "Phrygian tonality" rooted in *E*); Reinhold Brinkman [21] (who finds a pitch "domain" of the 5th *B—E* essential to the work's pitch structure); Edwin von der Null [22] (who claims an *E* major-minor caste for the piece); and Jim Samson (who refers to the movement's "residual tonality," with *E*b playing a "centralizing function in the piece as a whole. [23]And then the most forceful—if specious—argument of all is made by Wilbur Ogden. [24] He finds even a tonal *Exposition- Development-Recapitulation* for the work, all dominated by a tonic *G* established within the movement's first six measures.

Ex. 7.2 Opening, Schoenberg's *Opus 11, No. 1.*

---

[17] "The Magical Kaleidoscope: Schoenberg's First Atonal Masterwork, Opus 11, No. 1," 127.

[18] *Tonality in Modern Music*, 52.

[19] *Studien zur Entwicklung des dodekaphonen Satzes bei Arnold Schönberg,* p.XX.

[20] Perle: *Serial Composition and Atonality*, 12. Simms: *The Atonal Music of Arnold Schoenberg.* Wittlich: "Interval and Set Structure in Schoenberg's Op. 11, No. 1."

[21] Arnold Schonberg: *Drei Kalavierstucke Op. 11: Studien zur frühen Atonalität bei Schönberg.*

[22] *Moderne Harmonik.*

[23] *Music in Transition: A Study of Tonal Expansion and Atonality*, 1900-1920, 213.

[24] "How Tonality Functions in Schoenberg's Opus 11, No. 1."

So we are led to ask: "How could such a brief work elicit such contradictory explanations of such an elemental property?" Is it possible they are all right? Or is it not more likely that at least 50% of these conclusions are based on a flawed conception of what tonality (and thus of its absence) might be? After all, Schoenberg was convinced that his little piece was "relatively easy to understand." [25] And yet, if these contradictory interpretations flourish, lexical flaws—if not perceptual inadequacies—must flourish as well.

"Tonics Without Tonalities"

There are further mysteries embedded in serialist lore that revolve around rambunctious uses of the words *tonal* and *atonal*. Many are a result of the wish to find traditional—even tonal—conditions within compositions clearly hewn from 12-tone processings. [26]

Theorist David Lewin worked hard to reveal that some of the serial and atonal repertoire is blessed with NewAge versions of tonality. His vocabulary is impressive. He found "pitch-centered presences," "pitch-class axes," "antipodal centers," "harmonic bondings of pitch-classes," "antipodal axes," "pitch centers," and "centers of inversion" in that never-never world of abstraction, pitch-classes. All indicate tonalities-in-hiding. He was impressed, finding Schoenberg's mixes of rows and their inversions to be contributors to a new kind of structural

---

[25] *Style and Idea*, 79.
[26] Schoenberg himself spoke of future audiences who would recognize the *tonality* within music then known as *atonal*. (*Style and Idea*, 284)

wherewithal. In Lewin's words, for Schoenberg the result was "something quite analogous to the balance induced by a tonal center."[27]

Lewin's prose can be opaque, often because of his will to explain simple matters with the precision of space mission plans.[28] The sample of his lexical care quoted below involves a description of what are called "complementary sets."

> If P is a collection of notes, the complement of P is defined to be the collection of all notes not in P. Thus, in the sense in which I use the word "note," if P contains X notes, the complement of P contains 12 - X notes, and has no notes in common with P. I shall write P' to denote the complement of P. [29]

Or, translated: "I call a collection of notes *P*. All notes not in that collection I call *P'*."

Several of Lewin's discoveries spark memories of those 19th century thinkers who discovered the minor triad in the *Undertone Series*. [30] He finds row properties in Schoenberg's music derived from row structurings that, he suggests, are meaningful as heard music. [31] Of early works they are in #14 of Schoenberg's *Pierot Lunaire* as well as in the opening scene of *Moses und Aron*. In the latter he vouches for the "strong tonic character" of the chord *A-B-flat-E.* [32] It's a strange tonic chord, but as likely for that role as any of the competing *tonics* (*G, E, Eb, C*) claimed in the past for *Opus 11, No. 1*. It is impossible to know precisely what he means by the term "tonic," to what degree he attributes a perceived quality to it. (The Bebop jazz of Dizzy Gillespie and Charlie Parker often ended with more complex "tonic" chords than his *A-B-flat-E*.)

---

[27] ."Inversional Balance as an Organizing Force in Schoenberg's Music and Thought," 2.

[28] For this reason, I lack a comforting sense of confidence in attempts at explaining his discussions of serialist matters. I know of no writer in music whose prose is more difficult.

[29] "Re: The Intervallic Content of a Collection of Notes, Intervallic Relations Between a Collection of Notes and Its Complement: An Application to Schoenberg's Hexachordal System," 99.

[30] As noted earlier, turn the harmonic series upside down (which is meaningful only in the Land of Oz!) and a minor triad shows up in partials 3-4-5. (See Example 4.9.)

[31] Lewin allows that "we may think of these p-c inversions as possessing axes; each also may be regarded as having a pair of "antipodal centers."

[32] "Inversional Balance as an Organizing Force in Schoenberg's Music and Thought," 10.

We are told that similar echoes of tonal things occur in Schoenberg's later serial music as well. They are reminiscent, we are assured, of the "balances" induced by tonal centers of old. This motivation to uncover deep structural correspondences with past times leads into dark lands of discovery; Lewin's use of the word *tonic* wins as one of the century's catachrestic classics. Like Forte's *atonal*, it's a condition hard to pin down as an aural percept. But whatever it means, we are aware of its presence, according to Lewin, in Schoenberg's *String Quartet No. 3*.

He finds in that music a condition he names with a term worthy of Derrida: *tonic abstract texturing*. Or, expressed less colorfully, the work's row and its inversion offer "dual centers," p-c centers equivalent to "contextual pitch axes." [33] The row origins for this dual centricity, are found in the Quartet's set (S) and its transposed inversion (It5)

7.3: Quartet's Pitch set and its inversion

And thus, having promised "tonics", Lewin reminds us that

'tonic sense' in this piece is attributed not simply to the basic set,
but to the set, plus a basic pitch class inversion I, plus the abstract
Texturing that results when S is compared to I=I (S).

It all sounds a bit like a latter day riff on Schoenberg's touted *Grundgestalt*—with an equal sense of regret that the *aural* presence of such properties seem highly

---

[33] I have chosen my words carefully with the hope of not altering Lewin's claim.

suspect—if not wholly doubtful. As listeners we are left to wonder how these "antipodal centers" that do not exist except as imaged classes of things (like *pitch-classes*) can possess such real-world residues.

Even if true, there still persists a most basic question: "So what is *tonic*—if there be such?" What pitch conditions tie these passages in the Schoenberg *Quartet* to the same kind of aural presences in phrases by Haydn or Hindemith? There is the unequivocal suggestion that this form of tonicality consists of—or more consistent with Lewin's language "is embodied in"—the *p-c* duality *E-Eb* within the row's initial grouping of five. It has been called one of the "centers" for this Set/It5 match, followed by the *A-Bb* conjunction of the 7-note grouping. What are we to believe? Are there changing "dual centers" in these passages, brief encounters with varying contexts, one whose focus is on *E-Eb*, the other on *Bb-A*? Or is it a matter of just *Eb/E* as dominating axis, with its accompanying axis of *A/Bb*? And if any or all of this be true, is the Emperor not overdressed?

Like the *E-Eb* duplication, the 5 X 7 row compartmenting is not hard to see in the notes. But there is no evidence that what we *hear* projects any kind of oxymoronic tonicality, two pitch-classes as pitch Axes? Could this be a form of aural strabmismus, music's counterpart to cross-eyed vision? Are these fleeting "wiggles," as Lewin calls them, sufficient to launch a "tonic" Or even, as claimed, a "*sense* of tonic?" And just how does a "sense of tonic" differ from a "perception of tonic?" Equating this condition discovered in 12-tone *notes* with contexts of tonics apparent in tonal music seems far-fetched at best, a fatal case of *MetaMusic* at worst. Let us face a simple fact: a condition of *note-prominence* is not of the same realm as *tonicality* or *tonality* or *tonic*, or *pitch centricity*. [34]

Lewin's attempt to achieve linkage of dodecaphonic note conditions to structural imperatives of yore is admirable. If his ties were valid they could represent a welcome bond between past and present, a healthy trend toward theoretical reductionism. Theorist Ernst Kurth has suggested that these random

---

[34] As just one homely example, the first pitch of the old pop tune *Ghost of a Chance's* is overwhelmingly present. It is not the tune's tonic.

moments of tonic sense, these *Scheintonalitäts momente*, are but accidents of serialist methods. In a sentence worthy of *MetaMusic* fame, he suggests that they "result from temporary imbalances in the twelve-tone system's abstract counterbalancing of multiple tonal relationships." [35]

Who knows? He may be right.

There are good reasons (including my own listening results) to believe that some searches for fleeting "tonics" readily lead into sightings of sonic phantoms. Lewin's Search-and-Discovery approach is wholly consistent with the Deconstructionism popularized late in the past century and still engrained in some academic psyches today. Like Freudian psychology, it is an approach to knowing that separates words from their surface definitions, then seeks more profound meanings by analyzing surrounding text for other, deeper messages. Most disturbing is the trend to behave as though the actual sonic artifact is less important than the technical process at the base of its creation. As Allen Shawn has observed, too much writing about music today

> implies that the very purpose of the "foreground music," the purpose of what you hear, is actually to express the "background"—that what you hear is about the underlying structure, not the other way around. [36]

I have dwelt at length with these esoteric claims because they are classic examples of serialist descriptions that find questionable happenings in unlikely places. Richmond Browne thoughtfully itemized the most pressing problems encountered in Allen Forte's *The Structure of Atonal Music* in a review of 1974. His comments are broadly applicable to the unravelings of Lewin as well as to the "structural" discoveries of Babbitt. As Browne notes, the essential drawbacks are twofold:

> (1) the over generalizing of musical data (a problem inherent in the excessive reliance upon the notion of pitch class as the primary kind of

---

[35] "Suspended Tonalities in Schoenberg's Twelve-tone Compositions," 243-244.
[36] *Arnold Schoenberg's Journey*, 296.

musical equivalence), and (2) the difficulty of disentangling statements about musical equivalence from the thicket of mathematical terminology and private alphanumeric codes. [37]

With a different twist, George Perle argued a slightly different brand of serialized tonal resonances, of "pitch centricities," "tonics," and "tone centers."[38] He excuses the troubled marriage of *Pitch Center* with *Atonal Music* by slipping out a lexical side door hung in 1963 by Arthur Berger, [39] who adopted the designation "pitch-class priority." [40]

Berger wisely found no necessary relationship between what in the past was called *tonality* and the condition of a pitch-class operating with structural prominence. He claimed instead that "the centricity of a given pitch or collection of pitches is no less unmistakable in many of the 'tonal' sections of *Wozzeck*." [41] And that conclusion is easy to accept: given the latter condition of "tonal," one reasonably expects the former of "pitch centricity." They are dependent properties.

Like Lewin's resurrections of abstract notes as "pitch-class axes," Perle's are forced, perceptually beside the point. Regardless of the total pitch kinetics of a given locale, listeners would have to attend methodically to special pitches as they flit by, noting their recurrences (or their pitch-class resurrections) to fit them into hierarchies. It would constitute a frenetic context-on-the-go process, exceeding normal audition. Such picayune notions only further erode our understanding of words like *tonic* and *tonal center*, both of which are contextually defined. Criteria for what are *structural* pitches and what are not (aside from their tonal meanings) most often turn upon local rhythmic emphasis, textural deployments, loudness levels, or by simple quantitative dominance. None of those are *pitch* causes.

---

[37] Browne, *Loc. Cit.*, 395.

[38] Perle studied composition with one of the elders of the 12-tone canon, Ernst Krenek.

[39] In "Problems of Pitch Organization in Stravinsky," *Perspectives of New Music* 2 (1963).

[40] The coinage may have influenced David Lewin's judgment too.

[41] *The Operas of Alban Berg*, 130. The claim is easily confirmed; *Wozzeck* is unmistakably tonal in many of its passages, although Perle's reference to "collection of pitches" as an option of centricity seems strange if it was to imply a simultaneity.

Perhaps the word *prominence* rather than *centricity* might better fit the described conditions.

And there is at least one further consideration of import. Statistical *prominence* in traditional tonal music doesn't necessarily produce *contextual* dominance. Even the statistically evident reciting tones of Gregorian chant were structurally secondary to the *modus finalis*. The tonic of many a folk and pop tune is among the least heard pitches: they just show up in the most prominent places.[42] Hans Reichenbach shows pitch dominance for eighteen English folksongs in the Dorian mode. The note *D* (*Final*) is exceeded in duration by *A* (*Dominant*), 271 vs. 234.5. For this reason, those who go no further than counting notes to reveal *structural* dominances must remember Arthur Koestler's classic indictment: purely statistical data are like the Bikini bathing suit. "What they reveal is provocative, but what they conceal is crucial."

Both Perle and Lewin leave skeptics with nothing better than a latter day conundrum: "What is a tonic without tonality the tonic of?" Or for the grammatically sensitive: "If there can be such a form of pitch *centricity*, what species of sensate elements is centered?" Is it a pitch or a pitch-class? For tonality it is a pitch-class: the *C* that is the tonic of *C* major is all *C*s of the family of pc *C*.

This simple realization leads us back to the oft-repeated hunch that music *as sonic being* is not the controlling goal for many of the careful recountings of Serialism. Indeed, the artificial respiration that has kept that doctrine intact and upstage in academe is not fundamentally different from that which continues to dissect and ennoble the opaque literary gems of Gertrude Stein and Ezra Pound, the supreme minimalisms of Kandinsky and Agnes Martin. Tom Wolfe's insight was monumental: the *Art* of it all "has become completely literary: the composition exists only to illustrate the text." [43] *MetaArt* prevails.

A humorous twist of irony leads us to recognize a kinship between two quite different human practices: Serialism's elaborate stories of note

---

[42] "English and Gaelic Folksong," 271. He shows tallies for tunes in other modes too.
[43] *The Painted Word*, 3.

transformations are kissin' kin with the symmetries we earlier associated with the *Schizo* affliction in crossword puzzles. Both are irrelevant to the functional *essence* of their attached structures. The permutations and transformations and commutations of pc sets are of no commanding consequence to what is heard as music. Since those elements bear no powers as contextualizing factors, Schoenberg could have used different note recipes for shaping the opening chords of his *Opus 33a* without altering the aural essence of his music. [44] Those fancy elucidations of $n = pq$ elements and their partitionings are of no consequence—at least, not so long as they fail to project any scent of that pesky old attribute so basic to music called pitch context.

In the *MetaMusic* of Serialism the text gains the spotlight. Its words imply descriptions of real music, that such music is so complex that its understanding requires special indoctrination into the procedures that fostered its creation. A classic "description" of the genre is a single sentence in a discussion by Milton Babbitt of Schoenberg's *Concerto for Violin and Orchestra*. It personifies the implicit—and often ignored—concern for pre-compositional note juggling rather than audible result.

> The rhythmic character of this presentation most strikingly articulates—by a rest—the set into two halves, two distinct hexachords, and immediately suggests the fundamental role of hexachords in the set, and so in the work [45] . . .

We can profit from the wisdom of philosopher Andrew Ushenko in our positings of "structural" explanations for all art objects. Describing any medium, he observes that "to perceive the aesthetic effect we do not need to know the rules for its execution. Artistic truth is in art, not about art." [46] Or as painter Charles Demuth put it, "no writing, no singing, no dancing will explain them."

---

[44] Which is not to say that, after knowing the sound of Schoenberg's *Op. 33a*, we would not immediately recognize a *difference* of pitch content. We certainly would.

[45] *The Collected Essays of Milton Babbitt*, 224.

[46] *Dynamics of Art*, 183.

In closing let us draw a conclusion already touched upon lightly: classic tracts of the serialist world impose one knowledge domain upon another, one to which they are ill-suited. The most precise and thorough itemizations of *notes* cannot reflect contextual kinematics that govern any complex *pitch* perception, one of "moving" parts in time. For this reason the Babbitt and Lewin and Perle "explanations" are but bayings at a fictive moon, regardless of the precision of their discoveries and the care with which they are presented. Theorist Richmond Browne enunciated a similar conclusion in the summation of his review of Allen Forte's *The Structure of Atonal Music.* [47]

> I conclude that the goal I, they, we seek is the phenomenological experience of pitch orientation we learned under tonality to call music, and I conclude that it is an exaggerated quest to try to find, beneath the surface of non-tonal music, a potential source of pitch coherence which, if we could only work hard enough, would give us "tonal security." The essence of natural language and gestalt is that you don't have to (can't, in fact) look for it. It presents itself.

But—just to keep all conceptual doors open—let us bend over backwards to avoid forgetting at least one alternative perspective. Those of us who do not find relevant the dodecaphonic cant may only suffer as musical troglodytes. Just as many of us lack absolute pitch recall, we also may be incapable of the advanced hearing demanded by passages freighted with meanings exhumed from elaborate prefabrications. As our final chapter discloses, there are serious composers still seeking ways for mixing their sound bits before committing them to the tests of human ears. We may keep in mind, nonetheless, that these may be nothing more than further remnants of a failed Revolution.

---

[47] *Loc. Cit.,* 401.

Chapter 8

. . . AND THE BEAT GOES ON

Our preceding discussions urge one to suspect a wholly dormant condition: although the words continue to flow, the serialist jig is up. Composers have moved on to more dependable ideological supports. That conclusion is not wholly borne out by the facts. It is true that most American composers of art music have ignored rumors of an imposed "evolution," eschewing the idea that musical basics of our day need be radically different today from what they were for Monteverdi or Haydn. And yet, there are continuing strains of compositional play grounded in the serialist genes.

Most of this play is not *serialist* composition as such; its operations nonetheless retain prefabrication processes of bits and pieces as a core ingredient. The approach is wholly consistent—and confirming—of the perspective aired by Pierre Boulez four decades ago. In his words,

> Far from seeing the pursuit of a method and the establishment of a system as proof of a withering of the faculties, I see it on the contrary, as containing the most powerful form of invention, wherein the imagination plays an essential, determining role.[1]

Consistent with the esoteric musings of *MetaMusic*, these post-serialst recipes reside almost exclusively in academe, where art music, as Milton Babbitt predicted, has been "saved from extinction."

Most of these composers would question the idea that they be considered as within the "12-tone" or "Serialist" tradition, but they have a basis in common

---

[1] *Boulez on Music Today*, 162.

with that past; it is a pre-compositional plan for assembling pitch or time components (or more) prior to achieving full contexts, before launching into the "How does this sound?" stage of composing. Of course, some consider those preliminary deductions, with Boulez, as the mere beginning of that process. And yet, from what their descriptions imply, their initial steps lack any sense of holism, any sense of the interplay of several properties in time. Contexts await later deductions. It's far removed from the Chopin or Berlin or Gershwin or Copland days of sitting down at the keyboard to plunk out test runs of a newly audiated creation.

These predawn procedures are sometimes used only as a basis for limited sections of a work rather than as an assumed foundation for the whole. Over the years I have found most typical the career-reminiscence of acclaimed American composer Morten Lauridsen: "I used certain serial procedures in developing materials from short rows or motivic cells in several of my early works . . . but only as one of many compositional tools." [2]

All do not tread so lightly. A notable example is Professor Paul Nauert. [3] He's a thoughtful composer, openly intent about searching for artistic apotheosis via rationalized procedure. Indeed, he brings to mind those composers mentioned earlier by Boretz and Cone for whom the fabrication and articulation of a system is a major part of the compositional process. His way is neither unknown nor eccentric in the academic community. In fact, revelations of his stage-by-stage processings have been discussed in the primer of current NewAge theorizing, *Perspectives of New Music*, as well as in the *Journal of Music Theory*.

His approach is fascinating—if painfully complex and musically suspect. In a nutshell, it involves elaborate pre-compositional templates. In his own words, the goal is to establish "structures for organizing pitch materials and coordinating

---

[2] Morten Lauridsen, personal correspondence, Feb. 2008.
[3] Professor of Music, University of California, Santa Cruz. Prof. Nauert has an academic background in Electrical Engineering as well as in Music.

them with a particular conception of rhythm and form."[4] His methodology enjoys the same system-seduction syndrome of 12-tone technique, prodding our most basic questions of perceptual potency. And yet Nauert describes his prefabrications as if their musical fertility is a foregone conclusion: they are but inherent consequences of his own composerly insights that have been applied during the pre-creative labors.

In the beginning he seeks ways for creating widespread yet generalized contexts—regions larger than mere phrases—that will articulate a whole work. Setting partitions that entire work is the beginning step. In achieving that end (1) a temporal span with its unique articulations is established. Only then is (2) a pitch-filler template planned. Once achieved, those pitch-class contents are (3) woven into an overall rhythmic mapping. The two may end up as complementary, but they are not conceived as such from the beginning.

CHORDS: In explaining his step-by-step process Nauert observes that "chord changes can articulate a relatively small level of rhythmic structure," and thus sections can be fenced off in this process by confining them to chords [5] made of a common set of pitch intervals. There is no accompanying discussion of just how "small" these enclosed chord areas might be. The implication is that this will supplant a function formerly provided by tonality (or for serialists the 12-tone row). In other words, chords in one section are fabricated to project cohesion within that section yet contrast with chords of neighboring sections. Sounds reasonable as a plan—if one must stake out such matters independent of textures, melodies, rhythms and timbres.

PITCH FIELDS: These collections become the coordinating or "fixing" ingredients for the overall setup pre-established in his opening ploy. They provide the kind of harmonic *Gesamtqualität* dodecaphonists claimed for 12-tone rows. An unvoiced assumption for Nauert is that chords of any degree of complexity

---

[4] "Timespan Hierarchies and Posttonal Pitch Structure: A Composer's Strategies, "34.

[5] And thus use of the word *chord* subsumes pitches sounded in succession as well as together. In the former condition we must conclude that they form chords by intent rather than because segregated from other potential "chord" members.

can be perceived as similar *if their intervallic contents are similar*, a condition the Gibson studies reported in Chapter 6 found to be wishful thinking.

As an approach to composing music, it's not unlike "painting by the numbers," except that the "pigments" are secondary to the "stages" of creation: *Time*-stage is followed by *Pitch*-stage. And then, in addition to quarrying what he calls "melodic spans" from the "pitch-fields," Nauert sires his chords from the same DNA established in his melodic bits.

The note series of Example 8.1 shows the "pitch field" basis of Nauert's *Arabesque* for solo flute of 1994. Note that Field *B* is a transposed version of *A*, beginning on its fourth note.

Ex. 8.1: "Pitch Fields" basic to *Arabesque*

Pitch Field *A* prevails in this work until m. 42, where field *B* begins. Although the two fields share all but one pitch-class, we are left to assume that this subtle shift to Field *B* nonetheless projects *formal* separation to a listener. Pitch-class *B*, which does not occur in Pitch Field A, presumably ushers in that new Field B, with emphasis on it beginning in mm. 42-43. It's a conviction reminiscent of Babbitt's claim that the *G-flat-F* in m. 621 of the Schoenberg 4th *Quartet* projects *closure*.

Ex. 8.2: Excerpts from *ARABESQUE*

But the sectional fence claimed for *Arabesque's* m. 42 is by no means novel because it is made from new pitches; indeed, its first three, *A♯*, *G♯* and *E*, have been heard in the preceding section. Most salient, according to Nauert, is that the already familiar *F♯* is approached for the first time by the "new pitch" *B*, and in the following measure this unfamiliar *B* is preceded by the familiar *G♯–A♯*. That new *B* is assumed to provide a fresh stepwise extension to the *Ab* (*G♯*)-----*Bb* (*A♯*) dyad heard so often up to this point. It's all there in the notes, sonically subtle though it may be.

Clearly, Prof. Nauert's appraisal of the powers wielded by intervallic shards depends heavily on atomistic listening. In this respect his expectations seem to be in line with those of Babbitt. They could prove to be excessive when the listener is confronted with a complex rhythmic scenario. Achieving auditory fulfillment of this kind demands that a listener retrieve and hold on to fleeting bits; absolute pitch recognition would help, for sure-fire recognition, so perhaps he is composing music for an audience of rare talents. That "new" *B* in measure 43, ascending as it does to the "old" *F♯*, seems a weak signal for a new formal section, even when it is repeated in the following measure.

RHYTHM: Nauert's plottings of time are equally complex. They recognize five levels of articulation, from the shortest span of what he calls "rhythmic surface" to the longest of "field change." He refers to melodic groupings as "chord changes," so the term does not necessarily designate pitch simultaneities, thus leaving us to ask, "So how does a "chord" differ from an "arpeggiation?" Or how do *chords* differ from melodic *figurations*? The distinctions are unclear, perhaps even irrelevant for Professor Nauert. About some of the arpeggiations in his *Arabesque* he tells us [6]

> these might operate like the chord changes in *Arabesque*, articulating a small middle ground level of activity, or they might occur directly in the foreground, producing something like an unelaborated chorale. . .

Between these "two levels" of time, "middle ground" and "foreground," lies yet another. It articulates sections more slowly than the "chord changes" but more rapidly than that of the "field changes." Such midway levels are built from chords of contrasting interval content; and thus "a timespan within which specific chords have become familiar closes upon the arrival of an unfamiliar chord." [7]

Professor Nauert's approach is fastidious. It is filled with deductive operations fleshed out verbally by placebos reminiscent of set-theory such as *interval vectors, inclusion vectors, progression vectors, pc networks, vector angles, pitch fields, field changes, levels of articulation, interval angle.* A classic example of post-serialist operations, it suggests yet a new variant of *MetaMusic*: *How Done* seems to overshadow *What Results*.

In spite of his elaborate prefabrications, Professor Nauert seems to be concerned—down the road—with what his music may sound like. In one place he notes that "cultivating this sense of an extensible chord-type requires a certain discipline in the choice of each chord—if the boundaries of a type become too fuzzy, then crossing those boundaries won't mean much." [8] So chords are chosen for how they satisfy a predetermined form plan. At least one fact of success seems evident: this elaborate path for creative plotting can lead to pages overflowing with a wealth of notes, all lined up in a row.

Let us also observe that this approach is strikingly different from the old way of doing things in that it is alarmingly two-dimensional rather than holistic.

---

[6] *Ibid.*, 40.
[7] *Ibid.*, 41.
[8] *Ibid.*, 45.

Pitch/rhythm (space/time) are no longer wedded from the creative act's beginning in ways they inevitably must be wedded in the listening process. In this sense, the composer is not at this point acting out a perceiving-listener's role. Forays by composers of the past into pitch collections *separated* from rhythms, during the act of composing, was rare until the advent of Serialism. Pitches were imaged as temporal spans, a particular articulation of space layers in time, these usually wedded to appropriate timbres as an integral part of the imagery. So Nauert's approach is by all means a curious new—not to say eccentric—way of skinning the old creative cat.

His explanation for the relationship between any two of his partitioning "chords" demonstrates the lexical price paid by skirting traditional vocabularies, to bask in the kind of explanatory prose popularized by dodecaphonic masters. His explanation for the derivation of pattern ii from pattern i of Ex. 8.3 is less than pithy:

> chord (ii) is produced from chord (i) by transposing the uppermost element of each loop downward 16 semitones (x becomes y, u becomes z) and then swapping the transposed elements between the loops (y goes to the loop that contained u, z goes to the loop that contained x)." [9]

Those "loops" and their hexachordal source are shown next.

Ex. 8.3: "Loops"

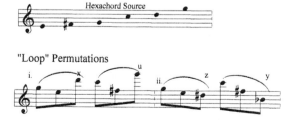

---

[9] *Ibid.*, 37.

Or to state it less grandly: "Chord ii replaces pc *D* with *B*-flat and *G* with *D#*, then uses each in the opposite triplet." Whatever may be the derivation process, in Nauert's judgment the result produces "a certain dizzy quality."

What do these arcane note transfigurations mean for a listener? They at least open another window on to the schizoid conditions some music ideologies have developed in American academe over the past thirty years. Indeed, the conceptualizing process seems to be thoughtfully systematic; concern for what may be its *auditory* import is tangential—when present at all. Its complicated steps represent a fastidiously simplistic way of approaching the creative act, an updated exemplar of G.B. Shaw's *Sardoodledom*. A listener's actual realization of the perceptual feats demanded by Nauert's approach appears to assume more perceptual finesse than the most resolute absolute-pitched convert might muster.

The Diesendruck Numeric Approach

All avant-garde prefabs are not so complex nor thorough, even when they too echo processes of the serialist persuasion. This is true of one used by composer Tamar Diesendruck, a veteran of several university faculties and recipient of a Goddard Lieberson Fellowship for composition. Her *Sudoku Variations* for piano is especially quaint, [10] employing for is time basis 9 X 9 solutions to a *Sudoku* puzzle. The matrix shown next was it deductive starting point, its source of elemental rhythmic content.

---

[10] It is not an approach employed in all of her music.

Matrix, *Sudoku Variations*

3	8	9	2	1	4	5	6	7
6	5	2	7	3	9	8	4	1
7	4	1	6	8	5	9	2	3
8	6	3	9	4	2	1	7	5
2	9	4	5	7	1	6	3	8
5	1	7	3	6	8	4	9	2
4	2	6	8	5	7	3	1	9
9	3	8	1	2	6	7	5	4
1	7	5	4	9	3	2	8	6

Professor Diesendruck's approach to meter uses each puzzle number as the numerator of a continuing eighth-note progression. Variation I (or "theme") consists of 3/8 8/8 9/8 2/8 1/8 4/8 5/8 6/8 7/8, Variation II of 6/8 5/8 2/8 7/8 3/8 9/8 8/8 4/8 1/8. Any meter occurs only once per variation, a variation lasts only nine measures and has the same number of beats.

An attempt at time/space coordination is made by using the same (or very similar) pitch collection for each metric unit, so that, for instance, 8/8 is associated with the figures from Variations I and III, while 3/8 is adjoined as shown from I and IX. The pitch collection for 8/8 is

Variation I, m.2

Variation III, m. 5

That for 3/8:

Var. I, m. 1

Var. IX, m. 7

According to Professor Diesendruck, the fundamental challenge for all of this numerical scheming resided in

> creating a sense of continuity and (occasional) closure while projecting each numeral with its own particular musical identity each time it appears, so the same material has to be convincing in any part as a phrase or section. [12]

As a reminiscence of most serial works—perhaps in a move to project a sense both of return to opening images and closure—the work's final variation employs the first set of 9 but in retrograde. So its total content is derived in a quaint way from that opening measure, perhaps more as an implicit salute to Machaut's *ma fa et ma commencement et* . . . than to a perceptually realized "home again" sense of closure.

Such pre-creative matrices may be of service to composers; only composers can make that judgment. But let us once again recall a central fact: they make an early end run around the kind of internalized creative ploys, the holistic approach past composers have trusted. Leonard B, Meyer identified those traditional composerly skills as "implicitly known images." They constituted a world of sound, a *style*. It was a developed feel for a basic way of doing highly complex things. Putting such matters into realistic terms, Meyer observed [13] that such composers

> know the constraints of a style not in the sense of being able to conceptualize them or state them as propositions, but in the sense of knowing how to use them effectively. As with knowledge of a language, what is involved is the acquisition of a skill, the internalization of the constraints as unconscious modes of perception, cognition, and response.

It's true. Even when gifted with those cognitive implants, composers need all the help they can get. But there is good reason to believe that a number series

---

[12] Quoted by August Brown, *Los Angeles Times* preview of the work on 24 January, 2007.

[13] Meyer, "Exploiting Limits: Creation, Archetypes, and Style Change," 180.

may impose impediments in the creative path to anything akin to *auditory* eloquence. It has a contrived origin, and in this a curious aesthetic potential looms large: The impulse of the listener may be to admire the conditions of the making—fulfilling a systemic plot—rather than admiring heard images. Perhaps Diesendruck's process isn't that remote. After all, it ties artistic creation to the common man: what could be more cross-cultural and down to earth than *Sudoku*?

Does such an imposed plan provide any semblance of perceptual wholeness, any sonic sense of context? Professor Diesendruck seems to think so. After all, "each line has the same number of beats. It feels random but it isn't random, you teach yourself to feel it." [14]

So perhaps our answer must be that old one championed by serialists for the row: it is a *felt*, an *indirect effect*. Indeed there are echoes of revolutionary writers of early 20th century inherent in Diesendruck's further claim that the numbers, as cues for musical meter, "lend a stream-of-consciousness feel to its consistently reappearing themes." [15] Again, one must test all claims by listening intently to the product, and that doesn't always help. [16]

Mixtures of East and West

The systematic prefabs of Nauert and Diesendruck are pikers when compared with those of Columbia University Emeritus Professor Chou Wen-chung. Composer Chou studied composition in the United States with Edgar Varese, but he adds rare cultural esoterica to serializations of musical properties, mixing the *I-Ching* symbolism of ancient Chinese tradition into his otherwise West-European creations. His approach is simple of basis if complex of realization. Indeed, readers may find my brief explanation here even more tedious

---

[14] August Brown, *Loc. cit.*
[15] *Ibid.*
[16] I heard the *Sudoku Variations* at a University of Southern California joint lecture-recital by pianist Elaine Chew and composer Diesendruck. I experienced no such "feel" of a "stream of consciousness."

than the serial musings of Babbitt and Lewin.[17] A more thorough explanation of his full regimen is available in a probing article by Mary Arlin.[18] But perhaps I can relay enough information to convey a sense of Chou's basic approach and its serialist genes. Let us delay any concluding estimates of his music's sonic delights, realizing that a number of prominent musicians, including the eminent conductor Richard Pittman, find Chou's music "delicate, and incredibly and meticulously constructed, and very beautiful in a rather unique voice."[19]

Chou's strategy uses numeric collections as a base for organizing pitch content, rhythms, and even loudness levels. It is not "12-tone," nor is it meant to be atonal; it nonetheless freely utilizes all pitch classes, and its operations are similar to those of the serialist tradition. A key to its uniqueness is the application of *Yin* and *Yang* determinations, first to pitch collections, from which are formed what he calls *Modal Complexes*. Even an initial grasp of the approach demands a basic acquaintance with the *Yin* and *Yang* designations, the alleged controlling forces of Chinese existence, often oversimplified in Western lore to a simple female-male opposition. These are the same *Yin* and *Yang* we encountered in Chapter 5 in our discussion of Leu Buhwei's concoction of the 12-note scale of ancient China.

Using binary arithmetic, if 0 = *Yin*, and 1 = *Yang*, then it follows for Chou that a succession of $1 - 1 - 1$ is a stellar representative of the *Yang* denomination ("Heaven" in *I Ching* terms), while $0 - 0 - 0$ ("Earth"), is that of *Yin*. And there are potential mixtures of those 1 and 0 elements. They translate into note collections by dividing the octave into three equal parts in two basic ways: by the

---

[17] Thorough discussions of system and music of *Windswept Peaks* are in the dissertation of Chang and in the article by Mary Arlin, as well as in several of Professor Chou's writings. I am indebted to Dr. Arlin for bringing composer Chou to my attention and providing a thorough basis for my limited explanations here.

[18] "*Befreitung von Fesseln: Die Kulturellen Wurzelin der Theoretischen Strukturen von Chou Wen-chung's Windswept Peaks.*"

[19] Originally on Pittman's website, the article containing this quotation has been removed.

(0 2 2) *Yin*, or (0 3 1) *Yang* interval successions shown in Example 8.5. [20] These prototypes can then be modeled into the eight permutations shown ini Ex. 8.6b; a "modal" permutation contains from six to nine different pitch-classes. These eight "trigrams" are basic. Stacking them two-by-two yields 64 permutations.

Ex. 8.5: Trichord templates for dividing octave

Passages from *Windswept Peaks* for Violin, Cello, Clarinet, and Piano illustrate his approach. Measures 34-44 reveal the orderings used to create one

---

[20] I have no idea why the one is proclaimed *Yin* while the other is *Yang,* nor could Dr. Arlin help when asked. Perhaps Feminist Susan McClary can clear up this mystery for us.

particular pitch fabric, the Violin part hewn from a trichord set of <1 – 0 – 1> <1 – 0 – 1>, the cello following a reverse version of the same set. The clarinet then leads with a <0 – 1 – 0> <0 – 1 – 0> set that is echoed in retrograde by the Piano.

Ex. 8.6a: Mm. 34-44, *Windswept Peaks*

8.6b "Modal Complexes" within 34-44.

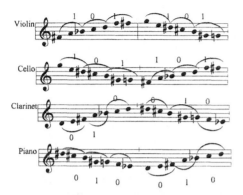

Such transformations can be stretched to fill an extended work. [21] I'll not delve more deeply into both the complexities and the breadth of Chou's numeric sortings that lead to final products, moving instead to a next realm of *Yin-Yang* structuralization.

Rhythmic schemes also are prefabricated from time-bits that are relatable to those note-bits of pitch. Just as three note trigrams made from such as < 0 1 0 > can represent the group *C − D − E   E − G − Ab   Ab − Bb - C*, durations can be plotted so that a note value divisible into six equal parts (as the octave is divisible) can yield combinations of equal durations. For example, 6 eighth notes can be organized into the following patterns: (Note the continued *Yin-Yang* designations.)

Yang		*Yin*
(3 + 2) +1 or 1 + (2 + 3)	and	(2 + 1) + 3 or 3 + (1 + 2)
(2 + 1) + 3 or 3 + (2 + 1)	and	(1 + 2) + 3
(1 + 3) + 2 or 2 + 3 + 1)		

---

[21] As Mary Arlin points out in her extended essay about this work, much of its second half consists of altered reappearances of materials in the first half, thus creating a semi-cancrizans ordering.

In notation these permutations can turn up in sequences, such as those of the violin and cello in mm. 34-44. Clarinet and piano follow suit with their own versions of 1 + 5 and 3 + 3.

Ex 8.7: Violin rhythms, mm. 34-44

While the cello in the same area follows the plan 2 + 4 3 + 3 5 + 1 4 + 2 3 + 3 4 + 2.

There are instances in Chou's rhythmic plan when the *durational*-count switches to that of an *articulation*-count. For example, a violin phrase later (m. 186) breaks the six 1/8 note durational model into six articulations, as shown next.

Ex. 8.8: Violin articulations, mm. 186-190

This echoed by clarinet as shown next.

Looking back at the music of Example 8.6a, note that the separate parts adhere rigidly to durational values. Those of violin and cello follow the same pattern as their pitch successions of < 1 – 0 – 1 > (Sun), while clarinet and piano parts project < 0 – 1 – 0 > (Rain) for both pitches and rhythms. This is not a casually assembled score!

In such an elaborate system the composer can work with established pitch and rhythm "modes" assembled at the creative beck and call of the musical moment. A built-in feature for Chou is that alleged symbolism of *I Ching*, which makes possible combinations of "close" or "distant" similarities of sonic images. We must leave to posterity any proof or disproof that designated emotional connotations of the *I Ching* are transmissible by the the sounds of these pieces, although I find that potential highly improbable.

But this is not the end of the Chou saga: loudness levels also enter the prefabrication process. As theorist Mary Arlin points out, they are as susceptible to systematic applications as pitch and rhythm. And thus Chou moves toward a realm of the "total serialism" pioneered by Boulez and others almost a half-century ago.

One can arrange eight loudness levels in order of increasing power and produce a blocking of values that can be represented numerically.

ppp	*pp*	*pp*	*p*	*mp*	*mf*	*f*	*ff*	*fff*
0	1	2	3	4	5	6	7	8

And looking again at Example 8.6a, you will find that all four instruments use the same stream of loudness values as those of the violin shown below.

m. 34	36	38	39-40	41	42-43
2-4	2-3	2-4	2-4	2-3	2-4

Dynamic levels associated with *Yang* are $4 + 2$, $5 + 1$, and $2 + 4$, thus differing by 2 or $2 + 2$ values. Those associated with *Yin*, on the other hand, bear lesser differences, changing only by one degree, as in $2 - 3$.

In ways similar to Professor Nauert's approach, Chou engages in an initial creative process far removed from the audiated images composers traditionally worked through in creating their music. They carry the same haunting message passed on by the late George Rochberg, who lamented the excessive attention to system at the expense of coherent heard content. Again, their overtones strongly echo the essence of G.B. Shaw's *Sardoodledom*.

These are fascinating regimens. They are not traditional *Serialism* as such, but they reflect the same calculations-by-recipe approach that the 12-tone method espoused. They force us to recall conclusions John Backus reached after studying an analysis in *Die Riehe* of Boulez's *Structures*. He forecast that one could make a life's work from such elaborate schema, such processes of "composition by numerology."

> By using different numerical rules—using a knight's move, for example, rather than a bishop's move along the diagonals—music for centuries to come could be produced. [22]

Many musicians outside academe today are unaware that such elaborate pre-sonic plottings play a leading role in the working lives of some contemporary composers. Perhaps it is but a "sign of the times," a continuation of that search for the NewWay begun back there around 1910. On the other hand, it may be the manifestation of an evolving culture, one in which objective calculation assumes a more secure role in the creative act, another manifestation of our hi-tech world. Whatever history may prove to be the accurate interpretation, let us listeners at all times try to keep our categories straight, separating the *Meta* part from the *Music*.

Revered American composer Roger Sessions long ago expressed remorse that such processes were a part of some composers' toolkits. In his opinion

> we must be concerned by the prevalent tendency to approach music indirectly, through preconceived ideas, instead of starting from a direct and naïve response . . . many of our composers go into action as theorists even before venturing to write music. The latter is then, properly speaking, not *music* at all, for music must begin with genuine and spontaneous expression, not with preoccupation about "style" or "tendency" or technique. [23]

And, heeding Sessions' concern, one may come closer to avoiding the pitfall of *MetaMusic*!

---

[22] "A Scientific Evaluation," 170.
[23] "Musicology and the Composer," 5.

Bibliography

Newspapers and Journals

Acta Musicologica
Advances in Infancy Research
American Anthropologist
Art News
Bulletin of Psychology and the Arts
Contemporary Music Review
Developmental Psychology
High Fidelity Magazine
Infant Behavior and Development
Journal de Psychologie
Journal of Aesthetics and Art Criticism
Journal of the Arnold Schoenberg Institute
Journal of Experimental Child Psychology
Journal of Experimental Psychology: Human Perception and Performance
Journal of Music Theory
Los Angeles Times
Music and Letters
Music Perception
The Nation
Nature
New York Review of Books
New York Times
Nineteenth Century Music
Parade Magazine
Perception and Psychophysics
Perspectives of New Music
Philadelphia Inquirer
Poetry
Poetry Review
Psychomusicology
Sammelbande der Internationalen Musikgesellschaft
Theoria
Toronto Star
transition

Primary Sources

Alderman, Pauline. "Schoenberg at USC." *Journal of the Arnold Schoenberg Institute* 5, November 1981.

Aristoxenus. *The Harmonics of Aristoxenus* (trans. and ed. by Henry S. Macran. Oxford, Clarendon Press, 1902.

Arlin, Mary, "*Befreitung von Fesseln: Die kulturellen Wurzelln der Theoretischen Stukturen von* Chou Wen-chung's 'Windswept Peaks.'" *MusikTexte: Zeitchrift für Neue Musik,* 118 (August, 2008), 69-82.

Ashton, Dore. *Twentieth–Century Artists on Art.* New York: Pantheon Books, 1985.

Babbit, Milton. *The Collected Essays of Milton Babbit.*, Ed. Stephen Peles, Princeton: Princeton University Press, 2003:
. . . ."Who cares if you listen," *High Fidelity Magazine* 8 (1958), 38-40.

Backus, John. "Re: Pseudo-Science in Music." *Journal of Music Theory* IV. 2 (Nov 1960), 221-232.
. . . . "*Die Reihe*—A Scientific Evaluation." *Perspectives of New Music* 1 (1962), 160- 171.

Balch, W.R. "The Role of Symmetry in the Good Continuation Ratings of Two-part Tonal Melodies." *Perception and Psychophysics* 29 (1981) 47-55.

Bassart, Ann Phillips. *Serial Music: A Classified Bibliography of Writings on Twelve-Tone and Electronic Music.* Berkeley: Univ of California Press, 1961.

Beumont, Anthony. (trans. and Ed.) *Ferrucio Busoni: Selected Letters.* New York: Columbia U. Press, 1987.

Bennighof, James. "Set Class Aggregate Structuring, Graph Theory, and Some Compositional Strategies." *Journal of Music Theory* 31 (1987), 51-98.

Bernstein, David W. "Schoenberg Contra Riemann: Stufen, Regions, Verwandt-schaft, and the Theory of Tonal Functions." *Theoria,* 6 (1992), 23-53.

Bernstein, Leonard. *The Unanswered Question.* Cambridge: Harvard University Press, 1976.

Berger, Arthur. "Problems of Pitch Organization in Stravinsky." *Perspectives of New Music* 2 (1963), 11-42.

Blacking, John. *How Musical is Man.* 1973. Seattle: U of Washington Press.

Boethius, Anicus Manlius, *Fundamentals of Music.* (trans. of *De Institutione Musica*, Calvin Bower), New Haven: Yale U. Press, 1989.

Boretz, Benjamin, and Edward Cone. *Perspectives on Contemporary Music Theory.* New York: W.W. Norton, 1972.

Boulez, Pierre. *Boulez on Music Today.* Cambridge: Harvard University Press, 1971.

Bowlt, John E. *Russian Art of the Avant-Garde: Theory and Criticism, 1902-1934.* New York: Viking Press, 1976.

Brinkman, Reinhold. *Arnold Schönberg: Drei Kalavierstucke Op. 11: Studien zur frühen Atonalität bei Schönberg.* Wiesbaden: Franz Stgeiner, 1969.

Browne, Richmond. "Forte's The Structure of Atonal Music" (Review). *Journal of Music Theory* 19 (1974), 390-409.

Bruner, C.L. "The perception of contemporary pitch structures," *Music Perception* 2 (1), 1984), 25-39.

Burkholder, J. Peter. "Schoenberg the Reactionary." Schoenberg and His World. (See entry "Frisch, Walter.")

Busoni, Ferruco. "Sketches of a New Aesthetic of Music," in *Three Classics in the Aesthetics of Music.* New York: Harper-Collins, 1962.

Butler, David,and Helen Brown. "Describing the Mental Representation of Tonality in Music." *Music Perceptions*, Rita Aiello, Ed. Oxford: Oxford U Press, 1994, 191-212.

Chang, Peter. *Chou Wen-chung and His Music: A Musical and Biographical Profile of Cultural Synthesis.* Ph.D. Dissertation, Urbana: Univ. of Illinois at Champaign-Urbana, 1995.

Chao, Mei-Pa. *The Yellow Bell.* Baldwin, MD: Barberry Hill, 1934.

Chen, Cheng-Yih. *Science and Technology in Chinese Civilization*. Singapore: World Scientific Publishing Co., 1987.

Chou, Wen-chung. "The Aesthetic Principles of Chinese Music: A Personal Quest." *Canzona* 7, no. 24 (June 1986), 74-78.

Cone, Edward T. *A View From Delft*. Chicago: Univ. of Chicago Press, 1989.

Cookson, William. *A Guide to the Cantos of Ezra Pound*. New York: Persea Books, 2001.

Copland, Aaron. *Music and Imagination*. Cambridge: Harvard University Press, 1952.

Dahlhaus, Carl. *Schoenberg and the New Music*. Cambridge: Cambridge Univ. Press, 1987.

Dasenbrock, Reed Way. *The Literary Vorticism of Ezra Pound and Wyndham Lewis*. Baltimore: Johns Hopkins U. Press, 1985.

Davidson, Lyle. "Tonal Structures of Children's Early Songs." *Music Perception* 2 (1985), 361- 374.

De Lannoy, Christian, "Detection and Discrimination of Dodecaphonic Series," *Interface* I (1972), 13-27.

Deliège, Irène, and John Sloboda (Eds.) *Musical Beginnings: Origins and Development of Musical Competence*. Oxford: Oxford U Press, 1996.

Dessanayake, E. *Arts and Intimacy: How the Arts Began*. Seattle: Univ. of Washington Press, 2000.
. . . .*Homo Aestheticus: Where Art Comes From and Why*. Seattle: Univ. of Washington press, 1997.

Deutsch, Diana. "The Processing of Structured and Unstructured Tonal Sequences," *Perception and Psychophysics* 28 (1980), 381-389.
. . . . "The Processing of pitch combinations," 349-411, *Psychology of Music,*(Editor, D. Deutsch). 2nd Edition, London: Academic Press, 1999.
. . . . "The Psychology of Music," in *Psychology and Its Allied Disciplines*. Ed. Marc Bornstein. Hillsdale: L. Erlbaum, 155-194.

220

Dibben, Nicola. "The Cognitive Reality of Hierarchic Structure in Tonal and Atonal Music," *Music Perception* 12 (1994), 1-25.
.... "The Perception of Structural Stability in Atonal Music: The Influence of Salience, Stability, Horizontal Motion, Pitch Commonality, and Dissonance." *Music Perception* 16 (1999), 265-294.

Dowling, W.J. "Recognition of Melodic Transformations: Inversion, Retrograde, and Retrograde Inversion." *Perception and Psychophysics* 12 (1972), 417-421.

Dutton, Dennis. "Aesthetic Universals." *The Routledge Companion to Aesthetics*, Eds. B. Gant and D,M. Lopes. New York: Routledge, 2001, 279-291.

Earle, Ben. "Taste, Power, and Trying to Understand Op. 36: British Attempts to Popularize Schoenberg." *Music and Letters* 84 No. 4, November 2003.

Eliot, T.S. "Literature and the Modern World." in Brooks, Purser, and Warren, Eds., *An Approach to Literature*, 3rd ed. New York: Appleton-Century-Crofts, 1952, 570-574.

Epstein, David. *Beyond Orpheus*. Cambridge: MIT Press, 1979.

Fair, Charles. *The New Nonsense*. New York: Simon and Schuster, 1974.

Fink, Robert. *The Origin of Music*. Saskatoon: Greenwich, 2003.

Fletcher, H. "A Space-Time Pattern of Hearing. *Journal of the Acoustical Soc. Of America*, 1930, 311-343.

Flint, F.S. "Contemporary French Poetry." *Poetry Review,* August, 1912. Reprinted in Cyrena Pondron, *The Road From Paris: French Influence on English Poets*, 86-145. Lanham, MD: The University Press, 1974.

Flynn, Daniel J. *Intellectual Morons*. New York: Crown Forum, 2004.

Forte, Allen. *Contemporary Tone Structures*. New York: Teachers College, Columbia U., 1955.
..........."Context and continuity in atonal work: A set-theoretic approach," *Perspectives of New Music,* 1963.
.... .Response to Review by Howard Boatwright of *Contemporary Tone Structures* in *Journal of Music Theory,* Nov. 1957, 201-205.
.... "A theory of set-complexes for Music" *Journal of Music Theory* 8 (1964), 136-139 + 141-142-183.
.... "The Domain and Relations of Set-Complex Theory," *Journal of*

Music Theory 9 (1965), 173-180.

. . . . "The Musical Kalaidoscope: Schoenberg's First Atonal Masterwork, Opus 11 No. 1." *Journal of the Arnold Schoenberg Inst.* 2 (Nov. 1981), 127-168.

Francès, Robert. *The Perception of Music.* (Trans. W.J. Dowling) Hillsdale: L. Erlbaum, 1988.

. . . . "*Recherches expérimentales sur le perecption des structures musicales.*" *Journal de Psychologie* 45 (1954), 78-96.

Frisch, Walter. *Schoenberg and His World.* Princeton: Princeton University Press, 1999.

Gass, William H. "Vicissitudes of the Avant-Garde." *Harper's Magazine,* October 1988, 64-70.

Gibson, Don. "The aural perception of non-traditional chords in selected theoretical relationships: A computer-generated experiment." *Journal of Research in Music Education* 34 (1986), 5-24.

. . . . "The Aural Perception of Similarity in Non-Traditional Chords Related by Octave Equivalence." *Journal of Research in Music Education* Vol. 36 (1988), 4-17.

. . . ., "The Effects of Pitch and Pitch-Class Content on the Aural Perception of Dissimilarity in Complementary Hexachords," *Psychomusicology* 12 (1993), 58-72.

Godwin, Joscelyn. *Music of the Occult.* Rochester: University of Rochester Press, 1995.

Goodman, Nelson. *Languages of Art: An Approach to a Theory of Symbols.* Indianapolis: Hacket, 1976.

Gombrich, E. H. *The Story of Art* (14th ed.). Englewood Cliffs: Prentice-Hall, 1984.

Gross, Paul R. and Norman Leavitt. *Higher Superstition: The Academic Left and Its Quarrels With Science.* Baltimore: The Johns Hopkins University Press, 1994.

Haimo, Ethan. *Schoenberg's Transformation of Musical Language.* Cambridge: Cambridge University Press, 2006.

Harvey, David. *The Condition of Modernity.* Oxford:: Blackwell, 1989.

Herzog, George. "Research in Primitive and Folk Music in the United States." *Bulletin of the American Council of Learned Societies* 24 (1936), 1-96.
.... "Speech Melody and Primitive Music." *The Musical Quarterly* 20 (1934), 452-466.

Hesse, Eva (Ed.). *New Approaches to Ezra Pound.* Berkeley: University of California Press, 1969.

Hindemith, Paul. *The Craft of Musical Composition* I. New York: Schott Music Corp., 1937/1945.

Hood, Mantle, *The Ethnomusicologist.* Kent, OH: Kent State Univ. Press, 1982.

Hornbostel, Eric von "African Negro Music." *Africa* I (1928), 30-62.

Hunt, Morton. *The Story of Psychology.* New York: Doubleday, 1993.

Imberty, M. "How do We Perceive Atonal Music? Suggestions for a Theoretical Approach." *Contemporary Music Review* 9, 325-337.

Janik, Allen, and Stephen Toulmin. *Wittgenstein's Vienna.* New York: Simon and Schuster, 1973.

Johnson, Paul. *Intellectuals.* New York: Harper and Row, 1988.

Jolas, Eugene. *Man From Babel.* (Eds. Andreas Kramer and Rainer Rumold). New Haven: Yale Univ. Press, 1998.

Kandinsky, Wassily, *Complete Writings on Art*, Vols. I and II. Kenneth C. Lindsay and Peter Vergo, Eds., Boston: G,K. Hall, 1982.

Keefe, Douglas H., Edward d M. Burns, and Phong Nguyen. "Modal Scales of the Dan Tranh." *Journal of the Acoustical Soc. of America* 84 (1988), 449-458.

Kerman, Joseph. *Contemplating Music.* Cambridge: Harvard Univ. Press, 1985.

Kimball, Roger. *Tenured Radicals.* New York: Harper and Row, 1990.
.... *The Long March.* San Francisco: Encounter Books, 2000.

Kodály, Zoltán (Ed.). *Studia Memoriae Belae Bartók Sacra.* Budapest: Hungarian Academy of Sciences, 1958.

Koestler, Arthur. *The Sleepwalkers.* New York: Grossett & Dunlap, 1963.

Kolinski, Mieczyslaw. "Recent Trends in Ethnomusicology." *Ethnomusicology* 11 (1967), 1-24.

Kramer, Lawrence. "The Mirror of Tonality: Transitional Features of Nineteenth Century Harmony." *Nineteenth Century Music* 4 (1981), 191-208.

Krumhansl, Carol L., Gregory J. Sandell, and Desmond C. Sargeant. "The Perception of Tone Hierarchies and Mirror Forms in Twelve-Tone Serial Music." *Music Perception* 5 (1987), 31-78.

Kurth, Richard, "Suspended Tonalities in Schönberg's Twelve-Tone Compositions," *Journal of the Arnold Schönberg Center* 3 (2001), 239-265.

Kuspit, Donald. The *Cult of the Avant-Garde Artist.* Cambridge: Cambridge U. Press, 1993.

Kwan, Kenneth, *Compositional Design in Recent Works of Chou Wen-chung.* Ph.D. dissertation, State University of New York at Buffalo, 1996.

Laborit, Henri. *Decoding the Human Message.* New York: St. Martins' Press, 1977.

Lecanuet, Jean-Pierre. "Prenatal Auditory Experience." In Deliège and Sloboda (Eds.) *Musical Beginnings: Origins and Development of Musical Competence.* Cambridge: Oxford University Press, 3-34.
. . . ., C. Granier-Deferre, and M.-C. Bushnel. "Human Fetal Auditory Perception" in Lecanuet, J.-P., W.P. Fifer, N.A. Krasnegor, and W.P. Smotherman (Eds.), *Fetal Development: A Psychological Perspective.* 239-262.

Leggio, James. "Kandinsky, Schoenberg, and the Music of the Spheres." 97-128 in *Music and Modern Art*, Ed. Leggio. New York: Routledge, 2002.

Lerdahl, F. *Tonal Pitch Space.* Oxford: Oxford University Press, 2001.
. . . . "Atonal Prolongational Structure." *Contemporary Music Review* 4 (1989), 64-87.

Levin, Flora. *The Harmonics of Nichomachus and the Pythagorean Tradition.* University Park, Pa.: American Philological Association, 1975.

Levis, John H. *Foundations of Chinese Musical Art.* New York: Paragon Reprints, 1954.

Lewin, David, *Generalized Musical Intervals and Transformations*. New Haven: Yale University Press, 1987.

. . . ."Inversional Balance as an Organizing Force in Schoenberg's Music and Thought." *Perspectives of New Music* 7 (1968), 1-21.

. . . . .Certain Techniques of Re-Ordering in Serial Music," *Journal of Music Theory* 10 (1966) 267-287.

. . . ."Re: The Intervallic Content of a Collection of Notes, Intervallic Relations Between a Collection of Notes and Its Complement: An Application to Schoenberg's Hexachordal System." *Journal of Music Theory* 4 (1960), 98-101.

. . . . "A Theory of Segmental Association in Twelve-Tone Music," *Perspectives of New Music* 1 (1962), 89-101.

Lewis, Wyndham. *W. Lewis on Art; Collected Writings 1913-1956*. New York: Funk & Wagnalls, 1969.

Liber usualis. S. Joannis Evangelistae Desclee & Socii, 1950.

Lockspeiser, Edward. *Music and Painting: A Study in Comparative Ideas From Turner to Schoenberg*. New York: Harper and Row, 19073.

McClain, Ernest. "Musical Theory and Ancient Cosmology," *The World and I*, February 1994, 371-391.

Maergaard, Jan. *Studien zur Entwicklung des dodekaphonen Satzes bei Arnold Schönberg*: Copenhagen, 1972.

Malevich,Kazimer. "From Cubism and Futurism to Suprematism: The New Painterly Realism," in *Russian Art of the Avant-Garde Theory and Criticism 1920-1934*. John Bowlt, editor and translator. NY: The Viking Press, 1976

Marcuse, Herbert. *One Dimensional Man*. Boston: Beacon Press, 1964.

Marks, Robert. "The Music and Musical Instruments of Ancient China." *The Musical Quarterly* 18 (1932), 593-607.

Martinez, M.E. "Cognitive Representations, Distinctions, Implications and Elaborations" in *Development of Mental Representation* (Eds. Kathleen R. Tyner and Irving E. Sigel), New York: Erlbaum Associates, 1999, 13-31.

Medawar, Peter. *Pluto's Republic*. London: Oxford University Press, 1982

Mengozzi, Stefano. "Virtual Segments: The Hexachordal System in the Late Middle Ages," *The Journal of Musicology* 23 (2006), 426-467.

Meyer, Leonard B. *Music, the Arts and Ideas*. Chicago: U. of Chicago Press, 1967.
........................""Exploiting Limits: Creation, Archetypes, and Style Change." *Daedalus*, Spring 1980, 177-205.

Milton, Joyce. *The Road to Malpsychia*. San Francisco: Encounter Books, 2002.

Morris, R.D. "A similarity index for pitch-class sets." *Perspectives of New Music* 18 (1979), 445-460.

Nauert, Paul. "Timespan Hierarchies and Posttonal Pitch Structure: A Composer's Strategy." *Perspectives of New Music* 43.1 (2005), 34-52.
.... "Field Notes: A Study of Fixed-Pitch Formations," in *Perspectives of New Music* 41 (2003), 6-65.
.... "The Progression Vector: Modeling Aspects of Post-Tonal Harmony," in *Journal of Music Theory* 47 (2003), 103-124.

Nettl, Bruno. "An ethnomusicologist contemplates music universals," *The Origins of Music*. (Eds. N.L. Wallin, B. Merker, and S. Brown). Boston: MIT Press, 2001, 463-472.
.... *Music in Primitive Culture*. Cambridge: Harvard Univ. Press, 1956.

Nichomachus, of Gerasa. (See Levin, *The Harmonics of Nichomachus. . .*)

Nketia, J.H. Kwabena. *The Music of Africa*. New York W.W. Norton, 1974.
.... *The Music of Ghana*. Evanston: Northwestern University Press, 1963.

Nüll, Edwin von der. *Moderne Harmonik*. Leipzig: F. Kistner & C.F.W. Siegel, 1932.

Ogden, Wilbur. "How Tonality Functions in Schoenberg's Opus 11, No. 1," *Journal of the Arnold Schoenberg Institute,* Nov. 1981, 169-181.

Ortega y Gasset, Jose. "The Dehumanization of Art" (1925). Trans. Helen Weyl, in *The Dehumanization of Art and Other Essays on Art, Culture, and Literature*. Princeton: Princeton U. Press, 1968

Payne, Anthony, *Schoenberg*. London: Oxford U. Press, 1968.

Perl, Jed. *Gallery Going: Four Seasons in the Art World.* San Diego: Harcourt Brace-Jovanovich, 1991.

Perle, George. *Serial Composition and Atonality.* Berkeley, Univ. of California Press, 1968.
.... *The Listening Composer.* Univ. of California Press, 1990.
.... *The Operas of Alban Berg*, Vol. I. Berkeley, U of Cal. Press, 1980.
.... *TwelveTone Tonality.* Univ. of California Press, 1980.

Picken, Laurence. "The Music of Far Eastern Asia: China." *Oxford History of Music* I, Oxford: Oxford Univ. Press, 1957, 83-134.

Pikler, A.G. "The Diatonic Foundation of Hearing." *Acta Psychologica* 11 (1955), 432-445.
....   "A History of Experiments on the Musical Interval Sense," *Jour of Music Theory* 10 (1966), 55-95.

Pinker, Steven. *How the Mind Works.* New York: W.W. Norton, 1997.
.... *The Language Instinct.* New York: Harper Perennial Classics, 2000.
.... *The Blank Slate.* New York: Penguin Books, 2002

Popper, Karl. *The Unended Quest.* New York: Open Court Press, 1982.

Pound, Ezra. *Gaudier-Brzeska: A Memoir.* New York: New Directions, 1974.
.... *The Cantos of Ezra Pound.* New York: New Directions Publ., 1993.

Pousseur, Henri. "The Question of Order in New Music." *Perspectives of New Music*, Fall-Winter 1966, 93-111.

Rahn, J. *Basic Atonal Theory.* New York: Longman, 1980.

Reichenbach, Hans. "The Tonality of English and Gaelic Folksong." *Music and Letters* 19 (1938), 268-279.

Regelski, Thomas. "Scientism in Experimental Music Research." *Philosophy of Music Education Review* 4 (1996), 3-19

Reti, Rudolph. *Tonality in Modern Music.* Springfield: Crowell-Collier, 1962.

Rochberg, George. 1973 *The Aesthetics of Survival.* Ann Arbor: U. Of Michigan Press, 1984.
.... "Reflections on Schoenberg." *Perspectives of New Music* 11 (1973), 56-83.

Rosenberg, Harold. *The De-Definition of Art.* Chicago: U. Chicago Press, 1972

Rosza, Miklos. *Double Life.* New York: Wynwood Press, 1989.

Sachs, Curt. *The Rise of Music in the Ancient World.* New York: W.W. Norton, 1943.

Samson, Jim. *Music in Transition: A Study of Tonal Expansion and Atonality. 1900-1920.* Cambridge: Dent, 1993.

Satyendra, Ramon. "An Informal Introduction to Some Formal Concepts From Lewin's Transformational Theory." *Journal of Music Theory* 48 (2004), 99-141.

Schellenberg , E.G., and S. E. Trehub. "Childrens' Discrimination of Melodic Intervals." *Developmental Psychology* 32 (1996), 1039-1050.

Schiff, David. "Sound Check" (review of book by Alex Ross). *The Nation,* October 29, 2007, 25-30.

Schillenger, Joseph. *Kalaidophone.* New York: Witmark & Sons, 1940.

Schoenberg, Arnold. *Theory of Harmony* (trans. Robert D.W. Adams). New York: Philosophical Library, 1948.
. . . . *Style and Idea,* Ed. Leonard Stein. London: Faber and Faber, 1975
. . . . *Arnold Schoenberg, Wassily Kandinsky.* London: Faber & Faber, 1984

Schoffman, Nachum. "Schoenberg's Opus 33a Revisited," *Tempo* 146 (1983), 31-42.

Searle, John. *The Rediscovery of Mind.* Boston: MIT Press, 1992.

Shawn, Allen. *Arnold Schoenberg's Journey.* New York: Farrar, Strauss and Giroux, 2002.

Simms, Bryan. *The Atonal Music of Arnold Schoenberg.* New York: Oxford U Press, 2000.

Singer, Irving. "The Aesthetics of Art for Art's Sake." *Journal of Aesthetics & Art Criticism* 12 (1954), 343-359.

Smith College Studies in Modern Languages, Vol. II (1921), No. 4.

228

Strauss, Joseph N., "The Myth of Serial Tyranny," *The Musical Quarterly* 83 (1999), 301-343.

Stravinsky, Igor. *An Autobigoraphy*. New York: Norton Library, 1962.
. . . . *The Poetics of Music* (Trans. Arthur Knodel and Ingolf Dahl). Cambridge: Harvard U Press, 1947.

Stevens, Anthony. *Archetypes: A Natural History of the Self*. New York: Morrow, 1982.

Subotnik,. Rose Rosengard, ""Toward a Deconstruction of Structural Listening: A Critique of Schoenberg, Adorno, and Stavinsky," in *Explorations in Music the Arts, and Ideas* (Eds. Eugene Narmour and Ruth Solie). Hillsdale: Pendragon Press, 1988. Pp. 87-122.

Thompson, William Forde and Richard Parncutt, "Perceptual Judgments of Triads and Dyads: Assessment of a Psychoacoustic Model, *Music Perception* 14 (1997), 263-280.

Thomson, Virgil. *American Music Since 1910*. Holt, Rinehart and Winston, 1971.

Thomson, William, "From Sounds to Music" *Music Perception* 21 (2004), 431-456.
. . . . *Schoenberg's Error*. Philadelphia: U. of Pennsylvania Press, 1996.
. . . .*Tonality in Music: A General Theory*. San Marino: Everett Books, 2001.
. . . . "The Problem of Tonality in Pre-Baroque and Primitive Music," *Journal of Music Theory* 2 (1958), 36-46.

Tokita, Allison McQueen. "Mode and Scale: Modulation and Tuning in Japanese Shamisen Music" in *The Ashgate Research Companion to Japanese Music*. Farnham: Ashgate, 2008.

Trainor, L.J."The Effect of Frequency Ratio on Infants' and Adults' Discrimination of Simultaneous Intervals," *Journal of Experimental Psychology*: Human Perception and Performance 23 (1997), 1427-1438.

Trainor, L.J., and B.M. Heinmiller. "The Development of Evaluative Responses to Music," *Infant Behavior and Development* 21 (1998), 77-88.

Trainor, L. J., Christine D. Tsang, and Vivian H.W. Cheung. "Preferences for Sensory Consonance in 2- and 4-month old Infants. *Music Perception* 20 (2002), 187-194.

Trehub, S.E., "In the Beginning There Was Music." *Bulletin of Psychology and the Arts* 4 (2004), 42-44.
. . . ., M. Endman, and A. Thorpe. "Infants' Perception of Timbre: Classification of Complex Tones by Spectral Structure." *Journal of Experimental Child Psychology* 49 (1990), 300-313.
. . . . .and L.J. Trainor. "Singing to Infants: Lullabies and Play Songs." *Advances in Infancy Research* 12 (1998), 43-77.

Ushenko, Andrew. *Dynamics of Art.* Bloomington: Indiana University Press, 1953.

Watson, John B., *Behaviorism.* New Brunswick: Transaction Press, 1925/98.

Watson, Steven. *Gertrude Stein, Virgil Thomson and the Mainstreaming of American Modernism.* New York: Random House, 1998.

Werner, Eric. "The Oldest Sources of Octave and Octoechos," *Acta Musicologica* XX (1948), 1-9.

Wen-chung, Chou, "The Aesthetic Principles of Chinese Music: A Personal Quest." *Canzona* 7, No. 24, (June 1986), 76-93.
. . . ., "Towards a Re-Merger in Music" In *Contemporary Composers on Contemporary Music* (eds. Elliott Schwartz and Barney Childs. New York: Holt, Rinehart and Winston, 1967. 308- 315.

Werner, L.A., and G.C. Marean. *Human Auditory Development.* Boulder, CO, Westview Press. 1996.

Wertheimer, Max, "*Musik der Wedda*" in *Sammelbande der Internationalen Musikgesellschaft* 11 (1909-10), 300-309.

West, M.L. *Ancient Greek Music*, London: Oxford U Press, 1992.

Wilcox, John. "The Beginnings of L'Art Pour L'Art," *Jour. of Aesthetics and Art Criticism* 11 (1953), 360-377.

Wilding-White, R. "Observations re Tonality and Scale Theory," *Journal of Music Theory* V (1961), 275-286.

230

Winckel, Fritz. *Music, Sound and Sensation, a Modern Exposition*. (Trans. by Thomas Binkley from *Phänomene des musikalisches Hörens*) New York: Dover Publications, 1967.

Wilson, Peter. A *Preface to Ezra Pound*. New York: Longman, 1997.

Wiora, Walter, "Older Than Pentatony," in *Studia Memoriae Belae Bartók Sacra*, Boosey & Hawkes, London 1959, 183-206.

Wittlich, Gary, Ed. *Aspects of Twentieth-Century Music*, Englewood Cliffs: Prentice Hall, 1975.
. . . ."Interval and Set Structure in Schoenberg's Op. 11, No. 1," *Perspectives of New Music* 13 (Fall-Winter, 1974).

Wittgenstein, Ludwig, *Tractatus logico-philosophicus*. London: Routledge, 2001.

Wolfe, Tom. *The Painted Word*. New York: Farrar, Strauss and Giroux, 1975.

Wuorinen, Charles, "*Pierot lunaire*, Op. 21," Notes for the CD Arnold Schoenberg: Pierrot Lunaire; The Book of the Hanging Gardens. Elektra Nonesuch, 1990.

Yasser, Joseph, *A Theory of Evolving Tonality*. New York: American Library of Musiclogy, 1932.

Ying, Hsu Wen. *Origins of Music in China*. Paper delivered at the annual conference of the Society of Ethnomusicology, Seattle, Oct. 29, 1970.

Zarlino, Gioseffo. *On the Modes* (trans. Vered Cohen). Part IV of *Le Istitutioni Harmoniche*, 1558. New Haven: Yale U. Press, 1983.

Zentner, M.R., and J. Kagan. "Infants' Perception of Consonance and Dissonance in Music." *Infant Behavior and Development* 21 (1998), 483-492.
. . . . "Perception of Music by Infants," *Nature* 383 (1996), 29-37.

Index

William Thomson

Dr. William Thomson is Emeritus Professor and former Dean of the School of Music at the University of Southern California. Dr. Thomson is an Associate Editor for the publications *Music Perception* and *Empirical Musicology*.